CONFESSIONAL CRISES AND CULTURAL POLITICS
IN TWENTIETH-CENTURY AMERICA

RHETORIC AND DEMOCRATIC DELIBERATION
VOLUME 5

EDITED BY CHERYL GLENN AND J. MICHAEL HOGAN
THE PENNSYLVANIA STATE UNIVERSITY

Editorial Board:

Robert Asen (University of Wisconsin–Madison)
Debra Hawhee (The Pennsylvania State University)
Peter Levine (Tufts University)
Steven J. Mailloux (University of California, Irvine)
Krista Ratcliffe (Marquette University)
Karen Tracy (University of Colorado, Boulder)
Kirt Wilson (The Pennsylvania State University)
David Zarefsky (Northwestern University)

Rhetoric and Democratic Deliberation is a series of groundbreaking monographs and edited volumes focusing on the character and quality of public discourse in politics and culture. It is sponsored by the Center for Democratic Deliberation, an interdisciplinary center for research, teaching, and outreach on issues of rhetoric, civic engagement, and public deliberation.

Other books in the series:

Karen Tracy, *Challenges of Ordinary Democracy: A Case Study in Deliberation and Dissent*

Samuel McCormick, *Letters to Power: Public Advocacy Without Public Intellectuals*

Christian Kock and Lisa Storm Villadsen, eds., *Rhetorical Citizenship and Public Deliberation*

Jay Childers, *The Evolving Citizen: American Youth, the Deliberative Impulse, and the Changing Norms of Democratic Engagement*

CONFESSIONAL CRISES AND CULTURAL POLITICS IN TWENTIETH-CENTURY AMERICA

DAVE TELL

The Pennsylvania State University Press | University Park, Pennsylvania

Some material in this book appeared, in a different form, in Dave Tell, "The Secular Confession of Jimmy Swaggart," *Rhetoric Society Quarterly* 39, no. 2 (2009): 124–46. Reprinted by permission of Taylor & Francis Ltd, http://www.tandfonline.com/.

Library of Congress Cataloging-in-Publication Data

Tell, Dave, 1976–
   Confessional crises and cultural politics in twentieth-century America / Dave Tell.
      p.   cm. — (Rhetoric and democratic deliberation)
Summary: "Examines the role of confession in American culture. Argues that the genre of confession has profoundly shaped (and been shaped by) six of America's most intractable cultural issues: sexuality, class, race, violence, religion, and democracy"—Provided by publisher.
Includes bibliographical references (p.   ) and index.
ISBN 978-0-271-05629-6 (pbk. : alk. paper)
1. Confession—Psychology—History—20th century.
2. United States—Social life and customs—20th century.
I. Title.

BF634.T45 2013
306.0973'0904—dc23
2012017706

Copyright © 2012 The Pennsylvania State University
All rights reserved
Printed in the United States of America
Published by The Pennsylvania State University Press,
University Park, PA 16802-1003

The Pennsylvania State University Press is a member of the Association of American University Presses.

It is the policy of The Pennsylvania State University Press to use acid-free paper. Publications on uncoated stock satisfy the minimum requirements of American National Standard for Information Sciences—Permanence of Paper for Printed Library Material, ANSI Z39.48–1992.

For HANNAH, JACK, *and* ASHLYN

CONTENTS

Acknowledgments ix

Introduction: Confessional Crises and Cultural Politics 1

1 Confession and Sexuality: *True Story* Versus Anthony Comstock 20

2 Confession and Class: A New *True Story* 45

3 Confession and Race: Civil Rights, Segregation, and the Murder of Emmett Till 63

4 Confession and Violence: William Styron's Nat Turner 91

5 Confession and Religion: Jimmy Swaggart's Secular Confession 119

6 Confession and Democracy: Clinton, Starr, and the Witch-Hunt Tradition of American Confession 146

Conclusion: James Frey and Twenty-First-Century Confessional Culture 180

Notes 192

Bibliography 213

Index 227

ACKNOWLEDGMENTS

The project now known as *Confessional Crises and Cultural Politics in Twentieth-Century America* was ten years in the making. Although I often felt alone in front of my computer, the truth is that the past ten years have been filled with support from every quarter. Without that support, I don't imagine I would now have a book; if I did, it wouldn't be on confessional culture; and if it were, it would have been a far inferior rendition.

My foremost intellectual debt belongs to Ned O'Gorman. Ned was there in the Penn State copy room when, one year into the project, I was ready to call it quits. On that occasion, Ned saw merit in the project and encouraged me to press on. Since that time, through countless phone conversations, late-night drinks, and marked-up drafts, Ned has remained committed to the project. He has also challenged my thinking about the role of confession in American culture more than anyone else. While I have often resisted his challenges, that doesn't mean I haven't profited immensely from them.

A select group of people has amazed me with their depth and continuity of support. These people have read multiple drafts, written countless letters on my behalf, or otherwise gone beyond the call of duty in their support of *Confessional Crises*. In this category are Rosa Eberly, Mike Hogan, Shawn Parry-Giles, and Ned O'Gorman.

Without colleagues willing to critically engage with portions of the manuscript (in some cases its entirety!) and offer resistance and feedback, *Confessional Crises* would have suffered. In this category, I am indebted to Jack Selzer, Steve Browne, Steven Mailloux, David Zarefsky, Jim Aune, Chuck Morris, John Murphy, Cara Finnegan, John Lucaites, Bjorn Stillion Southard, Davis Houck, Jeff Drury, James Darsey, Carolyn Miller, Calvin Troup, Pete Simonson, Jerry Hauser, Mike Edwards, Roger Stahl, Robert Hariman, Mitch Reyes, Nicholas Thomas, Roseann Mandziuk, Jeremy Engels, and David Frank.

Beyond these, still others contributed material support to *Confessional Crises*. Here my debts run to Barbara Biesecker, Devery Anderson, Jeffrey Motter, Matt Newcomb, Sara Ann Mehltretter, Susan Wise Bauer, Brian Jackson, Debra Hawhee, David Timmerman, Greg Spencer, Nathan Crick, Josh Gunn, Scott Wible, Trevor Parry-Giles, Susan Zaeske, and Ben Henderson.

A special thanks goes to those who made the University of Kansas an ideal spot to write this book. I have shared both drafts and life with these colleagues, and am better for it: Shawn Alexander, Robin Rowland, Ben Chappell, Beth Innocenti, Jay Childers, Anthony Corbeill, Henry Bial, Donn Parson, Sharon O'Brien, Kristine Bruss, Kundai Chirindo, Greta Wendelin, Mary Lee Hummert, Rob Topinka, Jason Barrett-Fox, Thomas Heilke, Brent Steele, Sally J. Cornelison, Laura Mielke, Amy Devitt, Frank Farmer, Christopher Forth, Jason Roe, Jill Kuhnheim, H. Faye Xiao, and Allan Pasco. The Pie and Theory Reading Group has been a breath of fresh air. Kansas librarian Julie Petr deserves standout recognition; without her capacity to find rare documents I would have been lost. Finally, thanks go to KU's General Research Fund, whose consistent support made summertime research possible.

At the center of my Kansas experience has been the Hall Center for the Humanities, which provided me a residential fellowship and two semester-long workshops to refine my argument under the best conditions possible. Here my debts extend to Victor Bailey, Kristine Latta, Jeanie Wulfkuhle, and Cindy Lynn.

The Humanities Grant Development Office at KU has done more for the intellectual narrative of *Confessional Crises* than I ever dreamed possible for an institutionalized office. HGDO is far more than grant support—it is also thought support. Without the supportive resistance of the HGDO, *Confessional Crises* would have been underfunded and underdeveloped. Thanks go to Kathy Porsche and Sally Utech.

Kendra Boileau and the whole team at Penn State University Press have been fantastic. Freelance copyeditor Nicholas Taylor was a pleasure to work with.

Very few friends outside the academy ever asked me about the specifics of what I was writing. But I'm quite thankful for the few that did: Jamie and Darcy Kidd, Matt and Kori Podszus, Marc and Jenea Havener, Bill and Sue Tell (my parents!), and Jeff and Aubrey Tell.

Finally, *Confessional Crises* is dedicated to Hannah, Jack, and Ashlyn. Even if *Confessional Crises* becomes a best seller, it could never compensate these three for the endless support, encouragement, and relief they have provided.

INTRODUCTION:
CONFESSIONAL CRISES AND CULTURAL POLITICS

In contemporary America, the rise of reality TV, the proliferation of daytime talk shows, the endless parade of celebrity confessions, and the insatiable market for fake memoirs such as James Frey's *Million Little Pieces* have pushed the genre of confession to the forefront of the public mind. Writing in the January 2010 issue of the *New Yorker*, the distinguished cultural critic Daniel Mendelsohn suggested that the outrage over the recent "onslaught" of Frey-styled "phony" confessions indicates a "large and genuinely new anxiety" about what sorts of texts should count as confessions.[1] Thus did Mendelsohn add his voice to what has become a widespread sentiment: we no longer live simply in a confessional culture. This much is well known and well documented.[2] Rather, we live in a culture defined by *confessional anxiety*: an anxiety born of an uncertainty about which texts should count as confessions, and compounded by the conviction that such classifications matter a great deal.

Confessional Crises and Cultural Politics in Twentieth-Century America demonstrates that these anxieties are nothing new. In fact, anxieties over precisely which texts qualify as confessions have been a staple of twentieth-century American life. They have manifested themselves in what I call *confessional crises*. Confessional crises are the public debates incited when a text that contains no apparent confessional characteristics is labeled a confession for patently political purposes. For example, in 1956 NAACP Executive Secretary Roy Wilkins argued that *Look* magazine's story on the racially charged murder of Emmett Till was a confession. Despite the fact that the story was written in the third person, that it contained no apology, no remorse, no admission of sinfulness, and, in short, *none* of the standard markers by which a text is typically identified as a confession, Wilkins recognized that if the *Look* story circulated as a confession, it would provide him leverage with which to pressure Mississippi Governor-Elect J. P. Coleman to reconvene a grand jury.

Wilkins thus acted on a central assumption of *Confessional Crises*: that the classification of a text as a confession is not an idle, academic task. To the contrary, at least to Wilkins's mind (and mine), to call a text a confession or to deny the same is always a political act (i.e., an act that stresses or reinforces the established social order). In the case at hand, the possibility of justice for Emmett Till turned on the question of whether the *Look* story counted as a confession. And conversely, the *Look* story counted as a confession for Wilkins only because of his racial politics. In these respects, the January 1956 debate over the *Look* article was a paradigmatic confessional crisis: because cultural politics were inextricably interwoven with the contested classification of *Look*'s story, it instigated a widespread discussion of confession, its boundaries, and its proper place in public life.[3]

Confessional Crises and Cultural Politics in Twentieth-Century America is about precisely this imbrication of confession and cultural politics. As we shall see, the two will simply not leave each other alone. I argue that six recurrent issues in American cultural politics—sexuality, class, race, violence, religion, and democracy—have been deeply informed by the genre of confession, and the genre of confession, in turn, is a product of its historical allegiances with these same issues. The strength of the bond joining confession to cultural politics is best judged by the sheer time, energy, and expense activists like Wilkins have spent ensuring that only the correct texts are called confessions. And here Wilkins is only a type. In the pages that follow, I tell the stories of countless partisan actors who—from all points on the political spectrum—have redefined the genre of confession in order to make it better serve their political needs. Their efforts have been pursued with such vigor and such passion that they have transformed both the nature of genre criticism and American culture writ large. Genre criticism, the once-staid activity of deciding how texts should be classified and what such classifications mean, has over the course of the twentieth century been invested with the pathos, energy, and hostility familiar to students of cultural politics. On a wider level, as I document in the conclusion, twenty-first-century American culture is now shot-through with confessional anxieties and hyper-attuned to the political stakes of labeling texts as confessions.

I pursue these arguments by examining the controversy over the *Look* article and five similar episodes in which partisan political investments sparked public debates over whether particular texts counted as confessions. The first two were incited by the 1919 publication of Bernarr Macfadden's *True Story Magazine*. Although *True Story* is now widely recognized as the founding text in the confession industry, its origins in cultural politics have been all but forgotten. *True Story*, and the confessions that once filled its pages, were a direct result of Macfadden's conviction that "confessions" were a powerful weapon—both in his lifelong feud with Anthony Comstock over sexual politics, and in the development of capitalism. These articulations of confession with sexuality and class sparked widespread public debates over *True Story Magazine*, the genre of confession, and its place in public life. Over the course of the century, at least four more events triggered similar crises. In October 1955, Emmett Till's acquitted killers sold their story to *Look* for $4,000; in 1967 the white Anglo-Saxon southern Protestant William Styron claimed that he "entered the consciousness" of a black slave to write *The Confessions of Nat Turner*; in 1988 the televangelist Jimmy Swaggart's church (the Assemblies of God) fought to control the meaning and dissemination of his confession; and in 1998 the Clinton administration and Kenneth Starr's Office of the Independent Counsel publicly debated whether Clinton's various speeches on Monica Lewinsky counted as legitimate confessions.

Despite all the differences among these episodes, they share decisive commonalities. In each instance, cultural politics demanded the reclassification of a text as a confession. Further, in each instance this reclassification sparked vigorous public debates over what we might call *confessional hermeneutics*, a shorthand term I use to designate the collaborative but always contested activity of deciding which texts do, and which texts do not, qualify as confessions. *Confessional Crises and Cultural Politics in Twentieth-Century America* is premised on the belief that these debates—or in my terms, these confessional crises—teach us four specific lessons about the politics of confession.

First, these debates underscore the intense political power of labeling a text as a confession. Simply by repeating Wilkins's strategy of claiming politically convenient texts as confessions, scores of partisan advocates have brought new force to their arguments. Thus it is hardly surprising that confessional crises have been clustered around twentieth-century America's most intractable issues—not only race, but also sexuality, class, violence, religion, and democracy. Indeed, the central argument of this book is that confessional hermeneutics—the act of determining precisely which texts count as confessions—has been one of the most powerful, and most overlooked, forms of intervening into American cultural politics. *Confessional Crises* thus offers what Steven Mailloux has called a "specifically *rhetorical* form of cultural studies": a form premised on the assumption that historical acts of interpretation "extend and manipulate the social practices, political structures, and material circumstances in which they are embedded at particular historical moments."[4] In other words, Mailloux argues that the interpretation and classification of texts is not innocent; rather, it is itself a form of cultural intervention. Herein, I argue that the interpretation and circulation of six specific texts *as confessions* has concretely shaped the public understanding of six intractable issues: sexuality, class, race, violence, religion, and democracy.

Second, if confessional hermeneutics is a powerful mode of cultural intervention, the converse is also true: American cultural politics have massively influenced what texts count as confessions. In surprising but concrete ways, *Confessional Crises* demonstrates that political commitments have shaped and reshaped the boundaries of the confessional genre. While the work of Robert W. McChesney and others have made the intrication of the media and political culture commonplace, it remains far too easy to think (mistakenly) that the genre of confession exists apart from the political struggles of American culture.[5] It remains far too easy to think that the confession is an autonomous genre, its boundaries marked off by a secluded professoriate. Quite the opposite. *Confessional Crises and Cultural Politics in Twentieth-Century America* stresses the political economy of confession; it stresses the fact that, historically speaking, the boundaries of confession have been subject to revision by activists interested primarily in cultural politics. The NAACP, Black Power, Mississippi's Citizens' Councils, two major New York publishing houses, a right-wing fundamentalist church, President Clinton's administration, and the Office of the Independent Counsel—these are just a few of the twentieth-century organizations (all of which are treated herein) that have sought to advance their politics by retrofitting the confession, adjusting its boundaries so that it would better serve their politics.

Third, the confessional crises of twentieth-century America suggest that virtually any text can circulate as a confession. Because political exigencies have consistently proved more pressing than checklists of textual characteristics, partisan advocates of all stripes have consistently done what Wilkins did: blatantly ignored textual characteristics and labeled any text a confession, so long as doing so promised political advantage. Indeed, the most conspicuous characteristic of the confessional crises I examine is that they were incited by texts that did not look like confessions at all: a magazine, an expose written in the third person, a novel, a legal interrogation, and an investigative report—in sum, texts that were turned into confessions despite their substantive and formal characteristics rather than because of them. Taking the long view, and looking at the sheer diversity of texts that have been turned into confessions solely on the promise of political gain, it becomes apparent that there are, theoretically speaking, no limits to the confessional genre. Questions of composition, authorship, sincerity, formal features, and substantive content have proven almost irrelevant—so long as it is politically advantageous, it seems that any text can be claimed as a confession and circulated as such. For this reason, understanding the politics of confession in twentieth-century America requires an incredibly broad definition of the genre. In order to better understand these politics, I have counted as a confession any text that has been called a confession.

Fourth, America's confessional crises suggest that the power of confession resides in its claim to authenticity. Returning once more to Wilkins, he needed the *Look* article to be a confession because he recognized that the label itself was a powerful mode of authenticating the text. The label "confession," in other words, gave the *Look* account a claim to truthfulness it would not otherwise have; so categorized, the racial atrocities *Look* described could not be dismissed as mere partisan maneuvering. Taking the long view once more, Wilkins is hardly alone. Historically speaking, partisan advocates have claimed dozens of texts as confessions in order to bring the political cachet of authenticity to both important causes and trivial pursuits.

Confessional Anxiety

In 1966, Supreme Court Justice Byron White dissented from *Miranda v. Arizona*, claiming that it was based on "a deep-seated distrust of all confessions."[6] In the intervening years, it seems that this distrust has multiplied tenfold. Indeed, evidence of the confessional anxiety mentioned at the outset abounds. In the last twelve years alone, prestigious academic presses (e.g., Chicago, Princeton, Oxford) have joined forces with established commercial houses (e.g., HarperCollins, Simon and Schuster, Penguin) to turn the confession and its related genres into one of the most talked about rhetorical practices of our time. From Peter Brooks's *Troubling Confessions* (Chicago 2000), to Aaron Lazare's *On Apology* (Oxford 2005), to Susan Wise Bauer's *Art of the Public Grovel* (Princeton 2008), to Ben Yagoda's *Memoir: A History* (Riverhead 2009), to Andrew Potter's *Authenticity Hoax* (HarperCollins 2010), to Suzanne Diamond's *Compelling Confessions* (Fairleigh Dickinson 2011), studies of confession, its history, its relatives, and its relevance have been appearing with increasing speed. If Peter Brooks's comment that "our social and cultural attitudes toward confession suffer from uncertainties and ambivalences" remains applicable, this is certainly not for lack of effort.[7]

Words like "nervousness," "confusion," "uncertainty," "irritation," "unreliability," "ambivalence," and "anxiety" punctuate the literature on confession at regular intervals, constant reminders of the psychological perils that attend a confessional culture. The very title of Peter Brooks's *Troubling Confessions* is telling. Brooks gives eloquent voice to the confessional anxieties that plague contemporary America. He argues that confession is a "difficult and slippery notion" and implores his readers to exercise caution and restraint before demanding a confession: "Our sense of what confession is and does hovers in a zone of uncertainty." For this reason, Brooks wonders whether we would not be better served if every confessional text came pre-labeled with its own warning: "This is a confession, handle with care."[8] Voicing a related anxiety, *Book World*'s Jonathon Yardley worries about the sheer number of "confessions." The market is so saturated with them, he notes, that "it is just about impossible to separate what little wheat there may be from the vast ocean of chaff."[9]

Further, an array of popular books situate the "uncertainties and ambivalences" over confession within a larger set of anxieties over the notion of authenticity. David Boyle's *Authenticity: Brands, Fakes, Spin, and the Lust for Real Life* (HarperCollins 2004), Andrew Potter's *Authenticity Hoax*, and David Shields's *Reality Hunger* (Knopf 2010) each document the growing cultural sensitivity to anything marketed as authentic—confessions, memoirs, autobiographies, reality TV. As David Shields put it, the "very nearly pornographic obsession with [James Frey] and similar cases reveal the nervousness on the topic."[10] On Mendelsohn's account, our culture's confessional obsession reveals not nervousness, but irritation. The uncertainties surrounding confession, he argues, have given rise to a "critical and public irritation" with confessional writing—an irritation that has recently "reached a new peak."[11]

Yardley, Shields, Mendelsohn, Potter, Brooks, and Yagoda—these are not writers who otherwise share much in common. Their shared impulse to emphasize the anxieties of confessional culture is telling. Taken together, their common testimony is powerful evidence that despite our cultural fascination with confession, and despite the outpouring of books on the subject, we are not yet comfortable with the cultural power of this now-ubiquitous rhetorical form. Given this palpable discomfort, perhaps it is time to approach the study of confession with questions and methods designed to account for these anxieties.

Confessional Crises and Cultural Politics in Twentieth-Century America does just this. It is, to my knowledge, the first *reception history* of confession. Reception history has a deep and varied intellectual history. Nowhere, however, have the trajectories of rhetorical criticism and reception history been better articulated than in the work of Steven Mailloux. For this reason, I lean heavily on his 1998 volume *Reception Histories: Rhetoric, Pragmatism, and American Cultural Politics*. In this text (along with the earlier *Rhetorical Power*), Mailloux argues that the primary task of a reception history is the placement of historical acts of interpretation within larger questions of cultural politics.[12] Following Mailloux, I examine historical interpretations of texts as confessions and attend to the political climate that influenced (and was influenced by) these classifications. As such, my primary concern is neither establishing the formal characteristics of the genre nor adjudicating what counts as a confession. Rather, my primary concern is with the historical relationships binding schemas of classification to investments in cultural politics.

As a reception study, *Confessional Crises* is the only study of the genre that does not begin with a predetermined, substantive definition of confession. From the smart, conservative work of Susan Wise Bauer, to the smart, nontraditional work of Michel Foucault, every significant study of confession in the last fifty years begins with a predetermined definition. For Bauer, a confession is an admission of sin; for Foucault, it is a discourse of identity. For both thinkers, however—and in this they are representative of the wider field—the boundaries of their studies are determined in advance by their definition of confession. Their efforts have certainly been productive. Bauer can measure the reach of secularization, and Foucault can explain confession's complicity in identity politics. But by virtue of their methodology, neither of them can do what *Confessional Crises* does: explain the power of the genre by focusing a wide range of texts—serials, novels, exposes, interrogations—that, for political reasons, became confessions *despite* their textual characteristics. Thus *Confessional Crises* is uniquely attuned to the *public* power of confession in ways that the works of Bauer and Foucault could never be. Rather than drawing a definition of confession from religious traditions (Bauer) or from the confluence of legal and psychiatric traditions (Foucault) and then measuring public discourse against it, I assume that public discourse is trustworthy: I count as a confession any text that has been called a confession. From this perspective, *True Story*, Styron's novel, and the Starr Report are just as much confessions as Jimmy Swaggart's bleary-eyed apology or Clinton's defiant admission of an improper relationship with Monica Lewinsky. Although these texts share little at the level of formal characteristics, they share a decisive commonality at the level of popular reception: each was reclassified as a confession for political purposes.

From certain perspectives, my willingness to treat as a confession any text that is called a confession will smack of critical naiveté—of taking public discourse at face value instead of submitting it to careful scrutiny. In his recent study of apology, for example, Aaron Lazare began by charting the popular "misuse of the word 'apologize.'" From Lazare's perspective, the public is "confused" and their use of the word "apologize" cannot be trusted. As a means of correcting popular confusion, Lazare provided a definition of a "true apology" and then demonstrated the shortcomings of popular usage.[13] From my perspective, however, understanding the *public* anxiety that now surrounds the genre of confession requires respecting the *public* use of the term. In this respect, *Confessional Crises* is indebted to Raymond Williams. No one has more eloquently made the case for granting credence to the actual words used by men and women to describe their experience. In his landmark 1958 *Culture and Society*, Williams explained that he was seeking to understand culture, industry, class, democracy, and art by paying attention to what was labeled "culture," "industry," "class," "democracy," and "art." His account of his personal commitment to the words used by people to capture their experience is unsurpassed:

> *I feel myself committed to the study of actual language: that is to say, to the words and sequences of words which particular men and women have used in trying to give meaning to their experience.* It is true that I shall be particularly interested in the general developments of meaning in language, and these, always, are more than personal. But, *as a method of enquiry*, I have not chosen to list certain topics, and to assemble summaries of particular statements on them. I have, rather, with only occasional exceptions, *concentrated on particular thinkers and their actual statements, and tried to understand and value them.*[14]

There could hardly be a better description of my own methodology. I have granted credence to the statements of particular individuals—even when they applied the word "confession" to the unlikeliest of texts—and tried to understand these statements in their political contexts. Following Mailloux, I have called this methodology a reception study: rather than focusing on formal characteristics or the authors' designs, I am focusing on how texts were talked about by people who encountered them.

Significantly, because it is a reception study *Confessional Crises* is uniquely situated to speak to the palpable confessional anxieties of our time. *Confessional Crises* tells the stories of how the genre of confession has, over the course of the twentieth century, been constantly retrofitted and refashioned, constantly pressed into the service of various political agendas. And after a century of activists claiming any text as a confession merely to serve the political need of the hour, is it any wonder that contemporary America is shot through with anxieties about which sorts of texts count as confessions? In other words, *Confessional Crises* demonstrates that the anxieties the *New Yorker* called "genuinely new" are more likely the product of a long history. At the least, we can say with certainty that such anxieties have been cultivated by a century of opportunistic partisan actors willing to turn virtually any convenient text into a confession.

Confessional Crises has no pretensions of being a panacea; it certainly will not quell America's confessional anxieties, and it may exacerbate them. But by showing where they came from and why they arose, by unveiling the powerful political impetus to play fast and loose with the genre of confession, by demonstrating the political incentives pushing activists to call any self-serving text a confession—and thereby undermine any sense of certainty about what precisely counts as a confession—*Confessional Crises* may help us better understand our current confessional culture and its attendant psychological anxieties. It certainly suggests that the answer to our confessional anxieties does not lie in a Lazare-styled pursuit of a "true" or correct definition of confession. Nor does it lie with Peter Brooks's desire for clearly labeled confessional texts. So long as confessional hermeneutics remains an ideological resource, and so long as partisan advocates have a vested interest in claiming a wide variety of texts as confessions, no system of labels can be definitive and no "true" definition of confession stands a chance.

Politics and Confession

If, as *Confessional Crises and Cultural Politics in Twentieth-Century America* suggests, the history of confession is the history of a wide variety of texts being claimed as confessions on the promise of political gain, we need to ask new questions of the genre. It is not enough to ask after the boundaries of confession, to ask which texts are and which texts are not confessions. Nor is it sufficient to ask which textual features should characterize every confession. Although these questions have long occupied scholars, they are premised on the historically untenable assumption that the confession is a stable, ahistorical category characterized by recurring textual features. Working from the Mailloux-inspired assumption that every act of classification is "historically contingent, politically situated, institutionally embedded, and materially conditioned," *Confessional Crises* suggests that the important question to ask of every confessional text is a variation of the question that the early pragmatists famously directed to truth: "Truth for whom?"[15] Following the lead of Edward Schiappa and David Zarefsky, we should not ask if a text *is* a confession, but we should ask whom a text serves as a confession.[16] *Confessional Crises*, in other words, is a political rather than a categorical inquiry. I have no interest in generating an authoritative list of texts that have been categorized as confessions. I have a keen interest, however, in exploring why particular activists have insisted on particular lists, why particular political positions seem to require particular but improbable texts to count as confessions.

In a broad sense, there is nothing revolutionary here. Confessional inquiry has been driven by political questions for a long time. The question of power is why Foucault took up the genre in the 1970s, and it is why Brooks and Bauer have done so in the last fifteen years. All three of these influential scholars predicated their work on the premise that the study of confession would provide insight into the redistribution, abuse, or recovery of political power. To date, however, all inquiries into the politics of confession have assumed that such politics are a function of the genre's recurrent textual features. The works of Bauer and Foucault are again instructive and representative. Their work demonstrates just how thoroughly confessional inquiry has internalized the mistaken assumption that if we are to understand the politics of confession, we must first isolate the textual features that constitute a true confession. In virtually every study, in other words, a confession does what it does because it is what it is.

Consider again the work of Susan Wise Bauer. She argues that in twentieth-century America, "the public confession came to serve a very particular purpose. It became a ceremonial laying down of power, made so that followers could pick that power up and hand it back." After defining confession in these terms, the remainder of *The Art of the Public Grovel* evaluates how particular leaders used or misused the public confession in order to regain power: Ted Kennedy failed at Chappaquiddick, Jimmy Swaggart succeeded, and President Bill Clinton gradually perfected the art. What distinguishes Kennedy from Swaggart, the early Clinton from the late? Rhetorical artistry. Kennedy, Bauer tells us, did not recover his power because he "misread his audience" and therefore rationalized his actions rather than "admitting to moral blame." Swaggart, by contrast, responded to his scandal with a "model confession." He never "engaged in any blameshifting," he never excused his behavior, he offered nine "clear statements of fault" and "eight pleas for forgiveness." Consequently, "when Swaggart laid his power down, his congregation picked it up and handed it back."[17] In sum, for Bauer the power of the confession hinges on the artistry of the confessant—the ability, as it were, to say the right things at the right time.

Within confessional studies, the primary alternative to the instrumental tradition in which Bauer works is found in the work of Michel Foucault, who argues that the confessant makes her- or himself vulnerable to an insidious form of social control—a form of control he famously labeled disciplinary power. Just as much as Bauer, however, Foucault assumed that the power of the confession hinges on its substantive content. On two separate occasions, Foucault provided a survey of the history of the confession.[18] The critical movement in each of these surveys was the gradual disengagement of confession from a judicial code of prohibitions. For a long time, Foucault explained, the substantive content of confession was determined by the illegal acts of the penitent: adultery, fornication, debauchery, and so forth. Beginning in the sixteenth century, however, the substantive content of the confession was increasingly calibrated to the *thoughts* rather than the *actions* of the penitent.[19]

This is the decisive turning point in Foucault's account of confession. It is precisely when the substantive content of confession shifted from the disclosure of actions to the disclosure of thoughts that confession became a technology of social control.[20] If the content of confession had never shifted from actions to thoughts, then the genre would have remained a relatively benign practice. If every confession was modeled on *The Life of Benvenuto Cellini* or Clinton's *My Life*—texts in which there is little more than a recounting of past events—Foucault's explanation of confession would be wholly irrelevant. I say this not to minimize the force of Foucault's account, but to emphasize that its force is dependent on a particular, substantive definition of confession.

Thus, just as much as Bauer's instrumental approach, Foucault's critical approach is marked by a dependence on the substantive features of the confession. In both traditions, the political power of confession is calibrated to the textual characteristics of confessional prose. For Bauer, the capacity of a confession to recover power hinges on the avoidance of "blameshifting" and the outright admission of guilt; for Foucault, the application of power hinges on a shift from confessing actions to confessing thoughts. Neither approach to confession, however, accounts for the unmistakable power of texts that have circulated as confessions *despite* their textual characteristics.

For example, Bauer's schema could not account for the power of the Starr Report; Foucault's logic could not account for the power of Bill Clinton's August 17 confession; and neither schema could explain the power of *True Story Magazine*, *Look*'s article on Emmett Till, or *The Confessions of Nat Turner*—all texts that wide segments of the population called confessions. Because confessional studies writ large has followed Bauer and Foucault, tuning confessional power to textual forms, the field is still unable to explain the power of confessions that do not look like the models they posit. More pressing still, working from the influential models of Bauer and Foucault, the field is unable to explain the complicity of the genre with cultural politics. How is it that the genre of confession has intervened into such issues as sexuality, class, race, violence, religion, and democracy? In my view, these interventions have little to do with the rhetorical artistry of an individual speaker or the subtle coercions of disciplinary power. They result, rather, from the classification and circulation of texts as confessions.

What is needed, and what *Confessional Crises and Cultural Politics in Twentieth-Century America* provides, is an account of confession's power predicated not on any particular set of textual characteristics, but rather on the simple act of claiming a text as a confession or refusing to do so: a reception history. As Steven Mailloux has argued, reception studies are a rhetorical version of cultural studies. They are rhetorical because they attend to the specific ways that texts have been interpreted and classified; they are cultural because they work from the assumption that interpretation and classification are beholden to cultural norms. Under the heading of "rhetorical hermeneutics," Mailloux describes a reception study as follows: "Rhetorical hermeneutics is a form of cultural rhetoric study that takes as its topic specific historical acts of interpretation within their cultural contexts. It promotes a rhetorical history that embeds the act of interpretation in its most relevant critical debates (and there may be several) and locates these ongoing arguments within the rhetorical traditions of relevant institutional discourses."[21]

In *Confessional Crises*, I embed six historical acts of interpretation in their most relevant cultural debates: sexuality, class, race, violence, religion, and democracy. Throughout, I am at pains never to separate the always-shifting genre of confession from these wider cultural debates, through which particular understandings of confession were made relevant in particular moments. In this sense, *Confessional Crises* offers the first *political economy* of confession.[22] Stressing the relationship between the boundaries of the genre and the cultural politics of an age, I argue that the reclassification, declassification, and circulation of texts as confessions has been a potent means of influencing American cultural politics.

Confession and Authenticity

In addition to providing a history of texts that have been reclassified and circulated as confessions, *Confessional Crises and Cultural Politics in Twentieth-Century America* provides insight into why activists have so consistently turned to confessional hermeneutics as a technique of cultural intervention. One answer stands out from the lot: the sheer power of authenticity. It has driven both the reclassification of texts as confessions and the refusal to acknowledge the confessional status of a given text. Although Peter Brooks has claimed that the confession bears a "special stamp of authenticity," the reality is more complex.[23] *Confessional Crises* suggests that the simple act of labeling a text as a confession can either endow a text with an aura of authenticity or divest a text of authenticity. On the one hand, from the onset of the "modern confession industry" in 1919 forward, politically motivated citizens have been turning the unlikeliest of texts into confessions simply to cash in on the political cachet of the authentic. There is perhaps no better, more concise evidence of the political power of the link between authenticity and confession than this: when Twentieth Century-Fox sought to turn William Styron's *Confessions of Nat Turner* into a feature-length film, the Black Anti-Defamation Association insisted only that the film "must not bear the title of William Styron's book lest it lend validity to his falsification of history."[24] Fox complied.

On the other hand, while the political cachet of confession's "special stamp of authenticity" may be lucrative, it is also fragile. To the extent a confession is compelled or coerced, it is disqualified as an authentic expression. The very fact of the Miranda rights—not to mention their prominence in American popular culture—is evidence of just how tenuous is the link between confession and authenticity. Legally speaking, if a confession is not obtained in the proper manner, if the proper rituals are not observed, a confession will not be treated as authentic. Indeed, a coerced confession is definitively inauthentic, the product of an abusive power relation rather than an authentic expression of the self. On this score, labeling a text a confession de-authorizes both the text in question and the abusive power that produced it. The best evidence for the cultural power of the coerced confession is, again, the confessional crises of twentieth-century America. These demonstrate that, with as much intensity as partisan actors turned texts into confessions to cash in on the power of the authentic, they also turned texts into confessions to cash in on the power of the conspicuously inauthentic. Thus it was that the *New York Times* called on, of all people, the playwright Arthur Miller to explain the Starr Report—the choice itself suggesting that Starr's seven volumes constituted a forced confession and, as such, were inauthentic and could not be trusted.

Confession, then, is a volatile genre, and confessional hermeneutics is a dangerous activity. Labeling a text a confession may either endow it with an unmatched aura of authenticity or divest the text of authenticity and suggest that the power that compelled it is abusive. In either case, however, the power of the genre is calibrated not to textual features or recurrent formal characteristics, but rather to the sheer act of classifying a text as a confession. In each of the following chapters, we will see how confessional hermeneutics lends the power of authenticity, or sometimes the stigma of inauthenticity, to the embattled actors of American cultural politics.

Confessional Crises

There have been at least six confessional crises in twentieth-century America. In the pages that follow, I dedicate a chapter to each of them. Here I briefly introduce each one, and indicate the specific political questions that turned debates over whether particular texts count as confessions into large-scale political brouhahas.

Confession and Sexuality: True Story Magazine *Versus Anthony Comstock*

The first confessional crisis I examine was incited by the publication of Bernarr Macfadden's *True Story Magazine*. When the magazine first hit the newsstands in May 1919, it was the culmination of Macfadden's lifelong crusade against his sworn enemy, Anthony Comstock, the "Great Mogul of American Morals." Macfadden detested no one as much as he did Comstock, and *True Story* was designed as Macfadden's ultimate rebuttal of Comstock's pernicious influence over American sexuality. To Macfadden's mind, the confessions he published monthly in *True Story*, if they could only be properly understood, harbored the capacity to revolutionize conceptions of American sexuality. For this reason, Macfadden expended countless columns refining the genre of confession, educating the public on its proper deployment, and ensuring that the form itself could be placed in the service of his own, restrictive sexual politics.

Confession and Class: A New True Story

In chapter 2 I interrogate Bernarr Macfadden's 1930s claim that *True Story* constituted an ideal connection between producers and consumers. Because it was written by its readers, Macfadden explained, *True Story* not only carried advertisements to the masses, it also carried the masses—their subconscious desires, anxieties, and consumer impulses—back to business executives. Although this argument was an essential component in the gradual recognition of *True Story* as a distinctively confessional magazine, it must not be taken at face value. To make this claim, Macfadden redescribed the working class, telling business executives that workers were now defined by their expendable income, political docility, and overall contentedness. Macfadden, in other words, turned the working class into picture-perfect American consumers. The results were immediate: in addition to *True Story* becoming widely recognized as a confession magazine, the advertising dollars now flowed in. Yet—and this is my point—the very same strategy that turned *True Story* into a confession magazine and a commercial success also blinded a wide swath of Americans to the actual conditions of the working class. Because they were rendered invisible by Macfadden's rhetorical strategy, the actually existing working class paid the price of *True Story* becoming a confession magazine.

Confession and Race: Look's "Shocking Story" of Emmett Till

On October 28, 1955, the journalist William Bradford Huie signed a series of contracts with the murderers of Emmett Till. The contracts gave Huie the right to publish the killers' story of Till's murder in *Look* magazine, to quote the murderers at length, and to accuse them publicly of abduction and murder. However, the contracts did not give Huie the right to publish the killers' story *as a confession*. Because of this last point, Huie's "Shocking Story of Approved Murder in Mississippi" does not read as a confession. And yet nearly every reader of Huie's "Shocking Story" has followed the judgment of the renowned African American journalist James L. Hicks. Writing for

The Afro-American, Hicks claimed that "in the magazine article [the killers] simply confess that they killed Emmett Till."[25] How is it that "Shocking Story" is nearly universally remembered as a confession? More pressing still, why did both the NAACP *and* Mississippi's Citizens' Councils—two organizations that were deeply antagonistic, even offensive, to each other—*both* argue that Huie's "Shocking Story" was a confession?

These are the questions that animate chapter 3. Their answer lies in the combustible mixture of confession and the politics of the Second Reconstruction. For civil rights activists, if the "Shocking Story" was a confession, it provided them the leverage they needed to advocate for President Eisenhower's proposed Civil Rights Commission. For segregationists and southern apologists, the "Shocking Story" performed a different, but equally vital, service: it provided a sanitized version of Till's murder and a much-needed response to *Brown v. Board.* Thus with all parties standing to gain from Huie's rendering of the murder, how could it not become a confession? The South saw in the "Shocking Story" a chance to consign to oblivion the extent of the violence visited upon Emmett Till; the north saw documentable evidence of southern hypocrisy. For these reasons both sides had a stake in turning the article into a confession to better authorize the story and better advance their politics. The result was that, despite its manifold inaccuracies and partisan origins, Huie's version of Till's story became the authoritative account for nearly fifty years.

Confession and Violence: William Styron's Confessions of Nat Turner

Twelve years after the death of Emmett Till, the question of confession was once again at the center of American racial politics. On October 9, 1967, William Styron published *The Confessions of Nat Turner,* a historical novel based on Nat Turner's 1831 insurrection. Styron's white critics argued that his novel was a confession, his black critics argued it was not, but both sides returned to the generic question repeatedly, approached it from a variety of angles, and marshaled a wide range of resources to support their generic claims. The question I pursue in chapter 4 is why? Why were both sides preoccupied with the genre of the novel, and what does this preoccupation teach us about the genre of confession and the question of violence? In order to answer these questions I suggest the following: In the context of the 1960s, to take a position on the genre of the novel was, simultaneously, to take a position on two hotly contested, racially coded debates: first, a historiographical debate over the relative violence of American slaves; second, a postcolonial debate over the capacities of rhetoric to bridge the experiences of black and white Americans. Chapter 4 thus demonstrates how the genre of Styron's novel came to function as a heuristic within these larger debates over the role of violence in America's past and present.

Confession and Religion: Jimmy Swaggart's Apology

Twenty-one years after Styron's novel was released, Jimmy Swaggart incited another confessional crisis when, on February 21, 1988, he publicly confessed to the more than eight thousand people crowded into his Baton Rouge Family Worship Center. Although thousands may have witnessed Swaggart confess, precious few knew precisely why he chose February 21 to do so. Reverend Marvin Gorman, the across-town pastor whom Swaggart had publicly disgraced two years earlier, was getting his revenge by blackmailing Swaggart into making a confession. It might have played out in a church, but this was old-fashioned power politics. Armed with pictures of an escorted Swaggart entering and leaving a pay-by-the-hour motel, Gorman demanded Swaggart's confession.

Yet Swaggart had financial incentive not to confess. By 1988 he was raising more money than any other televangelist.[26] Moreover, his ministry was expensive and could not, as the *Houston Chronicle* put it, "afford his absence."[27] Swaggart was thus in a fix. On the one hand, he faced the photo-armed Marvin Gorman, who was demanding a public confession. On the other hand, the disclosures involved in a traditional, Christian confession threatened the economic stability of his ministry and, by extension, the spiritual vitality of numberless souls. How Swaggart negotiated this situation is the question of chapter 5. I argue that his response has much to teach us about the secularization of confession and, more generally, the place of religious discourse in public life.

Confession and Democracy: Bill Clinton Versus Kenneth Starr

By September 1998, Bill Clinton had confessed to an inappropriate relationship with Monica Lewinsky so many times that the news media began listing the confessions catalogue style. The listing of confessions, however, is never an innocent exercise. For, as I demonstrate in this chapter, the political debate over the guilt or innocence of Bill Clinton was indexed to a rhetorical debate over the definition of confession. For this reason, the seemingly innocent activity of listing certain texts as confessions was weighted with a new importance: to choose which texts counted as confessions was, in effect, to weigh in on Clinton's guilt. Chapter 6 asks which political positions required which texts to count as confessions. I argue that the Clinton administration radically expanded the list of texts that counted as confessions. It then aligned particular types of confession with the needs of a democratic polity and condemned other types of confession as a product of the invasive politics of Kenneth Starr. The result was not only the exoneration of Bill Clinton, but also a compelling redescription of public confession undertaken in the name of democracy itself.

Conclusion: Confessional Crises and Citizen Critics

Taken together, these six case studies bear witness to the power of the genre of confession. In each instance, the simple act of labeling an otherwise nonconfessional text as a confession was an important (and always contested) tactic in American cultural politics. The sheer diversity of texts that have been turned into confessions is a trenchant reminder that the cultural power of public confession cannot be explained with recourse to textual characteristics or formal properties. The only way to study the politics of confession in twentieth-century America is to study what people call a confession, no matter how unlikely a candidate it seems. For no established formal definition of confession—not Augustine's, not Rousseau's, not Freud's, not Foucault's—could possibly encompass Styron's novel or Starr's report. Each of these texts *became* confessions because confessional hermeneutics was driven not by academic questions regarding recurrent formal characteristics, but by patently political motives. This suggests that although the temptation to posit a substantive definition of confession is strong, it is a temptation that must be resisted. By determining in advance what counts as a confession, we will be closing ourselves off to the mainspring of confession's cultural power, a power that includes the ability to turn virtually any text into a confession.

In the pages that follow, I tell the stories of how and why politically motivated journalists, celebrities, writers, politicians, and ordinary citizens turned themselves into ad hoc literary critics, or what Rosa A. Eberly has called "citizen critics."[28] These "citizen critics" recognized clearly that confessional hermeneutics was an activity fraught with political ramifications. For this reason, these citizen critics have repeatedly refused the proprietary claims of the academy over the practice of genre criticism. At least when it comes to the genre of confession, there has simply been too much at stake to leave such demarcations to academics. As few academics have, these activists understood that confession is a product of its political economy and, accordingly, that the re- or declassification of a text as a confession is a particularly powerful mode of intervening in that economy.

As a means of reflecting on this last point, the conclusion to *Confessional Crises and Cultural Politics in Twentieth-Century America* examines the twenty-first-century confessional crisis incited by James Frey's *Million Little Pieces*—a brouhaha about which the *New York Times*' Frank Rich was fantastically wrong. Wrote Rich, "No one except pesky nitpickers much cares whether Mr. Frey's autobiography is true or not, or whether it sits on a fiction or nonfiction shelf at Barnes & Noble."[29] The fact of the matter, of course, is that nearly everyone cared. The controversy over Frey's so-called memoir was no different from the confessional crises that on six occasions punctuated twentieth-century American life. In every instance, the genre of confession demonstrated an incredible capacity for transforming political activists into literary critics and making virtually everyone care about the shelf on which a text is placed. I close with the story of Frey and the competing ways his book was classified as a concrete reminder that confessional politics are present politics. The rhetorical strategy of advancing partisan aims by controlling which texts count as confessions is alive and well. If, however, we are to understand Frey and the contemporary confessional crisis for which he has so often been made to stand, it is imperative that we look first to our twentieth-century history of confessional crises.

I

CONFESSION AND SEXUALITY: *TRUE STORY* VERSUS ANTHONY COMSTOCK

In May 1919, the eccentric American health crusader, sexologist, and entrepreneur Bernarr Macfadden published the first issue of *True Story Magazine*—and thus "the modern confessions industry came into being."[1] Within years *True Story* had dozens of imitators; George Gerbner reports that by mid-century the confession magazine industry boasted some forty titles.[2] The eventual ubiquity of the industry, however, must not occlude the fundamental importance of *True Story*. As the *Saturday Evening Post* put it, "The $10,000,000-a-year, I'm-Ruined! I'm Ruined! school of belles-lettres owes everything to Macfadden."[3] The *Post* is hardly alone in this estimate: *Scribner's* christened Macfadden "Father Confessor," *Harper's* called *True Story* the "first of the 'confessions,'" and the cultural historian Ann Fabian credits Macfadden's *True Story* with "turning the compulsion to confess into a glorious commercial enterprise." A "commercial enterprise" it certainly was. Fabian notes that *True Story* transformed Macfadden from an "eccentric health advocate to [a] millionaire."[4]

However, while Macfadden's wealth did not last his lifetime, his reputation as "Father Confessor to the American masses" was largely a *posthumous* designation.[5] Although the sheer financial success of *True Story* ensured that it registered on the cultural landscape almost immediately, it was not initially recognized as a confession magazine. Before it was a decade old, the *New Yorker*, *The Nation*, the *Atlantic Monthly*, a variety of trade journals, and *Hygeia*, the journal of the American Medical Association, had each devoted ample space to Macfadden's *True Story*. Yet none of these periodicals saw anything particularly confessional about it. In 1924, for example, the *Detroit Saturday Night* published one of the longest, most vindictive critiques of Macfadden that would appear in the 1920s. In it, *True Story* was decried as a "magazine for morons," designed for "the undeveloped, semi-literate, half-baked mentalities that can find no pabulum in real literature."[6] Despite the general thoroughness of the attack, the *Detroit Saturday Night* never once described *True Story* as a confession magazine. On the other end of the spectrum, the *New Yorker* used a 1925 column to praise the "God-driven pen of Bernarr Macfadden." Although it took pains to introduce *True Story*'s eccentric publisher, explain its unprecedented mechanism for securing manuscripts, and describe its bizarre criteria for publishing them, it, too, never once described *True Story* as a confession magazine—it never even used the word.[7] Similarly, a year later the *Atlantic Monthly* suggested that although *True Story* was stylistically similar to the confession magazines, it nonetheless occupied its own discrete category.[8] In sum, *True Story* was a lot of things in the 1920s: it was wildly successful and, depending on the reader, suggestive, uplifting, pornographic, "God-driven," moralistic, yellow, enlightened, pulpy, or authentic. But it was rarely—if ever—confessional.

Despite this, nearly every invocation of *True Story* since the 1940s remembers its founding in confessional terms. In 1950, for example, the *New Yorker* published a second series of articles on Bernarr Macfadden, this time arguing that Macfadden's "climactic achievement" could be traced to May 1919—the beginnings of his "fantastic success with 'confession' magazines." A similar pattern can be seen in *Time*: a 1927 article on Macfadden and his magazines nowhere mentions the word confession; thirty years later a 1957 article made confession the definitive characteristic of *True Story*.[9] This is nothing less than historical revisionism; it took until the 1950s for the 1920s *True Story* to become a confession magazine.

This revisionism is particularly conspicuous in the academic literature. In 1958 George Gerbner published his influential "Social Role of the Confession Magazine," which provided social scientific justification for the conclusions of the *Saturday Evening Post*. According to Gerbner, the confession magazine was "born" with *True Story*. In 1964 Theodore White followed suit: "In 1919, Macfadden fathered *True Story*, first of the confession magazines."[10] Then, in 1968, the historian William Taft: "In 1919, Macfadden turned his attention elsewhere, creating the 'confessions' business with *True Story*."[11] More recently still, Roseann M. Mandziuk has identified the first five years of *True Story* as a site par excellence to interrogate the commodification of confession.[12]

More surprising than the revisionism of popular journalism or academic literature, however, is the revisionism of *True Story* itself. Although the 1920s *True Story* largely avoided the term confession, in 1948 *True Story* recalled its own origins in explicitly confessional terms.[13] Ernest V. Heyn, then the editor of *True Story*, argued that the May 1919 appearance of *True Story* was simply the latest "offspring" in a "long line of first-person revelatory literature." Heyn then positioned *True Story* as the rhetorical "offspring" of Augustine, Benvenuto Cellini, Jean-Jacques Rousseau, and Thomas de Quincey—confession writers all. Although his mid-century readers may have been surprised by Heyn's suggestion that Augustine was the "world's first writer of a true story," they would certainly not have been surprised by the suggestion that *True Story* was a confession magazine.[14] For, as I hope is clear, in the middle years of the twentieth century there was a concerted effort—carried out by popular monthlies, brown quarterlies, and *True Story* itself—to revise the historical record and establish thereby that *True Story* always was what it later, indisputably became: a confession magazine.

This revisionism has been staggeringly successful. If there exists a single essay, article, blog, monograph, or book that challenges the *Saturday Evening Post*'s 1941 claim that *True Story* founded the confession industry in 1919, I am unaware of it. However, if we are to understand the politics of confession, it is imperative that we recover the initial cultural uncertainty that attended Macfadden's *True Story*. As the original articles in *Time*, the *New Yorker*, and the *Detroit Saturday Night* suggest, before *True Story* was self-evidently a confession magazine, it was the object of a confessional crisis: a very public debate over the meaning of *True Story*, its generic classification, and its proper place in American life. By bracketing our lately born certainty that *True Story* has always been a confession magazine, we will be able to tell a story that has never been told: the story of the remarkable energy Macfadden expended refining the genre of confession and deploying it as a political weapon in American cultural politics—the story, ultimately, of how, why, and for whom *True Story* became a confession magazine.

By telling this story over the course of the first two chapters of *Confessional Crises and Cultural Politics in Twentieth-Century America*, I argue that it is possible to understand how the genre of confession became ingredient in American conceptions of sexuality (chapter 1) and the working class (chapter 2). From its founding in 1919 through its 1926 editorial change, *True Story*'s primary political obstacle was the still-lurking specter of Anthony Comstock. The "Great Mogul of American Morals," the founder of the New York Society for the Suppression of Vice, and a sexual puritan of the most austere type, Comstock was Bernarr Macfadden's sworn enemy.¹⁵ Macfadden's antagonism to Comstock's sexual politics was fundamental to *True Story*'s founding and, mutatis mutandis, fundamental to the development of the "confessions business." Indeed, sexual politics were so integral to the rise of *True Story* that they defined the genre of the "true story" and recast the boundaries the "confession"—genres that Macfadden used interchangeably—turning both of them into rhetorical genres inherently dedicated to the preservation of a conservative sexual politics. Were it not for his preoccupation with American sexuality, Macfadden would have had no interest in the confessional genre and his magazine would have never dominated the birth and development of the "confessions industry." In very material ways, the United States owes its confessional culture to the conservative, oftentimes contradictory, always-extreme sexual politics of Bernarr Macfadden.

1905–1919: Anthony Comstock, Bernarr Macfadden, and the Prehistory of *True Story*

True Story Magazine was, in a very concrete sense, a direct response to Anthony Comstock's crusade to protect American moral purity. Although Comstock died four years before *True Story* began, Macfadden's 1905 quarrel with the self-proclaimed "weeder [of] God's Garden" would leave an indelible mark on Macfadden. Indeed, Macfadden's later moralism—his insistence that *True Story* contributes to the moral improvement of its readers—can be traced directly to his early conflict with Comstock. The occasion was Macfadden's "Monster Physical Culture Exhibition" at New York's Madison Square Garden. Half beauty pageant and half athletic competition, the exhibition drew twenty thousand New Yorkers to opening night on October 9, 1905—five thousand of whom were turned away by the fire inspector.¹⁶ Although Macfadden had advertised throughout the city, distributing posters of union-suited women and leopard-skinned men, the most effective advertisement was the fact that Comstock, by then infamous for his New York Society for the Suppression of Vice, regarded these posters as "the height of pornography and public impudence."¹⁷ Four days before opening night, acting as a "Special Agent for the United States Post Office Department," Comstock confiscated five hundred pounds of the "vile handbills" (posters) and arrested Macfadden.¹⁸ Curious to see what could provoke such an action, New Yorkers turned out en masse to see a show that was in fact quite tame. The historian William Hunt reports that there were "no nudes.

No erotic dances. Nothing titillating."[19] Compared to Macfadden's *Physical Culture Magazine*, which had since 1899 featured photos of topless women and loin-clothed men as specimens of bodily excellence, the exhibition proceeded along rather puritanical lines.[20]

Although, legally speaking, nothing came of Macfadden's 1905 arrest, historians agree that it inspired his lifelong crusade against prudery in general and Anthony Comstock in particular.[21] This crusade, which would culminate fourteen years later in the publication of *True Story*, received its opening salvo with a series of editorials in *Physical Culture*. Titled "Comstock, King of the Prudes," Macfadden's editorials argued that Comstock was responsible for prudery, which was, in turn, responsible for American "moral perversion," the "mental and physical decay" of its citizens, and the "pitiful deterioration of the race that you see on every hand." Treating "Comstockery" and "prudery" as convertible terms, Macfadden explained their meaning: "'Comstockery' has been added to our vocabulary as meaning the sniffing out of evil where no evil exists." As evidence, Macfadden pointed to the contested posters of the Physical Culture Exhibition. The posters, which Macfadden insisted were "simply representations of very perfect human forms," triggered in Comstock's mind "the grossest suggestions that the human mind could possibly conceive." If anything was "impure, salacious, and obscene," Macfadden countered, it was the mind of Comstock, which was little more than a "sewer for mental filth." Prudery was the product of Comstock's inability to distinguish the filth of his mind from the objects of his attention: "His perverted imagination finds vulgar and depraved meanings in a most inspiring sentence, or contorts the outlines of the most beautiful picture or statue into a semblance of vileness." We should not be surprised, Macfadden concluded, that a "perverted imagination" finds perversion everywhere it looks.[22]

Macfadden, however, was concerned with more than the subjective character of obscenity and the contested purity of his own posters. Indeed, the exhibition and its posters soon vanished entirely from Macfadden's editorials. From his perspective, the larger issue was methodological. Although Macfadden professed (but did not practice) a sexual austerity as conservative as Comstock's, he disagreed sharply with Comstock's method for achieving that austerity. As a drawing that prefaced one of his editorials made plain, Macfadden's primary objection was Comstock's belief that censorship and suppression produced moral purity. In the Foucauldian terminology fashionable today, Macfadden accused Comstock of subscribing to the "repressive hypothesis": the belief that power controls sexuality by repression, censorship, or obstruction.[23] The drawing pictured Comstock tying blindfolds on American children only to see them stumble blindly off cliffs labeled "excess" and "secret vice."[24] In case the moral was not self-evident, Macfadden laid it bare: Comstock "seem[s] to think that by simply hiding, by merely refraining from discussing the important subject of sex, that [parents] eliminate all thoughts on the subject from the minds of their offspring." Otherwise put, Comstock "cries out emphatically against knowledge and in favor of ignorance."[25]

Although Macfadden was obviously without the insight of Foucault (he was, for that matter, without the insight of any intellectual thought), he responded in a Foucauldian manner. He argued that in order for power to better control sexuality (a goal he shared with Comstock), it must work *with* knowledge rather than against it. From Macfadden's perspective, Comstock was simply naïve: no matter how severe the censorship, ignorance was not an option. Either American youth would be taught sexual morals by their parents or they would be taught by "evil companions": "Take your choice, Mr. Comstock. There is no dividing line." Thus, for the sake of the country, and with a rationale that would later become a monotonous refrain in the pages of *True Story*, Macfadden argued that moral virtue required an open, frank discussion of the human body, its vulnerabilities, and its capacities: "If you want your boy or girl to have pure thoughts in reference to themselves and their bodily functions, teach them the truth, in all its details. Teach them the wonders of the sex principle. Teach them the objects and the divinity of sex. Let them learn that fatherhood and motherhood exist solely because of sex. That the world owes everything to sex."[26] Thus did "power and knowledge directly imply one another."[27] The knowledge of the body was an essential ingredient in the power that Macfadden hoped would control the body.

In a pithy phrase that nicely captures the theory underwriting Macfadden's moralism, Clifford Waugh explains that, for Macfadden, "nakedness stood for truth undefiled." To portray the human body, omitting none of its details, was to speak the truth. Because prudery/Comstockery relied on the blindfold, Macfadden made "prudery . . . public enemy number one among the curses to be annihilated by Physical Culture."[28] Waugh explains the logic: "The only answer was education, which, in [Macfadden's] mind, automatically necessitated the total elimination of prudery. To control, if not to eliminate venereal disease, the public needed knowledge, and Macfadden was determined to meet that challenge. From the lecture platform, in his books, and through editorials and articles, the Father of Physical Culture spoke out against venereal disease and prostitution. Insisting that knowledge was power, he attempted to 'lift the veil' which he believed was 'shrouding subjects of the utmost importance to humanity.'"[29] And this, Macfadden explained, was why the exhibition and its posters required scantily clad participants: for how could the excellencies of the human body be demonstrated "if the exhibitors are dressed with clothing."[30]

The First Confession

In the fall of 1906, Macfadden took a decisive step. Working on the assumption that "realism was necessary in order to awaken the public," he decided to use a "confession" as a technique in his moralistic crusade against Comstockery.[31] At Macfadden's urging, *Physical Culture* editor (and future *True Story* editor) John R. Coryell wrote a six-installment serial titled "Growing to Manhood in Civilized (?) Society: The Personal Confessions of the Victim."[32] The serial was little more than Macfadden's anti-Comstock editorials translated into the confessional form. It told the story of the adolescent son of wealthy, syphilitic parents who "neglected to tell him the facts of life."[33] Kept in ignorance by his "parents and teachers," the unnamed protagonist confessed that he learned of sex "not by the parent or responsible teacher, but by a class of purveyors whose work is all done in darkness and secrecy." Relying on the subjugated knowledge of the stable, the boy learned "lewd words" and "obscene stories" by the end of the first installment.[34] The remaining five installments then charted the boy's moral degeneration: stolen caresses, drunkenness, sexual liaisons, pornography, venereal diseases, prostitution, and extortion—all told in the first person.

All of this was expressly calculated to dramatize the social consequences of Comstockery. Indeed, the most interesting aspect of the story is that, at regular intervals spread throughout the story, the author breaks from the narrative and interjects a meta-level commentary on it. It is as if Macfadden had learned from his experience with Comstock and the posters that portions of the reading public, unless they are properly coached, will see "nakedness" as obscenity rather than as "truth undefiled." This time around, Macfadden was taking no chances. Although "Growing to Manhood" was only slightly more suggestive than the Physical Culture Exhibition—there were descriptions of caresses and allusions to much more—Macfadden surrounded these descriptions and allusions with a running commentary that sought to restrict their range of meaning. "I cannot say enough to make it clear that under the system of suppression of truth about the facts of sex life, all boys become little ravening sex-wolves; little beasts." The descriptions and allusions, in other words, were designed to demonstrate the futility of a system that would ensure morality via censorship: "Plain speech is sometimes necessary." Indeed, had sex been discussed in a "frank, open manner," the morality of the confessant might have been preserved:[35] "But for the foul stream into which I had been thrown at the behest of immemorial custom, my soul might have been as white as hers [a girl on the verge of yielding to his temptations]."[36]

If it was too late to rescue the protagonist of "Growing to Manhood," the protagonist insisted that is was not too late to save others. Indeed, the telling of the story was motivated by the sense that the protagonist was just one of the numberless victims of a repressive society: "I am but the mouthpiece of thousands upon thousands of the victims of your wicked, wicked system of life." Against this wicked system of life, premised as it was on censorship and hypocrisy, stood the confession, premised on frank disclosure: "I am daring to tear the veil from the hypocrisy of our lives. I am daring to say that we are growing up a race of erotomaniacs. We think of nothing but sex, we talk of nothing but sex."[37] Although Comstock was not mentioned by name, it is not difficult to read the story—both in its form and in its content—as an attack on the "Great Mogul of American Morals." In language that explicitly recalls Macfadden's editorials against Comstock, the protagonist concluded that his self-described debauched existence "was the natural product of the scheme of life which is based upon pretence, upon systematic hypocrisy and upon that prurient prudery which converts the beautiful, natural sex attraction into a nervous disorder."[38]

"Growing to Manhood" quickly landed Macfadden a $2,000 fine and two years of "hard labor." After an unknown person directed the attention of the post office inspector to the confession, the federal grand jury of New Jersey found the story "obscene, lewd, and lascivious" and convicted Macfadden of "sending improper literature through the mails."[39] Countering that "Growing to Manhood" contained a "most valuable moral lesson," Macfadden protested vigorously.[40] Beyond the legal appeals (which he filed), and beyond the efforts of the Free Speech League (which carried his cause all the way to the Supreme Court), Macfadden took his case to the American public, declaring his innocence in *Physical Culture* editorials and public lectures across the eastern United States. Supportive crowds turned out en masse in Baltimore, Boston, Cincinnati, and Washington. For the most part, these crowds could hardly have been surprised by what they heard. Macfadden rehearsed his well-worn arguments about the subjectivity of obscenity, the moral imperative of frank speech, and the virtue of his own prose.

However, Macfadden's defense of "Growing to Manhood" included one very new argument. He defended not only the content of the confession and the purpose behind it, but also the form itself. Although the day was still a long ways off when he would consistently deploy the confession as a technique in cultural politics, he was already convinced that true stories were a powerful weapon in sexual politics. As he wrote in *Physical Culture*, "The day will come when the laws of this land, I fully believe, will encourage the publication of literature of this kind, because the evils so faithfully described in it, are ruining young men and young women everywhere by the thousands, simply because of their ignorance of the former."[41]

Thus did Macfadden use the controversy incited by "Growing to Manhood" to argue a rhetorical point. Indeed, unlike his defense of the exhibition posters, his defense of "Growing to Manhood" was defined less by its opposition to Anthony Comstock and more by its support of a rhetorical style marked by openness, truth, and exposure. As he put it in a 1908 booklet released in defense of "Growing to Manhood," "Plain speaking is the best remedy" for immorality. In the case at hand, Macfadden argued that his "confession" was "designed to serve as a warning against [erotic impulses]—instead of stimulating immoral passion it tended to arouse loathing and disgust." In a critical, instructive line, Macfadden concluded, "Neither in language nor in purpose was there any obscenity."[42] Macfadden, of course, had long insisted on his spotless motivations; now, in a move that presaged his later defenses of *True Story*, he argued that the language of "Growing to Manhood"—which he described as "plain speaking"—was itself a moral good. Not because it provided the absolution of sins, but because it was an important tool in his fight for austere sexual norms.

If Macfadden believed that the American people needed a moral reeducation, he believed just as insistently that they needed a rhetorical reeducation. Although he referred to his style as "plain speaking," and although his lawyer Henry Earle judged the virtue of "Growing to Manhood" to be "too obvious to require comment," Macfadden knew full well that there was nothing plain about the plain style.[43] Indeed, when we consider not only the meta-commentary inserted into the text of "Growing to Manhood," but also the editorials, booklets, and speaking tour that explained and defended it, it becomes clear that, at least for Macfadden, the plain style could never stand alone. Its very plainness rendered it vulnerable to misinterpretation by men like Anthony Comstock. Macfadden's lawyer complained, "There are men in the community to whose minds the mere presence of a woman, however chaste in bearing, will cause impure thoughts, and so may a book, picture or statue which is not in fact obscene."[44] What was needed was not simply the plain style, but a shared set of protocols for reading the plain style. Thus he beseeched his *Physical Culture* readership, "Help me in the education of the public. . . . Help each person realize the necessity for exposing these depraved conditions in order to finally destroy them." This is nothing less than a rhetorical education—a set of instructions for interpreting true stories and plain styles. The public must realize, he intoned, that the exposure of "sexual affairs" was an essential step toward "clean morals."[45]

Macfadden lost his argument regarding "Growing to Manhood." The United States Court of Appeals for the Third Circuit denied his appeal and the Supreme Court declined to hear it. Although the newly elected William Howard Taft granted Macfadden a presidential pardon and spared him the "hard labor," he was still required to pay a $2,000 fine for his first confession.[46] Though he lost his battle for "Growing to Manhood," he never gave up his crusade for a "literature of its kind." Although it would have to wait ten years, Macfadden never lost his conviction that moral reform required rhetorical reform. By 1918 Macfadden was explicit: moral reform went hand in hand with confessions—provided, of course, that these were surrounded by a set of reading protocols that restricted their range of meaning.

From Comstock to True Story

According to Fulton Oursler, the origins of *True Story* can be traced to a conversation between Macfadden and Coryell in the winter of 1918. Oursler reports that Macfadden had "never forgotten the public interest" raised by Coryell's "Growing to Manhood." Whatever Comstock or the Third Circuit may have thought, "the public had understood its intention and recognized its sincerity." The proof of this was the scores of letters that began arriving in the offices of *Physical Culture Magazine*. These letters, most of which "had the conscious ring of public confession," confirmed over and again the importance of Coryell's story.[47] As Macfadden recalled, "Some of these confessions were so charged with the drama of human hearts, so gripping in their intensity, so thrilling in the amazing combination of circumstances which they described, that reading this mail became a most interesting, and intensely thrilling undertaking."[48]

More than simply thrilling and interesting, however, the letters were also didactic. Like Coryell's "Growing to Manhood," they preached "the folly of transgression, the terrible effects of ignorance, [and] the [tragedy of] girls who had not been warned by wise parents."[49] Macfadden described these spontaneous confessions as "documents written in the tears of strong men and beautiful women, documents which bared the hope and sorrow, the joys and the disappointments, the broken faith and the dreams that came true, of thousands of human beings like ourselves—documents that were somehow written on the parchment of human nature, a part of the fabric of life, and, *above all, documents containing lessons from our own days and years, lessons conveyed through episodes which had seared their meaning into the souls of people with the white-hot brand of personal experience.*"[50] Although it is unclear whether it was Macfadden or his third wife who first thought of making these letters the basis of a new magazine (both partners claim exclusive credit), all agree that they were the origin of *True Story Magazine*. The value of these letters resided in both their form (confessional) and their function (didactic); they were, as Oursler would put it, both "confessions" and "parables."[51]

It is important to note that from its very inception, *True Story* was a didactic, moralistic enterprise *and* that the success of this enterprise—from the perspective of Macfadden and his associates—was tied directly to the confessional form. Consider the narrative of Fulton Oursler; he argued that *True Story* is best understood as the institutionalization of the didactic project begun with "Growing to Manhood." He argued that the original impetus behind "Growing to Manhood" was Macfadden's frustration with the editorial genre. Realizing that editorials were ineffectual in "his campaign against prudery," Macfadden searched for a better way to instruct the masses. "What could he do to wake up the public?" Oursler asked. The idea of using a firsthand confession to instruct and elevate the masses then appeared to Macfadden "with all the force and brightness of an inspiration. The greatest teachers of mankind had found in the parable the direct and the most potent weapon. The human mind responded to the story more quickly than to any other appeal. Why not show, in story form, the tragic consequences of 'Wild Oats.'"[52]

This is what Coryell did with "Growing to Manhood," and it is what Macfadden did with *True Story*. Using precisely the same language he used to describe Coryell's story, Oursler claimed that *True Story* was "an entire magazine devoted to confessions, to modern parables."[53] The only difference between Coryell's "Growing to Manhood" and Macfadden's *True Story* was that the latter was an "entire magazine." And just as "Growing to Manhood" was intended as an attack on the moral theory of Comstock, so, too, was *True Story*. Although *True Story* never mentioned Comstock by name, it is often difficult not to read it as a direct response to Comstockery. Consider, for example, this 1925 editorial: "Life is filled with realities and the only way to face realities is to face them—to know the TRUTH. It is the prudes and puritans who are afraid to face realities, who are ashamed to know the truth. And it was the prudes and puritans who burned poor, defenseless old women in Salem as witches."[54] Oursler makes the anti-Comstock politics of *True Story* explicit: "Out of his conviction that frankness would end such misery, Macfadden had long ago invented an epithet. To him it had all the force of an imprecation. That epithet was 'Comstockery!' *This* True Story Magazine *was his answer to 'Comstockery' and all for which, in his mind, the epithet stands.*"[55]

The "origin of *True Story*," then, "lies directly in Macfadden's previous physical culture career."[56] That career had pitted him against Anthony Comstock. And although Comstock had been dead three years by the time the idea of *True Story* was broached, the magazine was nonetheless conceived as a response to the sexual moralism that was still carried on in his name.

Just as surely as Macfadden remembered the power of Coryell's confession and its public resonance, he also remembered the bitter fight it engendered (he did not stop appealing his $2,000 fine until 1939).[57] Oursler reports that Macfadden was fully cognizant that *True Story* would "stir up the old antagonisms" with those who had inherited Comstock's mantle. For, as he had written in 1905, Comstock "stands for mystery, secrecy, ignorance, [and] superstition."[58] Now, preparing to launch an entire magazine based on plain speaking, a frank style, and true stories—a magazine, moreover, designed expressly as an attack on Comstockery—Macfadden knew that "it would be the old fight all over again": "If he dared to offer in the pages of a magazine, the lessons of life dramatized in the form of realistic stories, their moral implications made plain, the world would question his sincerity, and all the battalions of prudery would soon be on the march against him."[59]

Thus Macfadden designed *True Story* in such a way that he could defend himself from these battalions. He surrounded his true stories with constant reminders of *True Story*'s didactic purpose and moral foundations. These reminders functioned as a rhetorical primer—coaching *True Story*'s readership in the protocols of reading confessions, teaching them to place promiscuity, suggestiveness, and sexuality itself in the service of a conservative politics. As Oursler put it, "The millions who buy the magazine, and who think by its precepts and advice, believe that it is just what it offers itself to be—a book of modern parables."[60]

1919–1926: *True Story* as a "Great Moral Force"

From 1919 to 1926, *True Story* sold itself as precisely this: a book of modern parables. This is no small accomplishment. In an era that witnessed the Christian Endeavor Society, legislation regulating the maximum distance between ankle and hem (three inches), and, of course, the continued flourishing of the New York Society for the Suppression of Vice, now under the leadership of John Saxton Sumner, the sheer fact that a magazine designed to speak openly of sexuality could be marketed as an outpost of moral rectitude is itself a significant feat.

Selling "nakedness" as "truth undefiled," however, required far more than confessions and an editorial policy that prescribed that the "shadow of a bed" must fall on "every page."[61] As Macfadden was painfully aware, these were all too susceptible to co-optation by those for whom they were obscene. Thus *True Story* literally surrounded its confessions with explanations and rationalizations. Indeed, one of the most remarkable things about the early years of *True Story* is its sheer fascination with itself. The first fourteen volumes (1919–26) dedicated incredible amounts of ink and space to explaining the "true story idea." While I interrogate and explain this "idea" below, I begin by simply stressing the sheer effort expended to ensure that no reader of *True Story* could miss the nearly puritanical morality of the confession.

True Story *as a Rhetorical Primer*

True Story's 1925 editorial comment that "it is well every now and then to emphasize the purpose of our policy in publishing only true-to-life stories" is a massive understatement.[62] Alongside its true stories, *True Story* constantly emphasized its policies, explained its convictions, and demarcated itself from the wider run of American magazines. All of these emphases, explanations, and comparisons served as a rhetorical primer, teaching its readership how to read a confession. It was an education advanced by numerous mechanisms.

First, from its inception in 1919 until it was printing two million copies of each issue in 1926, *True Story* reserved a page-length sidebar on page 2 of each issue for explaining the "true story idea." In November 1924 *True Story* gave this sidebar to an advertisement for the American Red Cross, and in the years that followed the space would occasionally be used to advertise future issues of the magazine. In every issue until November 1924, however, and the vast majority of issues thereafter, the page 2 sidebar was wholly dedicated to explaining the mission and mechanics of *True Story*. These columns explained how the magazine collected its material, announced increasingly lucrative prizes for the best story submitted in a particular year, and, above all, laid out the criteria that determined which submissions measured up to the "true story idea."

Second, in addition to the page 2 sidebars, each issue of *True Story* contained numerous invitations for readers to submit their own true stories. These invitations often took the form of full-page advertisements, in which, after a prize was briefly but conspicuously announced, the requirements, philosophy, and morals of *True Story* were explained at length. Complementing these full-page invitations, the early issues of *True Story* were littered with sidebar-sized invitations. Often filling the blank space between the end of a story and the bottom of a page, these smaller invitations performed a similar function: announcing prizes, the criteria according to which they could be won, and the moral undergirding of *True Story*.

Third, in addition to the page 2 sidebars and the ubiquitous solicitations, the "true story idea" was disseminated through monthly editorials. Beginning in August 1921, Bernarr Macfadden wrote a one-page editorial for each issue. Most often, these editorials were trite, cliché-filled meditations on banal topics—the product, as Robert Ernst put it, of "the simple intensity of a believer who had no fear of the obvious."[63] About twice a year, however, interposed between these cliché-ridden rehearsals of Benjamin Franklin–style truisms—such as "honesty is the best policy"—Macfadden used his editorial column to explain the "true story idea," to defend the magazine against its competitors, to celebrate its accomplishments, and to explain its morality.[64] These editorials were in substance virtually indistinguishable from the page 2 sidebars and the solicitations for manuscripts that filled the pages of *True Story*.

Finally, the success of *True Story* imitators forced Macfadden to dedicate even more space to explaining and defending the "true story idea." In 1922 W. H. Fawcett introduced *True Confessions*, which sold out its first issue and was "for years second only to *True Story* in circulation."[65] Although the competition did not immediately register in *True Story*'s pages, by the spring of 1924, *True Story* apparently felt the need to defend itself. "The public is being deceived today by magazines being produced in imitation of *True Story*," the editors of *True Story* protested. This deceit, they continued, constituted "one of the most contemptible literary frauds in the history of American journalism, and the editors of *True Story Magazine* feel that they have a responsibility in exposing this condition."[66] Expose it they did. From April 1924 forward, *True Story* marshaled all its resources in order to defend its home ground against impostors. In addition to using the page-two sidebar and Macfadden's editorials to parse *True Story* and its imitators, Macfadden published selected letters to the editor and a number of feature articles all dedicated to the comparative superiority of *True Story*. In addition to defending *True Story*, these defenses functioned, once again, to explain *True Story* to its readership: its philosophy was laid bare and its moral virtue rehearsed.

The cumulative result of all these interventions—the sidebars, invitations, editorials, and comparisons—was a highly self-referential magazine. It is only a slight exaggeration to say that for every true story published, *True Story* also published a corresponding rationale explaining why they published it. It is almost as if, between and beneath every confession, the editors of *True Story* felt compelled to make their editorial criteria explicit. If they couldn't do so using a full-page explanation, they certainly could (and did) use several sidebars per issue. I trust by this point the reason they did so is clear: *True Story* was a direct outgrowth of Macfadden's lifelong battle with Comstockery—a battle that had forced on Macfadden the realization that nakedness, rhetorical or otherwise, was almost by definition liable to be misunderstood. To counter this possibility, *True Story* refused to allow true stories to speak for themselves. Despite *True Story*'s much-rehearsed claim that it was simply an unfiltered conduit of the American working-class experience, the sidebars, the ever-present solicitations, the carefully selected and dutifully printed letters to the editor, and the denunciations of the broader confession industry all served to filter the American experience and ensure that no one could miss the purportedly obvious fact that *True Story*—like the confessions that filled it—was a moral venture.

Authenticity and True Story

At the heart of the "true story idea" was Macfadden's insistence that *True Story* was written *by* its readers, *for* its readers, and *of* its readers.[67] Inspired by the letters he received in response to Coryell's confession, Macfadden offered one cent per word for confessions. He solicited manuscripts thus: "Simply describe as directly as you can, without omitting necessary details, what you consider the most interesting experience of your life." Typewriting helpful but not imperative. The cultural historian Ann Fabian underscores the importance of this fact: "Macfadden's great innovation was to offer his readers a hand in the production of the artifacts they so happily consumed, to urge them at every turn to become writers as well as readers, producers as well as consumers."⁶⁸ The editors of *True Story* knew as much. As they put it in May 1920, *True Story* is a "unique and distinctive magazine because its method of obtaining its material is unique and distinctive. It depends upon folk just like yourself to provide the stories, short and long, that appear in its pages—rather than upon a relatively small group of professional writers."⁶⁹ In a 1922 article titled "What *Is* the *True Story* Idea?" the editors argued that the "success" of the magazine was "chiefly due to its readers' response to its invitation to bare their life stories on the printed page."⁷⁰ One year later, the editors were even more emphatic: "The very corner-stone upon which *True Story* is built—the *True Story* idea itself—is its encouragement to everyday men and women, and not to professional writers alone, to set down their life-stories in black and white."⁷¹

True Story's insistence that it is written by its readers justified the vernacular style of its prose. This is Macfadden: "It was the purpose of this new magazine to present, not the highly colored imaginative plots of men who made story writing a business . . . but to take the unvarnished, rude, and sometimes even illiterate words and phrases of people who were not selling their imaginations, but who were giving memories to the world for whatever these memories might be worth."⁷² Almost every call for manuscripts emphasized that rhetorical skill, grammatical facility, and literary training were not required. Consider this 1922 advertisement: "*True Story*, you know, is unique among other things for the opportunities it affords the untrained and unexperienced [sic] writer. One who has a story to tell need have no misgivings as to his brainchild failing of recognition because its parent lacks literary experience."⁷³ Four years later, the line is the same: "We do not want the fiction of professional writers. We want throbbing dramas from the hearts and lives of people who have lived them."⁷⁴ In sum, *True Story*'s claim that it was written by its readers was indistinguishable from its "unpolished," vernacular style.

True Story's relentless pursuit of unvarnished prose led H. L. Mencken to envision the "perfect" Macfadden magazine as follows: "There will be no word of more than one syllable, and no word at all that might be a picture. The news of the day will be told precisely as the gory fictions of the comic strips are not told—in a series of graphs, with an occasional balloon. And the vocabulary of the balloons will be restricted to such terms as even infants of three are hep to: blaah, bang, boom, shhhh, wow, woof, hell, damn, and so on."⁷⁵ For Mencken and his *American Mercury* readership, the monosyllabic character of *True Story* was evidence of thoughtlessness, immaturity, and infantilization. For *True Story*, however, "unvarnished prose" was evidence of authenticity and an essential step in turning *True Story* into a parable.

Indeed, it is impossible to understand *True Story* without stressing that the "unvarnished, rude and . . . illiterate" prose of the people was not merely tolerated by *True Story* in order to secure more manuscripts. Illiteracy was itself a positive good. It both testified to the authenticity of the working class and distinguished confessional prose from that composed by professional writers. According to Fulton Oursler's recollection, Macfadden expressly forbid his first editor, John Brennan, from "using a fancy pencil on a *True Story* manuscript": "I don't want these stories to have any polish that doesn't naturally belong to them." Oursler explained Macfadden's logic: "He did not care how crudely [the stories] might be expressed. *In that very crudity he sensed the qualities of strength and conviction.*"[76] In George Gerbner's account, *True Story* required a disregard for proper grammar; he quotes an unnamed confession writer thus: "In the breathless rush of words, grammar, syntax, correct antecedents went overboard. Where they didn't, I went back and threw them out. The story sold."[77] The reason the story sold is that, according to the "true story idea," grammar, syntax, and antecedents undermine what Gerbner called the "flavor of authenticity."[78] Although Gerbner did not make this explicit, Macfadden did:

> Fiction stories are inventions of the author's brain. The manuscripts which find their way to *True Story*'s pages are not inventions at all, and they were not born in the brain but in the heart. They reflect life because they are life. The fiction story is only what the individual author thinks of life. The True Story is taken right out of the life of the man or woman who sends it to us. The fiction writer in his eagerness colors the truth. He tries to add more reality but by his very effort he takes away reality. Because truth is stranger than fiction and the imagination cannot begin to compete with life.[79]

There could hardly be a more compact synopsis of the *True Story* conceit: professional writers invent fictions; *True Story* writers, strictly speaking, do not *invent* anything at all. They simply, as it were, transcribe life onto the written page, a task for which the paucity of their rhetorical skill suited them perfectly. The imperfections of their prose guaranteed the authenticity of their confession.

To ensure that *True Story* retained its "flavor of authenticity," Macfadden assembled an editorial board wholly ignorant of "ideas on structure, on technique, [and] . . . artistic narrative quality." Oursler recalls that Macfadden filled his storied "Reading Department" with "girls and boys who knew nothing whatever about the publishing business."[80] The *Saturday Evening Post* caricatured Macfadden's Reading Department as a "corps of editors consisting of cooks, housemaids, office boys, chauffeurs, janitors, filing clerks, housewives, night-club hostesses, stenographers, elevator men and typewriter repairers."[81] A well-documented legend even holds that Macfadden fired two of his editors for taking courses in journalism.[82] According to Macfadden's third wife, one member of his editorial board even wrote an essay titled "How I Was Demoted to Editor of *True Story* and Worked My Way up to Elevator Man Again!"[83] Finally, when *True Story* turned into an unprecedented success, the *Saturday Evening Post* concluded that Macfadden "was on the verge of proving that illiteracy was the highest culture and that blank minds should be ruling the world."[84]

As amusing as these anecdotes are, it is important that we not lose sight of their function. If Macfadden insisted on his editors' rhetorical ignorance, it is because this ignorance could guarantee the authenticity of the confessions he published. This much Macfadden made explicit. He argued that the fact that his stories were written by "folk who will write but one story in all their existence . . . serves as a guarantee of their truth."[85] Similarly, in an undated (but likely 1930s) speech given by Dorothy Kemble to explain the inner workings of Macfadden Publications, she explained how, precisely, the public could be sure that *True Story* printed true stories: "If you could see the manner in which hundreds of these stories are submitted, I think that your question would be answered. Sometimes they are submitted on old school pads, the type we used in grammar school, sometimes in note books or on the back of scrap paper. I have even seen some stories written on plain brown wrapping paper. But in order to make doubly sure of their authenticity, an affidavit is required."[86] For Kemble, the affidavit is repetitive. The unpolished presentation of the submissions—the fact that they are scribbled on school pads and scrap paper—is Kemble's primary evidence for the truth of *True Story*. It is as if the nuanced prose of the legal contract was made unnecessary by the unvarnished prose of the stories themselves. Mark Adams got it completely right when he claimed that Macfadden "equated crudity with verisimilitude."[87]

Thus far, the "true story idea" is this: the magazine prints only the rude prose of its readers, the quality of the prose guaranteeing *True Story*'s claim to be an unfiltered conduit of the American working-class experience. The equation of rude prose and authentic truth, however, was only half of the "true story idea." The other half was the equation of authenticity and Macfadden's own sexual politics. It is to this troublesome equation I now turn.

Authenticity, Moralism, and Sexuality

There is, of course, nothing self-evident about the equation of authenticity and sexual morality. In fact, many of Macfadden's detractors conceded that *True Story* may be an authentic reflection of American culture, but they were not about to conclude on these grounds that it was, as Macfadden claimed, a "great moral force."[88] To ensure not only that his readers would perceive *True Story*'s confessions as authentic, but that they would also understand authenticity in the proper sense, Macfadden deployed once more his endless sidebars, solicitations, and editorials. All of these were placed in the service of restricting the range of authenticity, of governing the scales on which it could register, and of assuring that it was placed in the service of a conservative sexual politics.

At this point it is essential to recall Macfadden's particular brand of morality. At the turn of the century, Macfadden's primary argument against Comstock was that social morality required that the truth of the "sex principle" be expounded in "all its details."[89] In the 1920s, Macfadden understood *True Story* in precisely these terms: it was an unflinching register of true life, and for this reason an unparalleled source of moral instruction. For example, in a 1925 editorial that recalls the argument of Coryell's "Growing to Manhood," Macfadden argued that American children will learn about sexuality one way or another: "If you refuse to satisfy youthful curiosity by giving them the truth properly and reverently presented, they often absorb from questionable associates vulgar and vile distortions of some of the most divine phases of life." And such "vile distortions" gleaned from the subjugated knowledges of "questionable associates" had grave social consequences: "They have made a hell on earth for literally millions of poor victims who have been reared amidst falsehoods." From this point, it is a short step to *True Story*'s moral value. As an antidote to the danger of such "vulgar and vile distortions," Macfadden celebrated *True Story* as a didactic source of "naked truth, reverently presented": "If you are armed with the truth you cannot be deceived by evil. You know the nature of its influence, and you have only yourself to blame if you fall by the wayside. *True Story* is a great beacon of light which sheds a brilliant radiance upon life's pathway. It shows you the way. It warns you of your dangers. It is a school of experience from which you can learn without suffering the tortures of the poor struggling victims that are caught in its meshes."[90] Macfadden's claim that *True Story* is a "school of experience" perfectly captures the magazine's moral conceit. It was a "great beacon of light" precisely because it set the "naked truth" in bold relief.

Throughout the pages of *True Story*, Macfadden returned over and again to the claim that experience, unfiltered and reverently presented, was an intrinsic moral guide for disillusioned American youth. In 1922, for example, he dramatized the instructive character of authentic experience by telling the story of a fiction reader's brush with death. The reader in question had patterned her life on ideals taken from novels and subsequently "paid the price that comes with ideals that are false." In *True Story* fashion, Macfadden then made the moral of the story explicit: because novels do not "teach life as it is," they are an unworthy source of ideals. *True Story*, by contrast, because its confessions have "truth for a background," will provide ideals that will "stand the storms and stress of life."[91]

A year later, Macfadden argued that although experience is unquestionably the "greatest teacher," there are some situations in which the price exacted by experience is simply too high. He provided the example of poison. Although lessons from experience are more powerful than lessons from books, it is not worth learning about poison firsthand. This, Macfadden argued, is the virtue of *True Story*: through it you can "learn from the faults and failures of other people." It provides all the benefits of learning from experience without the burden of experience itself. This is Macfadden: "Experience as it is dramatically presented to you in *True Story* is indeed an invaluable teacher. While you read with fascinating interest the dramatic details of the trials and struggles of the characters presented therein, you are learning from others through their personal experiences—the greatest of all teachers, and it is a fascinating pastime. *True Story* fills an invaluable need. It presents the truth as it is lived by those in your own sphere of life."[92] In short, Macfadden claimed, "*True Story Magazine* came into being with the sole ideal of living up to its name, to tell the truth about life, so that others might learn its lessons without enduring the suffering consequent upon so many of these personal experiences."[93]

The years made Macfadden only more insistent and more explicit about the moral value of *True Story*. In April 1924, he penned a two-page editorial titled "*True Story Magazine*: A Great Moral Force," in which he laid out the "high ideals back of this publication." He argued that *True Story* "readers are made better morally, mentally, spiritually and even physically through the influence of the stories published herein."[94] Rehearsing arguments forged in his early battles with Comstock, Macfadden argued that ignorance facilitates personal and cultural decay: "The Evils that were everywhere devitalizing the race, the tragedies that have crushed human lives often beyond recall were presented in such great detail that I could not fail to see the truth in all its appalling aspects. And standing out from these mountains of human catastrophes was the ever present excuse: 'I DID NOT KNOW!'" Americans "fell into Evil," Macfadden concluded, because "they did not recognize its character."[95]

Against the power of a misrecognized evil, "*True Story* lights life's pathway. It sheds brilliant rays of knowledge upon the road that everyone must travel." It "sets up warning signs," it decries "selfishness and greed," and it exposes the "tremendous force" of the "sex instinct." On this last, volatile subject, Macfadden emphasized that *True Story* "clearly indicat[es] the necessity of living in conformity with the great moral law laid down by Jesus of Nazareth": "THE WAGES OF SIN IS DEATH." *True Story Magazine*, Macfadden concluded, "clearly and emphatically put forth this great Biblical truth." By putting this truth in the form of "strikingly dramatic, intensely interesting stories," *True Story* provided "education in the form of entertainment." And, I might add, entertainment in the form of confessions in which no moral was left to the imagination of the reader.

So confident was Macfadden in the high moral calling of *True Story* that he set up a "ministerial advisory board." Composed of clergymen from a variety of faiths, the board was given full authority over every article slotted for publication in *True Story*. Although there is no way to verify this, Oursler claimed in 1929 that since the board's constitution not an article had been printed in *True Story* without the full approval of the ministers.[96] What can be verified is the energy Macfadden spent reminding his readers that each true story had already received clerical sanction. To publicize his ministerial board, Macfadden occasionally dedicated a page or two of *True Story* to reprinting quotations culled from ministers and other readers. Typically arranged in two columns under an oversized title that announced *True Story* as a "Great Moral Force," these quotations were presented as evidence of *True Story*'s moral virtue and they functioned as a constant reminder of how the bed shadows that filled the pages of *True Story* were to be read.[97] The quotations themselves are deeply repetitive; a small selection may stand in for the lot. A certain Mrs. O. H. England wrote, "The stories are morally refreshing, for while they take us through the tunnels of life, they always bring us safely back to the sunlight of duty's path. There is an uplifting afterthought and theme in its stories which distinguish them from and make them superior to any other stories of sex and life. After one reads some of the magazines of sex stories, there follows a feeling mental degradation and an inclination to conceal them from the eyes of our associates. But I am always proud to have my copy of *True Story* lying in a conspicuous place."[98]

Surrounding Mrs. England's excerpted opinion were twelve other quotations of similar length and similar substance. From a broader perspective, this page of quotations testifying to *True Story*'s "moral force" was itself surrounded, in the proximate issues, by more quotation-filled, minister-laden pages bearing witness to the "sunlit path" of *True Story*. Taken together, these quotations provide *True Story*'s readership with a massive and intrusive rhetorical primer. They provide instructions for reading authenticity. Lest authentic stories of human sexuality be interpreted as salacious or lewd, the rhetorical primer—provided by *True Story* in the form of ministerial letters to the editor—provided a hermeneutic according to which the bed shadows testified to their own darkness and pushed the reader toward duty's "sunlit path."

Finally, and perhaps most tellingly, Macfadden used the shortcomings of the other confession magazines as an opportunity to teach his readers about the genre of the true story and how it was to be read. In May 1924 he carefully distinguished *True Story* from its competition on the basis of its moral rigor. Given the "extraordinary demand" for true stories, Macfadden noted that imitators were inevitable. Moreover, he insisted, "we have no objection to them when their efforts are imbued by the high ideals that inspire our *True Story* product." Unfortunately, Macfadden noted that the competition was "unwholesome," "lewd and obscene": "Their idea of a true story is an all-around filthy tale that presents lascivious details of various kinds." Macfadden, for his part, claimed a very different definition of a true story, and a different definition of authenticity: "We believe that [true] stories should be made to assume an attitude of respect towards the highest type of morality, and that the outworkings of human instincts and emotions should be portrayed naturally, cleanly as well as dramatically. For twenty-five years the publishers of *True Story* have been engaged in publishing literature that has had a distinctly upbuilding influence upon its readers. It has helped to make their lives more wholesome, more satisfying and more successful."[99] Macfadden's claim—made in 1924, five years into *True Story*'s life—that he had been publishing "upbuilding" literature for twenty-five years is telling. It reveals that, from Macfadden's perspective, *True Story* was a continuation of *Physical Culture*, which, besides being founded in 1899, was expressly dedicated to fighting Comstock's morality by censorship.[100]

This is the "true story idea": the unvarnished prose guarantees the authenticity of the tales, and the authenticity of tales guarantees the propagation of moral virtue. If both of these equations were rehearsed ad nauseam, it is because both were highly contested. Macfadden was fighting not only the likes of Mencken, who argued that unrefined prose was a signal of unrefined thought, but also a Comstock-inspired reaction that decried *True Story* as lewd, suggestive, and even pornographic.[101] With such opponents as these, and with the meaning of confession in the balance, is it any surprise that Macfadden took extra care to ensure that the two million readers in his charge understood clearly the genre of confession and the sexual politics it served?

Conclusion: Confession and Sexuality

Lurking in the founding and development of *True Story Magazine* are three important lessons for rhetorical critics. First, in the 1920s the boundaries of the confession were redrawn along political lines. Why did Macfadden bar his first editor from using a "fancy pencil"? Why did he insist on unvarnished prose and stories composed of monosyllabic words? Answer: His own sexual politics. Macfadden's crusade against Comstock required him to emphasize the truth of his stories, and the unvarnished, monosyllabic form of his confessions was a powerful means of doing so. If, as I have elsewhere suggested, the equation of inarticulacy and authenticity has become a standard marker of our contemporary confessional culture, it is important to remember that this equation is never self-evident.[102] In the case of Macfadden and *True Story*, it was driven by his political agenda.

Second, if cultural politics influenced the very form of the confession, the development of the genre was itself ingredient in the shaping of American sexual mores. Greg Mullins has insightfully called Macfadden's *Physical Culture* a "well-muscled closet." On his reading, the magazine displayed erotic pictures of the nude male body, but diffused the erotic charge by restricting the range of the nude body's meaning to aesthetic or medical values.[103] Following the same logic, it is possible to understand *True Story* as a "confessional closet." It was a place where the confessional form itself was placed in the service of conservative sexual politics. Lest his readership miss this point, Macfadden surrounded every illicit story with sidebars, explanations, and rationalizations aplenty—all designed to reinforce the association between nakedness and Christian virtue. So long as Macfadden had his way, bed shadows, stories of sexual deviancy, and even experience itself confirmed the legitimacy of the most austere sexual politics. When we consider the reach of Macfadden's influence—that he reached two million, mostly undereducated, working-class readers throughout the 1920s—it is hard to fathom that his twin claims of providing both an unfiltered conduit of the American experience *and* a Christian moral primer did not collude with each other and thereby become ingredient in the production of the heteronormative sexual culture that was twentieth-century America. Although I do not know how we might measure *True Story*'s influence on this score, I do know how we can judge Macfadden: he turned his bountiful resources toward the naturalization of his own sexual politics, and for this he remains culpable. That Macfadden's most powerful instrument of naturalization was the confession stands as a reminder to rhetorical critics that genres and genre criticism must not be taken lightly. It stands also as a rejection of Rod Hart's trivialization of genre criticism. Hart put it this way: "To my way of thinking, no particularly exalted intellectual function is served by tucking each of the world's little speeches into its own little generic bed."[104] However, to Macfadden's way of thinking, the categorization of his magazine served an exalted *political* function. And to my way of thinking, the suggestion that the categorization of texts is innocent, pedantic, or trivial amounts to a studied refusal to look at a major form of cultural politics.

Finally, one of the most remarkable things about the development of *True Story* from 1905 forward, is Macfadden's keen awareness of what we might call the emptiness of authenticity. Although he never articulated it quite this way, on some level Macfadden knew that the meaning of authenticity was neither self-evident nor transcendent. Put rhetorically, he knew that no matter the context, it was insufficient simply to defend his magazine as authentic. In addition to such a defense, Macfadden carried the further burden of making authenticity serve his own politics. This is the reason why the early years of *True Story* are overrun with sidebars, editorials, and explanations. Macfadden knew that he had to not only provide confessions, but also provide a protocol for reading them correctly.

There is a general lesson here. Confession, like Macfadden's authenticity, is not a transcendent genre, the contours of which could be adduced equally well from any number of situations. Quite the opposite. Confession might be called an empty signifier. It means different things at different times as different people put it to different ends. The task for rhetorical critics, then, is not the delineation of the form; it is, rather, in charting how various delineations have served various partisan agendas. What is needed—and what I've tried to provide—is a *political economy of confession*: an analysis of the genre that grants primary importance to the political commitments that provoked and defined the genre of confession in a particular instance. For the moment we lift any confession out of the political economy which required and defined it, we risk thinking that there exists some transcendent form of confession against which particular performances can be judged. While such criticism may be able to explicate formal changes in the genre over time—and here I have Foucault in my sights—it could not, as a matter of course, explain the politics of confession.

In the 1920s, the genre of confession was situated vis-à-vis the development of *True Story* and Macfadden's lifelong crusade against Anthony Comstock's sexual politics. In this political economy, confession was defined in a very particular way and according to the strictest of politics. As a hedge against mistaking this 1920s vision of confession for confession in general, in the next chapter I chart the changes in confession, authenticity, and *True Story* that resulted from Macfadden's 1930s preoccupation with American class politics. As we shall see, when confession is situated in a new political economy, torn from its 1920s alliance with sexuality and articulated instead to a particular class politics, the form itself will dramatically change.

2

CONFESSION AND CLASS: A NEW *TRUE STORY*

By 1936, when the *New Masses* put an effeminate, busted, brassiered, fingernail-polished, phallus-fondling caricature of Macfadden on its cover, it had become commonplace to decry *True Story* as pornographic. To be sure, Macfadden's *True Story* was the subject of much debate. But, as chapter 1 demonstrated, in the early years of *True Story* this debate was restricted to issues of sexuality. By 1936, however, a new set of terms had been introduced into the debate over Macfadden's *True Story*. Tellingly subtitled "From Pornography to Politics," the *New Masses* article was less about sexuality than about class: "Millions of working-class and lower middle-class citizens absorb [Macfadden's] reactionary editorials and wallow in the politely-dressed filth of his confessionals."[1]

True Story's shift from being defined by its opposition to the sexual politics of Comstock to its later concerns with class politics started in 1926. In that year, William Jourdan Rapp began his sixteen-year tenure as editor of *True Story* and, by historical consensus, fundamentally altered the magazine. It was a momentous shift. No longer the haven of Macfadden's "anonymous, amateur, illiterates," *True Story* now recruited and published such writers as Henry Ford, Edward Corsi, and the YMCA figurehead Mrs. Frederic M. Paist.[2] Although the stories still "taught a strong moral lesson," that morality was no longer grounded in stories authenticated by unrefined prose. Rapp reasoned that public education was improving public literacy and thus gave his editors license to exercise a "heavier hand."[3] All these, however, were incremental changes. The biggest shift in the administration of *True Story* was its newfound pursuit of mainstream advertising. Until that point, the advertising in *True Story* was scarce and as unrefined as its prose. Seven years after its founding, and two years after achieving a circulation of two million readers, *True Story* still "carried less than a dozen full-page or half-page ads for national advertisers."[4] The advertising it did carry was hardly capable of generating revenue. Filled with advertisements for alternative medicines, self-help books, public speaking lessons, violet rays, and Macfadden's eight-volume *Encyclopedia of Health*, *True Story* was filled with products that would generate neither mass interest nor mass revenue.

Beginning in 1926 and continuing through mid-century, *True Story* campaigned for mainstream advertising dollars. It did so by taking the "true story idea" to American business leaders and advertising executives. This campaign, which Roland Marchand has aptly characterized as a "series of sociological sermons to the trade," took a number of different forms: from advertisements in mainstream newspapers such as the *Chicago Tribune*, the *New York Times*, and the *Boston Herald Traveler*, to trade journals such as *Printer's Ink*, to a number of short books published by Macfadden Publications.[5] Whatever the outlet, *True Story*'s campaign for advertising dollars aimed to convince American executives that whatever their personal misgivings about *True Story* or its working-class readership, the magazine was nonetheless an essential advertising space. As one advertisement put it, "Socially these people are strangers to you. Culturally, their tastes are quite different from your own. But economically they are your bread and butter."[6] The campaign was wildly successful. The pages that were once filled with marginal products incapable of generating revenue were by the 1930s filled with products of mass culture: the Fleischmann Company, Eastman Kodak, Lever Bros., Jell-O, Listerine, and Lux Toilet Soap.[7]

Aspects of this campaign were conventional. It will surprise no one, for example, to learn that *True Story* emphasized its circulation numbers, which by 1926 could compete with any monthly in the land. Beyond the numbers, *True Story* argued that because it was designed by and for a working-class audience, an advertisement placed in its pages would be particularly effective. A *Printer's Ink* advertisement put it this way: "To reach them, to sell them, advertisers need use ONLY ONE great national magazine, True Story." While "wage earners" "can't comprehend the more sophisticated 'silk worm' magazines written for the white collars," *True Story*'s "democracy of editorial appeal has made it the only great national magazine tapping 86% of America."[8] *True Story* even created new slogans and new logos to foreground its penetration of the "wage earning market": "*True Story*: The Only Magazine They Read" and "*True Story*: The NEW Market."[9]

Yet we must not take *True Story*'s claim to access a working-class readership at face value. This access was built on two mutually constitutive fictions: first, the fiction of a happy, docile, politically passive working class with expendable income, and second, the fiction of a magazine that perfectly expressed the deepest desires of this class. Macfadden Publications developed both fictions with vigor, dedicating countless columns to redescribing America's working class in self-serving terms. Beyond securing advertising dollars, the results of this campaign were twofold. First, these two fictions combined to solidify *True Story*'s status as a confession magazine. Macfadden Publications argued that because *True Story* was written by its readers, it functioned as an ideal connection between consumers and producers. In addition to carrying products to the masses, it also carried the masses—their subconscious desires, anxieties, and consumer impulses—back to business executives. This redescription of *True Story* eliminated any lingering doubts about the confessional status of *True Story*, for in the middle decades of twentieth-century America, a discourse that expressed subconscious desires could register only as a confession. It is no coincidence that it was in these years that the *Saturday Evening Post*—and the *New Yorker*, and *Time*, and virtually every other cultural organ—now instinctively saw true stories as confessions. In this chapter I stress that this widely shared mid-century instinct to see Macfadden's true stories as confessions was not instinctual at all: it was provided for by a particular political economy, the product of an advertising campaign that redescribed both *True Story* and its readership.

Second, and perhaps more important, this redescription of *True Story* and its attendant reification as a confession magazine had consequences on the well-being of the American working class. Indeed, I suggest that the progressive immiseration of the working class can be indexed to the progressive certainty with which *True Story* was understood as a confession magazine. Here's why: *True Story* was gradually reified as a confession magazine to the degree that Macfadden's two fictions were believed. And to the extent that his fictions were believed, that segment of the working class that remained discontent and impoverished was hidden from view. It was hidden by the well-funded and widely deployed fiction of a happy, well-remunerated working class, the desires of which *True Story* perfectly expressed. In other words, because *True Story* claimed to be the organ par excellence of the working class, and because it fundamentally misrepresented this class, whatever portions of the actually existing working class that did not match Macfadden's fiction were cut off from all sources of power, left to defend themselves in a world that—if Macfadden had his way—would not even know they existed.

True Story's Fictional Working Class

Macfadden Publications rested its argument for advertising dollars on the existence and purchasing power of what Macfadden referred to as a "new market" of consumers.[10] He titled this class of consumers "wage earners." "Wage earners" were so central to *True Story*'s advertising campaign that Macfadden Publications released two books dedicated to establishing their existence and explaining their relevance. In 1927 Macfadden Publications released *86% of America* and followed it three years later with *The American Economic Evolution*. These are fascinating texts. Both were addressed to "Business Executives" and both comprised short vignettes of the so-called wage-earning class. Sometimes these vignettes were anonymous, at other times—especially in *86% of America*—they were attributed to such personalities as Walter Chrysler, Henry Ford, Herbert Hoover, and Andrew Mellon. On a descriptive level, both claimed simply to explain the relevant contours of the class: their purchasing patterns and political tendencies, of course, but also their aesthetic sensibilities and economic ambitions. While *The American Economic Evolution* explicitly used these descriptions as evidence of the value of *True Story*'s advertising space, *86% of America* relied on ads in *Printer's Ink* to connect its analysis of the wage-earning class to the conclusion that "magazine advertisers MUST use *True Story*."[11]

In both the books and their accompanying newspaper advertisements, Macfadden Publications argued that an economic revolution had transformed the working class: "Almost without our being conscious of the fact, a revolution in industry has been taking place that is raising all classes of the population to a more equal participation in the fruits of industry, and thus, by the natural operation of economic law, bringing to a nearer realization the dreams of those Utopians who looked to the day when poverty would be banished and all men could enjoy a greater share of the good things in life."[12] Because the "good things in life" were now broadcast, Macfadden imagined an American citizen rebuking a "Frenchman" as follows: "There are no peasants here. Our proletariat are more prosperous than your bourgeoisie."[13] Despite the language of economic law, classless societies, and the rising of the proletariat, *True Story*'s "economic revolution" should not be confused with Marx's never-quite-materialized revolution. According to *True Story*'s model, the economic revolution had already happened—albeit "without our being conscious of the fact"—and equality was a present reality rather than a motivating ideal. Macfadden himself recognized the difference: "To-day, the New World offers the spectacle of a proletariat so prosperous that the term, itself, is paradoxical."[14] With no acknowledgment of enduring inequalities, Macfadden argued that contemporary America marks "the closest approach to *absolute equality* that the human race or any other form of animal life has ever known."[15]

Macfadden illustrated this purported equality with the story of a certain Jim Smith. Ten years ago "any Jim Smith" working in "any American factory" came home "sour and tired," he "joined strikes and threw brickbats." He was unhappy, exploited, and politically active. As the reference to "brickbats" suggests, this unreconstructed Jim Smith criticized authority and "along the way," Macfadden writes, "Coxeys and Debses sprang up." "Then came tremendous economic change" and a corresponding "*miraculous* change in the life of Jim Smith." Ten years later, his workday had been cut nearly in half, his earnings multiplied sevenfold, his body fresher, his leisure longer, his comportment more genial, and his political engagement tempered if not altogether eliminated. The new Jim Smith drives an automobile home to the suburbs, "he goes to shows, he studies, he reads and writes." No longer the brickbat-throwing, Eugene Debs–producing agitator, the new Jim Smith "has learned moderation."[16] Like "Jim Smith," "the Missus" had once "risked her manicure in the Monday wash tub; now she threw the switch and let George Washing Machine do it." Likewise, the doughboy now "found that his new job paid enough to shift the family quite a bit uptown."[17]

Between the two books, there are countless "Jim Smiths," "Missuses," and "doughboys," who together constitute Macfadden's "wage-earning class." As a class, they are happy, leisured, suburban, blue-collar commuters who have been transformed by their newfound disposable income. Macfadden concludes, "A great upsurge of the common people of America has found itself on an economic level never even hoped for out of all its past."[18] And if common people are surging upward, this is a signal that the worker's labor is both intellectually and financially lucrative: "We have, in short, released labor from much of the drudgery, conserved its energy for tasks requiring higher intelligence and in effect made of each worker a foreman of mechanical forces who earns and can be paid a foreman's wages."[19]

From the perspective of the twenty-first century, it is obvious that a classless society of intellectually stimulated, well-paid wage earners was a fiction designed to sell advertising. It is important to remember, however, that it was a fiction that once captivated an age. In 1926 the J. Walter Thompson Company—the "leading advertising agency in the country"—proclaimed the working class the "New National Market": "Millions of families regarded almost as recently as a few months ago as poor prospects for many kinds of merchandise, are now the best sort of prospects."[20] Likewise the Chevrolet Motor Company proclaimed in 1937 that "tens of thousand of [working-class] men on one single payroll have money for themselves and their families to spend."[21] Propped up by the likes massive advertising agencies and national brands like Chevrolet, the well-paid, eager-to-spend laborer proved a resilient image. The historian Lizabeth Cohen explains that while "hard times forced many Americans to struggle to find and keep work, to feed their families, and to hold on to their homes or pay their rent," the working class was nonetheless increasingly envisioned—by themselves as much as by policy makers—as a consumer class.[22] After all, as Richard H. Pells has noted in *Radical Visions and American Dreams*, in the 1920s "American society began to take on the look of a white-collar paradise, complete with chain stores, suburban housing booms, the dependence on recreation as an escape from work and on advertising as a guide to life."[23] So many were taken in by these appearances that by mid-century it became almost a sociological commonplace to celebrate the death of classes in American society.[24] Even the *New Republic*—along with *The Nation* the leading liberal organ of 1920s America—proclaimed in 1929, "To believe that a proletarian philosophy may be brought into being in this country where the germs of class-consciousness are scarcely discernible is to submit to self-delusion."[25]

The image of a spending, liberated working class may have been resilient, but historians agree that it was one-part fiction. Commenting on "*True Story*'s version of the fate of the factory worker," Cohen insists that "a truer story" needs to be told. Contrary to the mythology of *The American Economic Evolution*, Cohen argues that workers "did not enjoy nearly the prosperity that advertisers and sales promoters assumed they did." Addressing *True Story*'s narrative, Cohen continues, "If factory workers could have depended on these slowly rising wages from year to year and year round, they might have consumed more like Jim Smith. Instead, unemployment remained high throughout the decade, even for people with so-called steady work."[26] Likewise, Richard Pells writes:

> Largely hidden from view were the more unpleasant realities of life in the 1920s, particularly the rise in technological unemployment as machines replaced men in the factory, together with the decade-long depression in agriculture, mining, and textiles. For most Americans the 1920s was a period not so much of prosperity as of sheer survival, with little money left over after the bills were paid to enjoy the party others seemed to be throwing. And as the years wore on, it

became increasingly difficult for the average man to consume what the economy could produce—an ominous sign which the pitchmen of the "new era" chose to ignore.[27]

All ominous signs were certainly ignored by Macfadden Publications. In *86% of America* and *The American Economic Evolution*, 1920s America was an unqualified, classless paradise.

Although the "wage earner" was certainly fictitious, Macfadden and *True Story* refined this immensely popular fiction to full effect. In the pursuit of advertising dollars, the most important characteristic of the "wage earner" was his disposable income (the worker was always cast as masculine). "The real money of America has finally landed in the pockets of several million pairs of overalls," Macfadden proclaimed.[28] In 1926 alone, he reported, the "wage earners" grossed $3.6 billion.[29] And this money did not stay overalled for long; it went straight to "radios, motor cars, and up-to-date appliances":[30] "With bricklayers making $14 a day and other trades in proportion, it is easy to understand why their wives can afford to spend 41 billions of dollars a year for foodstuffs, nearly 6 billions of dollars a year for house furnishings, and proportionate amounts for other staples and moderately priced luxuries."[31] A *True Story* ad in the *Chicago Tribune* put it this way: "Money is everywhere. More money than America has ever known before. And more widespread. And deeper down. This present prosperity has penetrated and permeated stratum after stratum of American Society until today that great mass of millions once casually known as 'labor' now controls the destinies of every factory in the land." They control the factories, not only because of "an economic equality that has never been equaled," but also because their disposable income has provided them the purchasing power that keeps the "whir of production . . . at concert pitch."[32] For these reasons, the "wage earners" are "unquestionably the richest and readiest market to any manufacturer whose fortune rests on selling."[33] In short, they are the *"great consuming outlet."*[34]

True Story thus defined its readership as the ideal American consumer: leisured enough to desire the amenities of mass culture, moneyed enough to buy them, and temperamentally disposed not to challenge authority. That such a demographic did not in fact exist was, from the perspective of *True Story*, a problem easily solved. *True Story*'s solution was to redefine true stories themselves, to turn authenticity, truthfulness, and experience—all of which were catalogued monthly in the pages of *True Story*—into documentable evidence of a fictional class. If, in the 1920s, true stories advanced a moral lesson, in the 1930s the same stories were made to serve class politics by establishing the existence of a docile, spending working class.

The Mirror Function of True Stories

If *True Story*'s sheer circulation and its "democratic editorial appeal" guaranteed that it could carry the news of products from the classes to the masses, the fact that it was written by its readers guaranteed the return trip.[35] In other words, because *True Story* was written by its readers, and because its readers were defined as consumers (wage earners), the articles in *True Story* provided a picture of the very consumers who were the object of the producers' attention. In this way, Macfadden suggested, advertising in *True Story* was more valuable than advertising elsewhere, for the nature of the magazine ensured that the products filling the advertising pages could be uniquely calibrated to the desires of its readers: "Here at True Story Magazine, the *people* not only *tell* us what they want but they also *give* it to us. We *can't* make any mistake. If their emotions are changing, *they* change them. If they lean toward mystery stories, *they* give them to us. But that is not the best of it. When they get *tired* of mystery stories, *they* stop writing them. We never have to guess what they want nor when they are sick of it." Macfadden concluded that *True Story* reflected social and economic change "as perfectly as a rock or a tree is reflected in a clear, still lake."[36]

Macfadden thus defined *True Story* as the collective self-expression of the fictional wage-earning class. To make this case he reminded his readers that *True Story* "never has been what might be called an '*edited*' publication." For Macfadden, "editing" was a devil term, a synonym for tampering or falsifying. Rather than tamper with "the great mass of personal experiences," *True Story* simply "printed them": "Wherever you have any personal expression from a cross-section of hundreds of thousands of individuals, you have a great human composite that is telling the story of its age more clearly than any historian could ever do. For self-expression is always true expression when you let it alone." *True Story* thus constituted a "perfect mirror" of "human affairs." Indeed, what we might call the mirror function of *True Story* was itself the grounds of Macfadden's fictional economic narrative. While the early submissions to *True Story* had once recorded tales of "misery and privation and struggle," the more recent stories, "which come flowing in to us in an ever endless stream, are ending happily": "In the last decade the very character of these True Stories has so completely changed that we ourselves do not recognize our own publication."[37]

Macfadden was extraordinarily committed to the "mirror function" of *True Story*. A decade after *The American Economic Evolution*, he made the conceit the basis for his 1941 *History and Magazines*. This richly decorated coffee-table book begins with the premise that "magazines never 'just happen.'"[38] Rather, they are a reflection of the "social forces at work in America." To illustrate the point, *History and Magazines* provided a two-page chart that calibrated fifty-five prominent magazines to the social forces that "created" them. For example, the *New American Magazine* was a response to the American Revolution; the *American Review* was a product of nationalism; the *Saturday Evening Post* was created by the Civil War; *The Nation* by Reconstruction; *Cosmopolitan* and *Good Housekeeping* by industrialization; and *True Story* by World War I. "That is why," Macfadden concluded, "*through magazines*, it is possible to see a *dimension in history* beyond a chronological presentation of events, an insight into the effects of these forces upon the people who figured in them." In this sense, *True Story* was something of a first among equals. Although all magazines reflected history, only *True Story* was written by its readers, and thus, to a greater extent than the others, it placed in bold relief the "hopes, fears, troubles, [and] ambitions" of its readers. Unlike the other fifty-four magazines on the chart, *True Story* was not simply created by a particular social force; it was a register on which shifting social forces were rendered legible. And this, Macfadden argued, made *True Story* an invaluable tool for the American manufacturer: "For this reason the pages of *True Story*—as they change with America's great Wage Earner Group—offer a monthly insight into the history of that group—an insight more revealing than the statistics of their wages, bank balances or purchases. A few great writers of advertising copy have discovered that truth for themselves and use True Story as a guide to the contemporary desires of its readers."[39] It is difficult to overestimate the consistency with which the *True Story* advertising campaign returned to the magazine's "mirror function." The *Chicago Tribune* emphasized the certainty of the wage earner's new wealth. Because *True Story* provided "the perfect reflection of this entire new cultural development," it argued, "there is no more question about it than there is about the nature of man."[40] Similarly, in *The American Economic Evolution*, Macfadden argued, "Today, the true stories in True Story Magazine are so different from the same true stories of ten years ago that it is hard to recognize them as the self-expression of the same people."[41]

All this is a very different picture of *True Story* than the one developed at length in the 1920s *True Story* as a response to Anthony Comstock. Two easy points of comparison will dramatize the point. While both the 1920s *True Story* and the later advertising campaign talked endlessly about the "true story idea" and the magazine's astronomical circulation, these two things had very different meanings in different contexts. Consider first the relative fate of the "true story idea"—the fact that it was written by its readers. In the 1920s, this meant that the magazine was didactic, educational, and corrective; an intervention into sexual politics. The fact that it was written by its readers guaranteed that it recorded actual experiences, and actual experiences were valuable primarily for their moral function. As Macfadden put it in 1924, "We want to help others to a safe passage by showing them the pitfalls that beset life's paths. That is our supreme purpose."[42] By contrast, while the advertising campaign rehearsed the fact that *True Story* was written by its readers with as much monotony as the first fourteen volumes of the magazine, this fact now meant something rather different. No longer a guarantee of *True Story*'s moral uplift, it functioned now to guarantee that *True Story* was a reflection of society rather than an instrument in its reform. In short, *True Story* now revealed rather than reformed America. And as its function shifted from reformation to revelation, *True Story* was increasingly recognized in confessional terms.

Or consider *True Story*'s record-setting rise to a circulation of two million in only five years. Both the 1920s magazine and the 1930s advertising campaign boasted of this achievement endlessly, but they drew very different lessons from it. In the magazine, it was evidence of the popularity of moral instruction. In a May 1924 article titled "Two Million," for example, Macfadden interpreted the achievement as a "gigantic testimonial to the popularity of truth as an entertainer." But not just as an entertainer: "The little lives of ordinary folks have built a new literature. They are teaching a moral lesson which our young folks need, and we will be a better people because we learn from the experiences of others."[43] The account in *History and Magazines* could not have been more different. After noting that the quick rise to two million was still honored well after the fact, it explained the achievement thus: "We believe that these achievements have been possible because True Story presents to its readers a true picture of current life—a picture they find interesting, illuminating, and inspiring."[44] Thus was the didactic moralism of *True Story* in its early years replaced by romantic sentiments of national self-expression.

On an empirical level, Macfadden's claim that *True Story* provides a "true picture of current life" is simply not true. Here I am not concerned with any of the particular stories, and I have no stake in the much-rehearsed debate over whether the true stories were forged. Rather, I simply wish to stress that, as Pells and Cohen remind us, Macfadden's so-called wage earners were a fiction. Historically speaking, the American working class was never relieved of drudgery and never found itself plagued with too many amenities. Thus, even granting Macfadden's claim that his editors never touched up a story or hired a professional writer, it is still impossible that his true stories could bear witness to the historical veracity of a fictional class. Yet Macfadden needed this class. For, regardless of whether or not they actually existed, wage earners were the picture-perfect consumer, and as such, Macfadden's case for advertising dollars rested on their existence. Macfadden's solution was ingenious. He had learned from his bouts with Comstock that confessions were empty signifiers—they were always liable to misinterpretation. That is why he had turned *True Story* into a rhetorical primer, why in the 1920s he had surrounded each true story with a set of directions for interpreting it as a guide to moral virtue. Why not give advertising executives a similar lesson? Why not teach them to see in true stories the exact thing he wanted them to see—the ideal consumer? *He thus, as it were, inserted the wage earner behind the confession.* Without changing a single editorial policy, he told executives that if they squinted just right, if they learned to read *True Story* properly, they could see between the lines of his true stories millions of affluent, docile, and eager consumers.

This, however, was no simple task. On its surface, *True Story* was just so many stories of promises broken and kept, rendezvous arranged and regretted. Thus, with as much intensity as the early *True Story* provided a never-ending commentary alongside the true stories it told, the advertising campaign insisted that business executives must learn to reread *True Story*. A *Printer's Ink* ad for *True Story* was titled "Do You Know How to Read Your Newspaper?"[45] The implied answer was no. Consider *The American Economic Evolution*. *True Story* may "fairly shout" its reflection of American culture, the book argued, but such shouting will be audible only "if one will take the trouble to read between the lines." This was imperative. If only the printed lines were considered, "one story may be about sex and one about money. Another about chastity and another about divorce. But when you lay them out together at the end of any period, as any good sociologist would do, and then look underneath them for the *impelling* motive—the factor that *caused* the story, you get a picture of the true conditions of the time that could not be written in any other way." Macfadden constantly urged business executives to be sociologists; to be "student-minded"; to ignore the surface content of the stories; to "take the *settings* of these True Stories instead of the stories themselves"; to see the fortunes of the American worker "in big type, between the lines"; to "take the underlay" of true stories, "not by what they tell, *but by what they do not even realize they are telling.*" Macfadden was insistent on this: "You have to have wisdom enough to read between the lines to see what is going on. The writers of these stories themselves do not realize what is going on except as they have personal wisdom, here and there, to read between their own lines."[46]

Literally speaking, of course, there was nothing but blank space between the lines. But Macfadden used this blank space to his great advantage. Rather than rely on business executives to read between the lines correctly, he was quick to fill in that blank space with his fictional wage-earning class. Consider again Macfadden's *History and Magazines*. This book claimed to document the shifting anxieties of the wage-earning class by providing lengthy excerpts from *True Story Magazine* and a meta-commentary explaining the meaning of the excerpts. Initially, stories like "Haunting Memories" revealed that the wage earners were anxious about the "changing moral code." Later, stories like "Rotten Riches" demonstrated that the "problems created by too much money replaced . . . the problems created 5 years before by the changing moral code." In the depression years, stories like "Desperate Days" revealed the problems of "too little money," and stories like "When I Needed Her Most" revealed that wage earners had rediscovered the "power of faith and the strength of family life." When we remember that *History and Magazines* was written for advertising executives, it will come as no surprise that the most recent anxieties of the wage-earning class stemmed from the superabundance of consumables—"refrigerators, radios, nylon plastics . . . [and] fortified bread"—and a "Wage Earner Group" whose education, earnings, and employment "are at new highs."[47]

Macfadden not only insisted that advertising moguls "read between the lines," he showed them in great detail what they would see. Read correctly, *True Story* confirmed the elites' own vision of the world: a vision in which everyone was well-off, prosperity came to all who worked, and all the gadgets of mass culture were justified as a response to the authentic desires of the working class. In this vision, business executives were not coldhearted capitalists, blind to the immiseration of the working class. Rather, they were the benefactors of the working class, providing high pay and consumables to satisfy every desire. "You," Macfadden told "Business Executives," "*have been making a fairy tale come true.* . . . Within a period of ten years, you have done more toward the sum total of human happiness for at least one nation on earth than has ever been done before in all the centuries of historical time."[48] It is no wonder the executives believed him.

True Story as a Confession

Historically speaking, *True Story* was not a reflection of the wage-earning class. Quite the opposite, the wage-earning class was a fiction produced by *True Story* to attract mainstream advertisers. Macfadden may have claimed that the wage earners produced *True Story* and that *True Story* in turn reflected their desires, but the reverse is actually the case: *True Story* invented the wage-earning class and inserted them into the only place such a class might be found: the blank spaces between the lines. He then taught business executives that, if they squinted their eyes just right, they would see (between the lines) that *True Story*'s true stories, as trivial as they may seem, harbored a deep significance to those who knew what they were looking for. True stories could not be taken at face value; the ever-present bed shadows held meanings of which the participants and writers were unaware. True stories were a special kind of text, one whose full meaning could be disclosed only by the presence of an expert in reading between the lines. The 1920s had a very good name for such texts: confessions.

To be sure, such descriptions would not "evoke the Catholic Confessional," as Jacqueline Hatton has claimed, nor would they have "the conscious ring of the public confession . . . in an old-fashioned testimony meeting of Southern camp religionists," as Fulton Oursler has argued.[49] Macfadden's description of true stories, however, sounded a lot like the Freudian notion of confession: a discourse innocuous enough on its surface that revealed, upon trained inspection, subconscious desires and anxieties unknown to the speaker.

In his early *Studies on Hysteria* with Josef Breuer in 1893, Freud noted that his method of curing patients of psychic tension by inducing them to talk about their own experiences resembled something like the "Roman Catholic confessional." For the confession, even when "there is not a priest and even when no absolution follows," is nonetheless therapeutic. As Freud concluded, "Telling things is a relief."[50] In Freud's example, a flu-ridden twelve-year-old boy had only to tell the story of how he was propositioned to alleviate his vomiting: "As soon as he had made his confession he recovered completely." At this stage in Freud's thought, the confession was therapeutic merely by the recounting of events, the "telling of things." If Freud's reflections on confession had remained at this stage, they would be inconsequential in the history of confession and irrelevant in the reception of *True Story*. By the time of his 1899 landmark *The Interpretation of Dreams*, Freud's talking cure had become far more robust. Freud no longer asked his patients to recount traumatic events; rather, he asked them to verbalize in his presence whatever thoughts came to mind:

> I want him [the patient] to do two things: to pay attention to his psychical perceptions more intently, and to switch off the critical faculty he normally uses to sift the thoughts arising in him.... He must be expressly bidden to abstain from any critical judgment of the thoughts he forms and becomes aware of. He is told, that is, that the success of psychoanalysis depends on his paying attention to everything that passes through his mind, reporting it, and on not allowing himself to be tempted, for instance, to suppress one idea occurring to him because it appears to him unimportant or irrelevant to the subject.[51]

In this view, psychoanalysis depends on the uncritical and unqualified confession of every thought that passes through his mind. Unlike the passage in "Studies on Hysteria," in which the confession was delimited in advance by the traumatic event in question, the confession is now bound by no standards of relevance, logic, or consequence. Moreover, the burden of establishing relevance has also shifted, moving from the patient/confessant in 1893 to the analyst/confessor in 1899. Now the analyst discovers in the patient's unsorted stream of words a salience unknown to the patient.

I trust that the correspondences between Freud's confession and Macfadden's *True Story* are emerging. Both are the product of, as it were, "switching off the critical faculty." Both Freud and Macfadden asked people simply to share their life experiences no matter how trivial they might seem. When Macfadden's readers and Freud's patients complied, both men insisted that the experiences related harbored truths that were unknown even to the authors. "One story may be about sex and another about money," Macfadden insisted, but "any good sociologist" can look beneath these events and find the "true conditions of the time."[52] For Freud, analysis replaces sociology, but the process is the same: "We expect that the analysis of the dream will invariably uncover for us the real, psychically significant source of the dream in the life of the day, though our recollection of the real source has displaced its emphasis onto the unimportant one."[53] For both men, an expert—a sociologist for Macfadden, an analyst for Freud—could "read between the lines" and discern the meaningful in the trivial. And while Macfadden originally resisted labeling the reporting of life experiences as "confessions," Freud had no such qualms.

As it happened, the middle decades of twentieth-century America was Freud's time and *True Story* could not escape this context. As the historian Frederick Lewis Allen wrote in *Only Yesterday*, *True Story* was part and parcel of America's Freudian revolution. Although it was consumed by readers "who had never heard [of] and never would hear of Freud and the libido," it was nevertheless a product of what he called the "Freudian gospel." According to Allen, by the 1920s a distilled version of Freudianism, "filtered though through the successive minds of interpreters and popularizers and guileless readers," circulated widely among the "American lay public."[54] The historian John Loughery agrees, arguing that the 1920s through the 1940s should be understood as "Freudian America"—a time when Freudianism gradually became a "veritable religion."[55] Indeed, there is perhaps no better evidence of Freud's popularity than the energy expended to discredit him. The American Medical Association's Morris Fishbein dedicated an entire chapter of his 1932 *Fads and Quackery in Healing* to "Psychoanalytic Charlatans," especially Freud himself. Chief among Fishbein's complaints was the place of confession in psychoanalysis: The "ritual demands that the patient lie upon a couch in a dimly darkened office. There she—and the word falls naturally for it is usually a feminine patient—begins her long autobiography and there the psychoanalyst sits—we hope—listening and stimulating ever more and juicy revelations."[56] Beyond critiquing the element of pleasure in the production of confessional knowledge, Fishbein also suggests that the knowledge produced by such pleasure-laden controversies is untrustworthy: "The method falls short of having that exactness which scientific procedure requires."[57] That this critique of confession would be leveled against Freud in a book designed to protect the American public from "quackery" is an indication of just how deeply the Freudian model of confession had infiltrated "lay America."

From Freud's perspective, Fishbein was hardly alone. Peter Gay reports that Freud was incensed by the American medical establishment's tendency to be "particularly unbending" in their demand that psychoanalysis conform to the rigorous standards of medical science.[58] In response to this demand, Freud wrote "The Question of Lay Analysis" in 1926, a late essay in which he defended his lifelong view that the practice of psychoanalysis required no professional medical education. In this text, Freud once again connected the recounting of events with confession. After insisting that the patient "keep nothing back intentionally that comes into his head," he then acknowledged that this procedure was something of a supercharged confession: "Confession no doubt plays a part in analysis—as an introduction to it, we might say. But it is very far from constituting the essence of analysis or from explaining its effects. In [the Catholic] Confession the sinner tells what he knows; in analysis the neurotic has to tell more. Nor have we ever heard that Confession has ever developed enough *power* to get rid of actual pathological symptoms."[59] Freud's analytic confession is a form of religious confession: it is wider in scope and more powerful in effect than its cousin in the Roman Catholic Church. In Foucault's reading, this was Freud's crucial move: by supercharging the confession, by freeing it from the confines of the Catholic confessional, Freud turned the confession into "one of the West's most highly valued [and most reproduced] techniques for producing truth": "The confession has spread its effects far and wide. It plays a part in justice, medicine, education, family relationships, and love relations, in the most ordinary affairs of everyday life, and in the most solemn rites."[60]

The confession also, it seems, played a role in *True Story Magazine*. Freud's insistence that the neurotic "keep nothing back" in order that an analyst might find knowledge therein is structurally identical to Macfadden's insistence that illiterates record their experiences so that sociologists and executives could find therein the desires of the masses. Macfadden may have been hesitant to call *True Story* a confession, but the need for advertising dollars forced him to describe it in terms that—by the middle of the century—could only be described as confessional. Freud's vision of confession had infiltrated American culture, it had spread its effects far and wide, and it had registered with the American Medical Association as a dangerous form of quackery. Thus, when Macfadden—who shared space with Freud in Fishbein's list of "charlatans"—described *True Story* as the subconscious expression of the truth of the working class, he might as well have called it a confession magazine. It is no wonder that, at the height of Freudian America, the *New Yorker*, *Time*, and the *Saturday Evening Post* all suddenly recognized *True Story* as a confession.

Conclusion: Class Politics and the Genre of Confession

As an entry point into the intrication of class and confession, it may be helpful to recall the contours of Macfadden's so-called wage earners. As a group, they were defined by their political quietism. Macfadden's claim that his readership is politically passive takes us straight to the heart of the academic literature on confession magazines. Since Gerbner's 1958 essay "The Social Role of the Confession Magazine," nearly all academic critics of confession have weighed in on the relationship between confession and political agency. Gerbner argued that *True Story* functioned ideologically, obscuring from its readers the relevance of social protest. Although, in theory, he reasoned that *True Story* might provoke social action by allowing the readership to identify with the suffering, bewildered victims of life that populate the pages of *True Story*, he argued that this possibility was, in practice, carefully—even intentionally—precluded. If "one barrel" of the editorial formula exploits "anxieties" that might generate social action, "the other barrel is loaded with editorial ammunition designed to minimize the risks of this appeal by making social protest appear to be out of place, unrelated to the insecurities of working-class life." Gerbner concluded with a moving, much-quoted passage: "The flame of rebellion is first kindled, then controlled in scope and divorced from its broader social context, and then doused in jet streams of remorse, sacrifice, and compromise."[61]

Gerbner's questions and his conclusions have stood the test of time. Maureen Honey and Roseann Mandziuk, for example, both *confirm* Gerbner's questions and *qualify* his answers. They both agree with Gerbner that *the* question to be asked of confession magazines is whether they encourage or inhibit political dissent. They agree, further, that confession magazines have a hegemonic function. While, in Janice Radway fashion, they do note that *True Story* (in Mandziuk's words) "provides space for oppositional understandings," at the end of the day they both affirm Gerbner's claim that *True Story* functions to douse dissent.[62] As Honey put it, the confession magazines encourage the "dominated [to] participate in their own domination."[63]

I have no desire to quibble with Gerbner's legacy. In fact, after reading volumes of *True Story* there is more evidence for his thesis than could ever be assembled in one essay. It is true: as Gerbner, Radway, Honey, and Mandziuk have each argued, the confession magazine does indeed function to rob its readership of political agency. Indeed, although none of these advocates for the Gerbner-inspired docile-body thesis has considered them, Macfadden's monthly editorials are often little more than pleas for political quietism. He assured his readers that wealthy people are actually unhappy; he insisted that "revenge isn't sweet"; he pleaded with his readership to not "complain" or "criticize" others; and he argued that the "glorification that comes with fame" is "effervescent," "transient," and not worth pursuing.[64] These are only a selection, but I trust they make the point. Given this monthly plea for quietism, I believe that Gerbner and his followers have, if anything, understated their case: *True Story* was indeed out to produce docile subjects.

This, however, is only half the story. It is important to remember that, for Macfadden, a docile working class and a confession magazine were mutually constitutive fictions. Political passivity was an essential characteristic of the wage-earning class, and the wage-earning class, in turn, was an essential ingredient in *True Story*'s gradual reification as a confession magazine. If it is true, as so many have insisted, that confession magazines produced a docile class of consumers, it is also true—and this is my point—that this docile class was a necessary fiction in turning *True Story* into a financially solvent confession magazine. *True Story* was not an economically viable confession magazine, in other words, until Macfadden invented the fiction of the wage-earning class and inserted it into the blank spaces of his true stories. *True Story* could have been many things without the wage earner; in actual fact, it was a moralistic, sexually conservative magazine. But it was not—indeed it could not have been—widely recognized as a confession magazine without the wage earner. And this, of course, raises serious questions about the politics of confession. In the case at hand, *True Story* quite literally became a confession magazine at the expense of the working class. More precisely, it became a confession magazine by teaching American elites to misrecognize the working class, to look at them and see only what Macfadden taught them to see: a newly liberated, spending, politically passive, wholly autonomous wage earner—a fiction from first to last. And to the extent that this ideological definition of the working class rendered the actually existing working class invisible and thereby contributed to their further impoverishment, it is safe to conclude that the gradual immiseration of the working class was indexed to the gradual reification of *True Story* as a confession magazine.

Finally, all this helps us answer the all-important "why" question that Gerbner and his followers leave unanswered: why do confession magazines invest such energy in producing a docile class of consumers? For *True Story*, its financial solvency required it. Macfadden invented the fiction of the wage earner to start the advertising dollars flowing. It worked marvelously; Jell-O, Eastman Kodak, and others began buying space from Macfadden based in part on his claim that *True Story* was the subconscious expression of an untapped class of happy, suburban, docile consumers. And, perhaps as a hedge against the possibility that one day a business executive might realize that the happy wage earner was an invention designed to extract his or her money, Macfadden set out to make his readership over in the image of the wage-earning fiction.

3

CONFESSION AND RACE: CIVIL RIGHTS, SEGREGATION, AND THE MURDER OF EMMETT TILL

On October 23, 1955, the journalist William Bradford Huie met Roy Bryant and J. W. Milam in the Sumner, Mississippi, law offices of Breland & Whitten. One month earlier, a handpicked, all-white jury deliberated for sixty-seven minutes before declaring Bryant and Milam not guilty of Emmett Till's murder. Now, less than five weeks after their acquittal and in desperate need of the $3,000 Huie was paying, Bryant and Milam were telling Huie just how and why they killed Emmett Till. Huie could hardly contain his excitement. Following the secret interview, he returned to his room at the Holiday Inn and dashed off an exuberant letter to Daniel D. Mich, editorial director of *Look* magazine:

> I have just returned from Sumner where I spent an almost unbelievable day in Whitten's office—with Bryant and Milam. We have reached a verbal agreement on all points; and they have told me the story of the abduction and murder. This was really amazing, for it was the *first* time they have told this story of the abduction and murder. Not one of their lawyers had heard it. . . . Perhaps I am too close to appraise it—but I can't see how it can miss being one the most sensational stories ever published.[1]

At seven o'clock the following evening, Huie returned to Sumner and again met in "secret session" with Till's killers.[2] As he explained in another letter to Mich the subsequent morning, it was a "shattering" experience: "Two long sessions with these bully-boys have been shattering, even to a man like [Milam and Bryant's lawyer John L.] Whitten. It's an amazing, indefensible murder—and much of our story will be in the cool, factual, manner in which we lets the facts indict the 'community.' It will shake people in Mississippi."[3] Although Huie's correspondence with Mich breaks off at this point, he later suggested to the civil rights chronicler Howell Raines that he spent multiple evenings with Milam and Bryant during the week October 24–28, 1955: "They'd have to tell me the truth at night when I talked to 'em. The next day, I'd go out and *find* the places, *go* to the places they told me to—where they got the weight, the gin fan they put around the victims neck, all this sort of thing."[4]

The stories told in these "secret sessions" may well have been sensational, but they would have remained forever secret were it not for a final and decisive rendezvous. At 7:00 p.m., on Friday, October 28, Huie, the acquitted killers, and lawyers for both parties gathered once more at the law offices of Breland & Whitten for what Huie called the "signing ceremonies." Before Daniel Mich would print a word of Huie's story, he required "Consent and Release" forms from the (legally innocent) men whom Huie was about to publicly accuse of murder. He also required a release from Roy Bryant's wife, Carolyn, who was also named in Huie's story.[5] In exchange for these three release forms, Huie promised the killers 20 percent of the royalties and a $3,150 advance. In addition, Huie provided the law offices of Breland & Whitten—the practice that had defended the killers pro bono and then arranged Huie's secret sessions with them—10 percent of royalties and a $1,269 down payment.[6] Huie would later explain, "For me to publish the fact that they did commit that murder would be what we call 'libel per se,' meaning I am libeling these men when I say they murdered because they had already been tried and found not guilty of murder . . . therefore, I'll in effect pay them for the right to libel them."[7] When the three identical contracts were signed—one each for J. W. Milam, Roy Bryant, and Carolyn Bryant—the killers and their lawyers marked the occasion by sharing a bottle of whiskey.[8]

The documents that were signed that evening carried a number of provisions. First, they functioned as an affidavit, confirming the fact that the "secret sessions" actually happened. Second, each of the release forms gave Huie the right to publish an "article, story, literary or dramatic work based in whole or in part upon my life and any incidents or episodes therein . . . and, in particular, dealing with the death of Emmett Till in Sumner, Miss., including in the work the extent of my participation therein." On this point, the contracts were explicit and the rights they granted Huie were expansive: "This includes the right to portray me as one of those persons who abducted and killed the negro, Emmett Till." Third, although the contracts gave Huie the legal protection necessary to publicly accuse J. W. Milam of murder, this consent did not constitute a confession: "The foregoing consent is in no way to be regarded or considered as an admission by me, express or implied, that I am a killer or possessed of any other reprehensible characteristics, criminal or otherwise, which Mr. Huie may, in the work, attribute to me."[9]

Huie took this last point quite seriously. To his mind, if the legal "Consent and Release" form was not a confession, then neither could the story he published be a confession. Although the contracts did not specify this, Huie explained to numerous people that he had reached a "gentlemen's agreement" with the defense lawyers, J. J. Breland and John Whitten, that he would not publish the story as a confession. In an October 12 fund-raising letter to NAACP Executive Secretary Roy Wilkins, Huie emphasized just this point: "I would have to give my personal word to Breland & Whitten that I would not claim that Milam and Bryant had 'confessed'; that I would write the facts of the crime without ever stating that either of the defendants 'told' me anything; and that I would leave the defendants in a position in their own community where they could deny having talked with me—and where the book would not further 'jeopardize' them."[10] In a fund-raising letter to the Chicago newspaperman Basil "Stuffy" Walters, Huie again emphasized the importance of genre: "One point I may not have made clear: this story cannot be published as a 'confession.'"[11] Finally, in a letter to Mich, Huie reiterated the point: "I will agree that I will not claim that anybody has 'confessed' to me; and that while I may quote directly the words of the murderers at any point in the action, I will not quote them as having said *anything* to me." Huie then underscored the seriousness of the point by lecturing Mich on the nature of a gentlemen's agreement in the South. Although he admitted that the term sounded facetious, he assured Mich that it was literally a matter of life and death.[12] "I don't need to remind you," Huie wrote Mich upon sending him the unedited notes from his interviews, "that in this package I am sending you is information which, if delivered to Mississippi, could still put these boys in prison for 10 years. And if some of it should leak, I *might* get shot. So don't toss it around the office."[13]

Three months after the "signing ceremonies," Huie published his account of Emmett Till's murder in *Look*'s January 24, 1956, issue. Titled "The Shocking Story of Approved Killing in Mississippi," the story reflects Huie's generic commitments. There is nothing in the "Shocking Story" that reads as a confession. There are no admissions of wrongdoing, no promises of reformation, and no ethos of guilt or shame.[14] More important, Huie excised the only portions of the interview in which the killers admitted the killing. Although in later works based on the same interviews Huie would quote Milam as saying "I decided to kill him" and "I shot him," these quotations are conspicuously absent from the "Shocking Story."[15] Indeed, when John Whitten saw the drafts of Huie's follow-up 1957 piece for *Look*, he objected that, unlike the "Shocking Story," the 1957 "story ... goes beyond the revelations made in your original article by revealing for the first time that Milam and Bryant confessed the killing to you."[16] Huie's efforts to write the "Shocking Story" in such a way that it could not be construed as a "confession" apparently convinced James Baldwin, who after reading the "Shocking Story" insisted, "One cannot refer to [Milam's] performance as a confession."[17]

Baldwin's reading notwithstanding, nearly everybody else has followed the judgment of the celebrated African American journalist James L. Hicks, who, writing for *The Afro-American*, claimed, "In the magazine article [Milam and Bryant] simply confess that they killed Emmett Till."[18] That the "Shocking Story" now exists in the American imagination as a confession is indisputable: John Edgar Wideman, Bob Dylan, Stokely Carmichael, Christopher Metress, the historians Stephen Whitaker and David Beito, the rhetoricians Christine Harold and Kevin DeLuca—in short, all the influential accounts of Till's murder, both popular and academic, save James Baldwin's, remember the "Shocking Story" as a confession. In 2006 the Federal Bureau of Investigation added substantive weight to this consensus, referring several times to the "Shocking Story" as a confession in their official report on the death of Emmett Till.[19] The report lists the "Shocking Story," along with Roy Bryant's 1985 confessions and Leslie Milam's deathbed confession, in a section titled "Admissions."[20]

So how is it that despite Huie's excisions and Baldwin's objections, despite the contracts signed and the promises made, despite the intentions of the author, the killers, and their lawyers, the "Shocking Story" is nearly universally remembered as a confession? How, in other words, did the "Shocking Story" become a confession?

This is the question that animates this chapter, and the answer will come as no surprise: the "Shocking Story" became a confession because, politically speaking, it needed to be one. As I suggested in the introduction, to label a text a confession reveals more about the politics of the critic than about the contents of the text. The "Shocking Story" is no exception. What sets the "Shocking Story" apart from the other texts considered in this volume, however, is the sheer collusion required to turn it into a confession. Were it not for the unlikely cooperation of die-hard segregationists and equally committed civil rights activists, the "Shocking Story" may never have become a confession. This cooperation existed even at the level of the infrastructure that organized the racial politics of the so-called Second Reconstruction. Although they certainly did not recognize it, the NAACP and Mississippi's Citizens' Councils found themselves working toward the same goal in the spring of 1956. Both organizations had a stake in authenticating Huie's "Shocking Story"; moreover, representatives of both organizations pursued this goal by working to assure that the "Shocking Story" was received as a confession. With so much effort directed toward a common end, it is no wonder the "Shocking Story" solidified in the American imagination as a confession.

After explaining why both segregationists and civil rights activists alike stood to gain by the reification of the "Shocking Story" as a confession, I examine the long-term effects of their collusion. I argue that the nearly unmitigated attempt to treat the "Shocking Story" as a confession had the unfortunate effect of naturalizing Huie's version of the story. In the fifty-plus years between Till's death and this writing, there have been countless tellings of Till's story. But until the documentary filmmaker Keith A. Beauchamp prompted the FBI to intervene in the early twenty-first century, nearly every telling of Till's story relied on the narrative Huie provided. It is as if the label "confession" that came to adorn Huie's tale induced decades of subsequent storytellers to forget that the "Shocking Story"—like all the other shocking stories of Till's death—was little more than a partisan telling. In this chapter, we confront one of confession's more potent political weapons—its power to control public memory. In the case of Till and his remembrance, the fact that one version of his story was called a confession marked the death knell of the competing narratives. At least in this instance, the confession worked its power by obscuring the political maneuvering that produced it and the political ideology that motivated it. By recovering this maneuvering and this ideology, we can witness firsthand the power that confession has wielded in American racial politics.

Many Exposes, Only One Confession

On August 20, 1955, a black fourteen-year-old boy known to his friends as "Bobo" and to history as Emmett Till boarded a Chicago train bound for the Mississippi Delta. Although nearly every detail of Till's Delta visit is contested, the standard story runs as follows: Four days after his arrival in the town of Money, Mississippi, Till entered Bryant's Grocery and Meat Market on a dare from his friends. Bobo, the story goes, had been bragging about his biracial sexual prowess when one of his friends challenged him to prove it: "You talkin' mighty big, Bo. There's a pretty white woman in there in the sto'. Since you Chicago cats know so much about white girls, let's see you go in there and get a date with her."[21] Till went in and, depending on which account you trust, did at least one of the following: bought bubble gum, talked to the "pretty white woman," asked her for a date, used obscene language, squeezed her hand, put his arm around her waist and pulled her body tight against his, or—in what has become the most widely accepted version of the story—simply whistled at her.

The "pretty white woman" in question was Carolyn Bryant. In the early morning of August 28, Carolyn's husband, Roy Bryant, along with his half brother J. W. Milam, showed up at the house where the young Till was staying, forced him to dress, and took him away in Milam's 1955 Chevrolet pickup. Depending on which account you trust, Bryant and Milam then did at least one of the following: interrogated the boy and let him go, "whacked" him a few times with a Colt .45, beat him so severely that neighbors heard screams for mercy, castrated him and stuffed his penis in his mouth, drilled completely though his head with a brace and bit, or—in what has become the most widely accepted version of the story—beat him, stripped him, shot him in the head, attached his naked and lifeless body to a cotton gin fan with a length of barbed wire, and sank him in the Tallahatchie River. One thing we know for sure: the river wouldn't hold him. Three days after his abduction a local fisherman spotted Till's feet protruding from water. When the authorities arrived, they pulled the corpse from the water and, because the body had been beaten beyond recognition, Till's uncle was forced to identify his nephew by the Till family ring still clinging to his finger.

The immensely popular writer for the black press Olive Arnold Adams summarized the reaction to the murder and subsequent acquittal thus:

> It was a story with the impact of Pearl Harbor. In fact it was even more stunning, for it was difficult to fathom the kind of brutality displayed in this murder of a 14-year-old boy. . . . This was a cold-blooded, ruthless, base, utterly senseless sacrifice of human life, and you wanted to see what kind of atmosphere could breed such hatred. You agreed with the millions who said somebody ought to do something about Money,

[Mississippi,] but you knew that in order to do something about it, you had to understand the who—the what—the why."²²

Adams was right on both counts; the beating was brutal and people did want to understand. As Karen Halttunen has written, murder "demands that a community come to terms with the crime—confront what has happened and endeavor to explain it."²³ In the case of Emmett Till, this demand was widely felt. There were, within months of the trial, dozens of exposes each claiming to tell the true story of Emmett Till. The first was the "Inside Story" written by James L. Hicks, who provided a blow-by-blow, heavily dramatized account of both Till's murder and his own journey to Mississippi to investigate it. Emphasizing the truth of his story and the personal danger he risked obtaining it, Hicks regaled his readers with stories of taking his rented Plymouth up to ninety miles per hour on a lonely Mississippi highway to ensure that he could outrun any racial violence he might encounter.²⁴ His "Inside Story" began as follows: "Here for the first time is the true story of what happened in the hectic five-day trial of two white men in Mississippi, for the murder of 14-year-old Emmett Till of Chicago. This story has never been written before. . . . No one else has written it because no one else in the capacity of a reporter lived as close to it as I did."²⁵ In the months that followed the publication of the "Inside Story," Hick's boasts of originality, authenticity, and truthfulness would be repeated ad infinitum by journalists selling competing versions of Till's story. Ernest C. Withers, for example, promised the "first and only complete, factual photo story of the Till case," featuring "authentic pictures . . . designed to meet public demand."²⁶ Olive Arnold Adams promised to tell the "real story," which was "told in whispers" and not circulated in the mainstream press.²⁷ Finally, the award-winning journalist Ethel Payne published "Mamie Bradley's Untold Story" in the *Chicago Defender*, in which Till's mother Mamie claimed "to tell the story [of her son's murder] so that the truth will arouse men's consciences and right can at last prevail."²⁸

In addition to the various printed exposes claiming to tell the truth of Emmett Till, there was, within weeks of the trial, a vibrant, celebrity-driven lecture circuit committed to providing the public with a "comprehensive" and "detailed account of the recent murder of Emmett Till."²⁹ Speakers included the Honorable Charles C. Diggs Jr., the prominent African American congressman; Dr. T. R. M. Howard, president of the Regional Council of Negro Leadership; the NAACP leaders Ruby Hurley, Roy Wilkins, and Medgar Evers; and Till's mother, Mamie Bradley. This Till lecture circuit was a resounding success: 2,500 people gathered in Baltimore's Sharp Street Methodist Church, 16,000 people crowded into New York's Williams Church, 15,000 in Detroit, 4,000 in Cleveland, and Chicago's Metropolitan Community Church reportedly turned away 6,000 people who had come to hear Till's story told.[30]

In sum, by the time Huie arrived on the scene in October 1955, there was no shortage of exposes or inside stories. Yet Huie knew that the market was not so saturated that it could not accommodate one more telling of Till's story, provided it was a firsthand narrative. At least to his own satisfaction, Huie believed that it was precisely his ability to write Till's story based on the killers' confession that would set his apart from the rest. Reflecting on the experience some years later, Huie recalled, "I knew enough to assume that Big Milam and Roy Bryant would tell me everything they knew and felt. No other reporter had assumed this."[31] Huie also "knew," however, that the killers would tell him everything only if their lawyers told them to do so.[32] Thus, when he arrived in Mississippi, Huie went first to the law offices of Breland & Whitten: "I told Breland and Whitten that I didn't like the hypocrisy in this case; that I wanted the facts; and that I intended to write, step by step, hour by hour, the story of the abduction, the torture, the murder; and the disposal of the body." To obtain these facts, Huie recalled in a letter to the NAACP's Roy Wilkins, he simply confronted Breland and Whitten and demanded an audience with the killers: "I further told Breland & Whitten that I wanted them to deliver Bryant and Milam and Bryant's wife to me—in a secret rendezvous in Greenwood—and that I wanted them to tell me every last line of the truth."[33]

For reasons that will become clear, Breland and Whitten did precisely as they were told. They arranged the rendezvous, the killers told Huie "everything they knew and felt," and the "Shocking Story" was published three months later. It was, in Huie's modest estimate, "more explosive than UNCLE TOM'S CABIN—and a damn sight more honest."[34] It was the honesty part that Huie and *Look* emphasized. In an advertisement that ran in both the black *Chicago Defender* and the white *Daily Corinthian*, *Look* claimed that the "Shocking Story" told "for the first time . . . THE TRUTH about the Emmett Till killing":

> Headlines screamed across the nation. Millions of words were written about it. A trial was held. Yet *the truth* about the Emmett Till killing in Mississippi remained hidden—until now! Now *exclusively* in LOOK Magazine you can read the story—the story that the jury did not hear,

that no newspaper reader ever saw . . . the brutal step-by-step *full account* of what happened that fateful night. You'll read *how* Till was killed, *where*, *why*, and *by whom*! Don't miss this shocking story in LOOK. It will be magazine history the minute it hits the newsstands. Get your copy of LOOK *early*![35]

Ten days later, *Look* prefaced Huie's "Shocking Story" with an "Editor's Note" that further attested to the veracity of his tale: "The editors of LOOK are convinced that they are presenting here, for the first time, the real story of that killing."[36]

In January 1956, all this talk of truthfulness would have done little to separate the "Shocking Story" from the run of competing Till exposes. It is important to recall that there was no shortage of claimants to the truth of Emmett Till. In fact, the sensationalist language of expose and the promises of step-by-step detail were something of an Emmett Till commonplace. Writing in the October 8, 1955, *Cleveland Call and Post*, for example, James Hicks claimed that his story on Emmett Till "has never been written before" because "no one else in the capacity of reporter lived as close to it as I did."[37] He claimed to be a "stand-in at the trial" for *Afro-American* readers everywhere, someone with "on-the-scene" stories and "behind the scenes" reporting.[38] Hicks recounted his tales of frequenting local funerals, barbershops, and taverns to meet informants who risked their lives to tell him the truth.[39] Likewise, Adams's *Time Bomb* claimed to disclose "a heretofore unpublished version of the crime" and was prefaced with Dr. T. R. M. Howard's assurance that "her story of the Emmett Till case has come from Negroes 'in the know' in Mississippi."[40] Dr. Howard himself, speaking to a Baltimore audience of more than two thousand people, claimed that he received his own version of Till's story from "eyewitnesses who were never called to the stand."[41] Yet despite boasts of truthfulness that could rival Huie's, neither Hicks's serialized expose nor Adams's *Time Bomb* ever captured the confessional imagination quite like Huie's "Shocking Story."

If the widely observed conventions of sensationalism rendered *Look*'s claims to truthfulness rather insignificant, Huie's and Milam's well-publicized denials also militated against the long-shot possibility that the "Shocking Story" would become a confession. According to the *Greenwood Commonwealth*, Milam denied the story in the most emphatic terms possible: "I don't know a damn thing about it, and you can quote me on it. I never saw anyone named William Bradford Huie that I know of. There were 75 reporters at the trial and I didn't know all their names but I've never made statements like that to anyone. There's nothing I can do about someone's imagination, but I didn't have nothing to do with killing anyone."[42] Although black papers did not give Milam's denials as much coverage, excerpts of the denials were printed there, too. In a widely quoted *Afro-American* interview, Milam pinned the entire story on Huie: "He (Huey) [*sic*] surely can't quote me as saying all that because I didn't make any such statement. There is nothing I can do about somebody's imagination, but I didn't have anything to do with killing anyone."[43] The *Atlanta Daily World* stated the denial even more emphatically, suggesting that Milam and Bryant may sue *Look* for libel.[44]

Although Huie stood by his story and threatened to sue those who called him a liar, he also stood by his commitment to Breland and Whitten.[45] When Mississippi authorities asked Huie for help, he refused to disclose his sources: "If I can find out the truth certainly the state of Mississippi can. If the state wants the facts, they can get them."[46] Likewise, when *Time* magazine's Jean Franklin pressed Huie as to how he "got his beat," he replied disingenuously, "I made two trips to Mississippi; I walked down dusty roads at night; [and] I made two trips to Chicago." In other words, Huie always pretended that he didn't need to talk to the killers to write the "Shocking Story." His tale, although he insisted it was true, "stems from nothing more than a distaste for hypocrisy; and some ability to write simple declarative sentences which infuriate a certain number of people."[47]

Taken together, the conventions of sensationalism (the fact that nearly every expose claimed to be true and authentic) and the public insistence by Huie, the killers, and their lawyers that the "Shocking Story" was not a confession, render even more mysterious the article's later reification as a confession. To be sure, the "Shocking Story" did include quotations that, as Huie put it, "could have been gotten only from a participant in the crime."[48] Yet in the spring of 1956, it was hardly a foregone conclusion that the "Shocking Story" would become the definitive account of the murder for nearly fifty years. At the time, there were dozens of exposes competing for that mantle, and if Huie's account was aided by the fact that it contained direct quotations, it was hurt by the fact that it was the only version of the story that the murderers ever specifically disclaimed. In the end, it would not be the quotations that set Huie's story apart from the field, but the fact that activists for both Jim Crow and civil rights colluded in the act of turning the "Shocking Story" into a confession.

The "Shocking Story" and Civil Rights

The January 1956 publication of the "Shocking Story" put the tale of Emmett Till where it hadn't been in over two months: the front pages of black newspapers across the country. As the *Atlanta Daily World* put it:

> The Till murder case has taken on new national significance in the wake of a story published in the current issue of Look Magazine charging that one of the two men acquitted murdered Emmett because he bragged about his relationship with white girls, and wouldn't scare.[49]

This is the *Cleveland Call and Post*:

> [Huie's] sensationally-exploited expose on the Till Lynch–Murder, on which [Look] reportedly gambled the printing of an extra million copies, has met with immediate—and varied—reactions from the interested parties. Almost simultaneously with the story's release to newsstands throughout the nation, NAACP's Executive Secretary Roy Wilkins issued a demand that a Mississippi grand jury be convened to hear a new presentation of kidnap charges.[50]

The *Chicago Defender*:

> William Bradford Huie, Pulitzer prize winning newspaper man and author, confirmed this week, in a published article, what most of the world has believed since early September last year—that J. W. Milam and Roy Bryant killed 14-year-old Emmett Till of Chicago. Huie, who has done some spectacular reporting in other cases involving crimes against Negroes, made the charges this week in an article appearing in Look magazine.[51]

The *Philadelphia Afro-American*:

> Much surprise was expressed over the daring of *Look* in printing what is supposed to be the confession of the men, who have been cleared of murder charges.[52]

The *New York Amsterdam News*:

> The grease is still popping from Mississippi's legal fish-fry over the Emmett Till kidnap–murder case last summer, the latest loud pop

being William Bradford Huie's sensational expose in Look Magazine. Though purporting to represent actual confessions of the slaying by the two men acquitted by jury in Mississippi, the article cannot cause a special grand jury to be impaneled to reopen the kidnap charges against them.[53]

All these quotations—culled from some of the leading black papers of the era—register quite clearly the affective shock Huie's story caused among those committed to civil rights. Two of them—those from the *Call and Post* and the *Amsterdam News*—register the fact that the publication of Huie's story created a unique opportunity to fight for racial justice. Only the *New York Amsterdam News*, however, connected the possibility of racial justice to the genre of Huie's "Shocking Story."

Despite the fact that the "Shocking Story" "purports" to be a confession, the *Amsterdam News* protested, it cannot "cause a special grand jury to be impaneled." The reason it could not, the article continued, is because a grand jury could be convened only by Judge Arthur Jordan, who was refusing to do so. Judge Jordan never relented and he never reconvened a grand jury. But his refusal to do so did nothing to temper the efforts of civil rights advocates and the NAACP to connect the genre of Huie's story to the possibility of racial justice. Time and again, civil rights activists adopted the strategy of the *New York Amsterdam News*: they claimed that the "Shocking Story" was a confession and used this fact to demand political intervention. In this context, it is worth considering the efforts of two influential leaders of the civil rights movement, the journalist James L. Hicks and NAACP Executive Secretary Roy Wilkins. Both men played leading roles throughout the civil rights movement, and both were personally invested in the Till case. Although Hicks and Wilkins did not always see eye to eye, especially when it came to issues of leadership in the civil rights movement, they agreed on the genre of Huie's story. They both argued that the "Shocking Story" was a confession and that this fact alone demanded federal intervention into Mississippi injustice.

James L. Hicks—"ace AFRO correspondent" and future executive editor of the *Amsterdam News*—was one of the first to label the "Shocking Story" as a confession.[54] He did so in a January 21, 1956, open letter to U.S. Attorney General Herbert Brownell. This was the second such letter Hicks had addressed to Brownell. In November 1955, Hicks had written Brownell a letter documenting the guilt of the recently acquitted Milam and Bryant, but his letter was never acknowledged. Now, upon the publication of Huie's

"Shocking Story," Hicks redoubled his efforts to convince Brownell to intervene in the Till affair. Unsurprisingly, the bulk of Hick's second letter was concerned with the genre of the "Shocking Story." Hicks laid out a complex rationale explaining why, precisely, the "Shocking Story" counted as a confession. First, he began by noting that "Mr. Milam is quoted from direct quotes all through the article." Second, Hicks argued that under most any circumstances, this would expose the magazine to legal trouble: "Now, Mr. Brownell, you are a lawyer and you know that if a magazine or any publication charges a man with murder in direct quotes, that man can sue the magazine or newspaper for libel in any court in this nation AND FORCE THAT MAGAZINE OR NEWSPAPER TO EITHER PROVE HE COMMITTED THE MURDER OR COLLECT DAMAGES TO THE AMOUNT OF HARM HE HAS SUFFERED BY SUCH A CHARGE!" Third, Milam was not filing suit. Fourth, and finally, the magazine was not worried that he would. This systematic logic prepared Hicks to pose his central question: "Why is the magazine so confident?" To Hicks's mind, there could be only one answer: "An affidavit signed by J. W. Milam in which he admits to the magazine that everything in the article is true. That's the only kind of guarantee that any publication with the national standing of Look Magazine could accept under the circumstances." Lest Mr. Brownell hesitate to read between the lines, Hicks spelled it out for him: "In other words, Mr. Brownell, what I now say is that Milam and Bryant have confessed their killing of Emmett Till."

At this point, with the "Shocking Story" now functioning as a confession, Hicks immediately implored Brownell to take action. I quote the closing lines of the open letter at length because they beautifully illustrate the bonds that, at least for Hicks, tied the possibility of racial justice to the genre of the "Shocking Story": "In the magazine article [Bryant and Milam] simply confess that they killed Emmett Till. It seems to me only logical that whatever plan you had of dealing with them when you investigated my charges can simply be dragged out now and used with full speed ahead. It's your move, Mr. Attorney General." In the open letter of James Hicks, the genre of confession is a political tool of the first order. He was seeking redress, and he recognized clearly that if the "Shocking Story" counted as a confession, it provided him another opportunity to pressure Brownell for action.[55]

At the same time that Hicks was distributing his open letter, Wilkins was publicly appealing to newly elected Mississippi Governor J. P. Coleman. Like that of Hicks, Wilkins's appeal to Coleman was grounded in a careful textual analysis of the "Shocking Story": "Mr. Huie does not say this is the story of the events as related by the woman [Carolyn Bryant], nor does he say or imply in any way that another person who gave him the story of the actual crime and told him this story was the one which induced the kidnapping and killing. Who stands behind these 'facts,' Mr. Huie?"[56] The last sentence of the above quotation—"Who stands behind these 'facts,' Mr. Huie?"— was quoted dozens of times, and it captures Wilkins's sense that Huie had an inside source. As this sense became more and more explicit, Wilkins placed more and more pressure on Mississippi politicians. The pressure culminated in a widely disseminated January 9 telegram to Coleman pressuring him to reconvene the Leflore County grand jury (although Milam and Bryant had been acquitted of murder in Tallahatchie County, they could still be indicted for kidnapping in Leflore County). According to the *Cleveland Call and Post*, Wilkins's decision to publicly pressure Coleman "was taken as the result of an article published in the current issue of Look Magazine" that quotes Bryant and Milam "admitting the kidnapping and killing."[57] This is Wilkins:

> In view of the admissions of Roy Bryant and J. W. Milam, of the kidnap and killing of Emmett Louis Till last summer as published in the current issue of Look magazine, the NAACP calls upon you to convene the grand jury of Le Flore [sic] County for the purpose of a new presentment of the kidnap charges against these self confessed criminals. The whole nation is horrified and stands humiliated in the eyes of the civilized world that these vicious men should walk free and unashamed while boasting of their depravity.[58]

Although he was not Wilkins's intended addressee, Mississippi Judge Arthur Jordan of Leflore County responded, "No grand jury will indict anybody just on the basis of a magazine article."[59] New York's *Amsterdam News*, in turn, responded to Judge Jordan, claiming that his decision to ignore the "magazine article" was tantamount to ignoring the "actual confessions."[60]

This exchange between Wilkins and Mississippi politicians is instructive. Wilkins and the *Amsterdam News* believed that the "Shocking Story" was a confession. Accordingly, they also believed that a careful deployment of the "Shocking Story" could be a tool to redress the injustices of Emmett Till's murder. When Jordan and Coleman rebuffed Wilkins's requests, they rebuffed also his suggestion that the "Shocking Story" was anything more than a "magazine article." To Jordan's mind, the "Shocking Story" would "carry some weight" only if "William Bradford Huie, the author of the article, came to Mississippi to testify."[61] Barring this, there would be no reason to treat the "Shocking Story" as a confession.

Hicks and Wilkins, of course, lost these arguments. Neither Brownell, nor Jordan, nor Coleman ever intervened into the Emmett Till case. Hicks and Wilkins should not have been surprised. In a sense, they were destined to lose these arguments. Not only were they fighting an entrenched system of segregation, their appeals were predicated on their insistence that the "Shocking Story" was something it wasn't: an "actual confession." Judge Jordan was right—technically speaking, the "Shocking Story" was simply a magazine article written in the third person with no direction admissions of guilt. Legally there were no grounds for treating it as a confession without the testimony of Huie. Of course, Huie would offer no such testimony, and had he done so, he would have brought with him signed affidavits attesting to the one thing that Hicks's and Wilkins's arguments could not brook: that the "Shocking Story" was not an admission of guilt.

The ultimate futility of their arguments, however, takes nothing away from the force of my point here. Indeed it strengthens it. Hicks knew that he was fighting a system of segregation so entrenched that it would be unresponsive to counterarguments. He was so aware of the southern intolerance for his position that, along with the other black reporters, he formulated a plan to steal a gun from a bailiff and escape out the window of the courtroom if vigilantism prevailed.[62] Yet so convinced was he of the power that resided in labeling Huie's text a confession, he persisted in his argument despite his keen awareness that his ultimate recourse may only be physical violence. To his mind, it mattered not a whit that, technically speaking, the "Shocking Story" was not a confession. He ignored that fact and put his effort into turning it into one, because he knew that if he could pull that off, he might also be able to make the case for intervention. Thus was the genre of confession intertwined with civil rights politics.

The "Shocking Story" and Segregation

Jesse Breland, John Whitten, and the Citizens' Councils had no desire for federal intervention into Mississippi race relations. Yet just as much as the NAACP—an organization they deplored—the councils, too, had a vested interest in authenticating the "Shocking Story." Unlike the civil rights activists, none of the segregationists actually claimed that Huie's story was a confession. This is not surprising. They had just exonerated two murderers, and labeling the text a confession would—as Hicks and Wilkins well knew—call into question the status of Mississippi justice. Despite this, there is overwhelming evidence that segregationists did not simply put up with Huie as an independent member of the Fourth Estate. The evidence suggests that Breland and Whitten, *because they were segregationists, wanted* Huie to write his article. Huie knew this; he confided to Basil Walters that Breland and Whitten went along with his plan because they thought his story would help their segregationist cause: "Publication of this story, with all its revolting details, is exactly what Breland's group in Mississippi wants."[63] They wanted Huie to tell their side of the story, and they wanted him to do so with a force no one could question. To this end, they arranged the "secret sessions" with the killers so Huie could hear their partisan story, as it were, "firsthand." Legally speaking, Breland and Whitten had to arrange things such that the "Shocking Story" could not be a confession. Politically speaking, however, they had incentive to arrange things such that the "Shocking Story" would mistakenly be read *as* a confession. They wanted their own version of the story told, and they knew that the more it was mistaken for the killers' confession, the more power it would have.

On this point, it is important to emphasize that although Milam may have denied the Huie story publicly (because he had to), privately he signed off, literally, on every single page. When he and the Bryants signed the "Consent and Release" forms on the evening of October 28, they also initialed every page of Huie's draft. This much was in the contract: "I have also read and fully understand the general rough outline and notes which are to be the basis for the article or story which Mr. Huie proposes to write, which are attached hereto, initialed by me and hereby made a part of this Consent and Release."[64] In other words, under the watchful eye of their attorneys, the killers signed off on a particular version of Till's murder. Clearly, they had a stake in disseminating this version of the story—what Milam would later refer to as the "Mississippi" version.[65] From Huie's perspective, Milam and Bryant were merely "bully-boys," men who were pushed around by the likes of Breland and Whitten to do their dirty work. From Breland and Whitten's perspective, however, Huie must have appeared as one more bully-boy: a reporter who would disseminate their story, and pay them for the privilege of doing so.

Why did the segregationists have a vested interest in authenticating Huie's tale? Why did the murderers sign off on this version of the story?

Why did Breland and Whitten "want" Huie to publish it? Why did they arrange the meetings that would allow Huie not simply to tell their story, but to tell it with the force of quotations that "could have been gotten only from a participant in the crime"? Why, in short, did they arrange things such that Huie could write their story in such a way that it would be widely mistaken for a confession? Answer: The segregationists had a double-interest in authenticating Huie's story. The "Shocking Story" as confession served them in two basic ways: it provided them with a relatively sanitized version of the murder, and it functioned as a much-needed response to the despised judicial intervention into Mississippi racial politics that was *Brown v. Board of Education*.

Sanitizing Till's Murder

It is important to remember that Huie was a latecomer to the truth-saturated market of Emmett Till exposes. By the time the "Shocking Story" was published in January 1956, Hicks's celebrated and syndicated exposes had been running in papers across the country for nearly four months. When Huie's story was published, the story it told of Till's abduction and death conflicted sharply with the published accounts that had flourished theretofore. It conflicted on a number of smaller points—the amount of alcohol consumed, the precise place of the murder, and the extent of the violence perpetrated against Till—and on one major point: the number of accomplices to the murder. This last issue was in a league of its own. Although the other points of conflict were certainly weighty matters, the question of how many people were involved in the death of Emmett Till had concrete legal ramifications. On this question, there is evidence to suggest that Huie told the story Breland and Whitten wanted him to tell.

In Huie's October 12 letter to Roy Wilkins, he reported that there were "four in the torture-and-murder party."[66] Because only two had been acquitted in a court of law, Huie wasn't sure if he could name all four people in his story. He thus sought the advice of *Look* editor Daniel Mich: "If we do not have their [the two undisclosed murderers] releases, shall we name them in the story or not? Shall we quote them anonymously in any part of the action?"[67] By the time he wrote Basil Walters on October 18, he had worked out a solution. After telling Mr. Walters that he knew "all four" murderers by name, he suggested the following: "We can, if necessary, omit the names of the other two. We can even avoid all reference to them, though I would urge any publisher to state that they were present, to quote whatever they said at any point in the action, but not to name them."[68]

Five days later, on October 23, Huie abruptly changed his tune. In the letter he wrote Mich immediately after returning from the first "secret session" with the killers, he cut the "torture-and-murder party" in half: "Of this I am now certain: there were not, after all, *four* men involved in the abduction-and-murder: there were only two. So when we have these releases from Bryant and Milam and the woman, we are completely safe."[69] Now, it is impossible to know just what happened between October 18 and October 23. Perhaps Huie genuinely changed his mind. After all, when he drafted the October 23 letter, he had just spent a day in "secret session" with Milam and Bryant. It is certainly conceivable that he learned from them the truth of the killing and revised the size of the "murder party" accordingly. There is, however, evidence to suggest that Huie may have adjusted the size of the party to match the number of release forms he could obtain.

Consider the following: We know that Mich required "Consent and Release" forms if he was to publish Huie's story.[70] We know, too, that on October 21—three days after he claimed to know "all four" murderers, but two days before he lowered his estimate—he wrote Mich with information about the likelihood of obtaining releases. Conveying a phone conversation with Whitten, Huie told Mich that he could certainly obtain releases from Bryant and his wife—they are "in the bag"—but Milam's release would be both more difficult and more important: "You want Milam. All I can say at this point is that I *think* I can bring it off."[71] If Huie had doubts about Whitten's ability to secure a release from Milam, who had been tried and acquitted in a court of law and who, accordingly, would not be "jeopardized" by the story, how much more would those doubts apply to the killers who did not enjoy the protections against double jeopardy? Given these legal constraints, the possibility exists that Huie's "Shocking Story" featured a "torture-and-murder party" of two only because Whitten could secure only two releases.

Adding to this suspicion is the fact that, until Huie's "Shocking Story," it was widely rumored that there were more participants in the murder party than simply Milam and Bryant. Huie was hardly breaking new ground when he confided to Roy Wilkins that four were complicit in the death of Emmett Till. Before the September 19 trial, rumors of additional accomplices came from all sides. Till's uncle Moses Wright, for example, initially told the *Daily World* that three men and one woman arrived at his house to kidnap Till.[72] Likewise, Tallahatchie County Sheriff H. C. Strider issued a warrant for

Carolyn Bryant's arrest and Leflore County Deputy Ed Cothran claimed that there "was another man and we will get him before we are through."[73] During the trial, an eighteen-year-old black man named Willie Reed testified that he saw three other white men and three black men with J. W. Milam on the morning of Till's death.[74] Although the trial effectively squashed the legal validity of Reed's testimony, stories of multiple accomplices continued to resonate in the black press well after the trial. On October 7, for example, Dr. T. R. M. Howard claimed that four whites and three blacks constituted the murder party.[75] The next day, James Hicks used the front page of the *Cleveland Call and Post* to claim that there were three white men involved along with two "colored" men.[76] Four months after that, just after the publication of Huie's "Shocking Story," Olive Arnold Adams claimed that, "regardless of court records or 'confessions'"—a not too subtle jab at Huie—there were actually seven people in the murder party, four white men, one white woman, and two black men.[77]

The Federal Bureau of Investigation's 2006 report on the Emmett Till murder overwhelmingly confirms these early rumors of an exaggerated murder party. The report cites nine independent sources, eight of whom named between four and eight accomplices to the murder. The ninth, a source whose name was redacted from the report, claimed that the murder party consisted of ten to twelve people.[78] Most dramatically, the FBI report claims that before he died in 1981, Milam confessed the details of the crime to a "confidential source" over the course of three telephone interviews. During these conversations, Milam admitted that by the time Till was beaten and killed, "the group . . . included Roy Bryant, [J. W. Milam's brother] Leslie Milam, Hubert Clark, Melvin Campbell, 'Too Tight' Collins and [name redacted]."[79] This account was corroborated both by Leslie Milam's 1974 deathbed confession—in which he confirmed that "he had been personally involved in the murder of Emmett Till"—and Carolyn Bryant's more recent admissions to the FBI (the vast majority of which are redacted).[80]

In short, there is overwhelming evidence that Huie's initial position was the correct one: the murder of Emmett Till required the collusion of far more than two white men. The early investigative reporting of Hicks, Howard, and Adams has been proven correct by the confessions of two Milam brothers and Carolyn Bryant. How, then, could Huie meet in "secret session" with Milam and the Bryants on October 23 and then proceed to tell Mich that he was "certain" that "were not after all, *four* men involved in the abduction-and-murder: there were only two." It is possible that Huie was lied to that day. This is the position of Davis Houck and Matthew Grindy.

In their outstanding account of the white press coverage of the Till affair, they conclude that Huie was "bamboozled and *Look* hoodwinked."[81] In other words, Houck and Grindy believe that Huie's "Shocking Story" relates the narrative it does because Huie mistook Milam's "Mississippi" version of Till's murder for gospel truth. As Sharon Monteith put it, "Huie failed to scent all the bullshit in Milam's account."[82]

However, given Huie's October 18 insistence that he knew all four murderers by name; given his "urging" on the same day that the names be published, given that he made no secret of this information, sharing it with Wilkins, Walters, and Mich; and finally, given his October 21 anxieties about whether he could obtain the requisite signatures, it is certainly within the realm of possibility that Huie constricted the size of the murder party until it consisted only of those who were willing to sign the Consent and Release forms.

Ultimately, whether Huie acted out of ignorance or self-interest is a moot point. The fact remains that he *did* put only two people in the murder party. In so doing, he virtually assured that no further legal indictments would be pursued. Given the rumors flying about at the time, and given the fact that the FBI has recently confirmed these rumors, it is not hard to see why Breland and Whitten "wanted" Huie to write their story—and why they did everything possible to ensure that when written, it would have all the force of a confession and thereby take the country by storm.

J. J. Breland Versus Brown II

Besides the limited murder party, the segregationists had a second reason for signing off on the "Shocking Story." Emmett Till was murdered fourteen months after the Supreme Court handed down *Brown v. Board of Education* and three months after *Brown II*, the enforcement order that demanded school integration "with all deliberate speed." The state of Mississippi was on the defensive. The staunch racist Frederick Sullens used the editorial page of his *Jackson Daily News* to publicly announce Mississippi's resistance: "Human blood may stain southern soil in many places because of this decision, but the dark red stains of that blood will be on the marble steps of the United States Supreme Court building. White and Negro children in the same schools will lead to miscegenation. It means racial strife of the bitterest sort. Mississippi cannot and will not try to abide by the decision."[83] This sentiment was not confined to Sullens. In July 1955, the whole of the state legislature "passed a constitutional amendment to abolish the public schools in Mississippi should the colored people seek integration."[84] The "archsegregationist" Mississippi Senator James O. Eastland expressly called for citizen resistance: "I know Southern people will not surrender their dual school system and their racial heritage at the command of this crowd of racial politicians in judicial robes."[85]

If Mississippi as a whole was on the defensive, the northern Delta felt particularly embattled. Stephen Whitaker argues that while Mississippi functions synecdochically for the entirety of the "Deep South," Tallahatchie County—the site of Till's trial—functioned synecdochically for the state of Mississippi: it is, as it were, the deepest of the "Deep South."[86] Unsurprisingly, the most organized form of resistance to *Brown* sprang up in the Delta—a place the historian Neil McMillen described as a "natural birthplace for a white supremacy movement."[87] Formed in 1954, the Association of Citizens' Councils of Mississippi (ACCM) was a "loose confederation of statewide segregation associations."[88] Although the councils were formed as a means of organized resistance to *Brown v. Board*, and although local chapters tended to spring up in precisely those counties in which the NAACP filed school integration petitions, they were not a one-issue organization. Beyond preserving school segregation, the ACCM was dedicated more generally to "the denial of socio-political equality to the black man."[89] This involved defending the myth of southern womanhood, proscriptions against interracial sexuality, and an exclusively white franchise. As both McMillen and the Till controversy demonstrate, these issues were often inextricably bound up with school integration.

More than any other portion of the state, the northern Delta experienced the *Brown* decisions as impositions—indeed, attacks—on their "southern way of life." In 1963 Whitaker ranked the "Free State of Tallahatchie" as a one of the three most insulated counties in the country. Along with Cook County, Illinois and Shelby County, Tennessee, Whitaker claimed that Tallahatchie County operated wholly "independently of outside restrictions."[90] This independence did not just happen. If the Delta whites were xenophobic, as Stephen J. Whitfield has claimed, they were trained to be so.[91] The FBI reports that the "white citizens of Mississippi were bombarded daily with news surrounding the end of segregated schools, efforts by blacks to register to vote and heated calls for the defense of their segregated life."[92] For these reasons, the councils thrived in the Delta. Founded in Indianola (the birthplace of Carolyn Bryant), and soon thereafter headquartered in Greenwood, by the time Till died the ACCM reported "60,000 members in 253 Councils."[93]

When we remember that Milam and Bryant were tried in Tallahatchie County—ground zero in the fight over a "southern way of life"—it is hardly surprising that the murder of Till was intricately bound up with the anxieties produced by the *Brown* decisions. What is surprising is that this intrication took time. Whitfield notes that in the immediate aftermath of the murder, there was no impulse to justify the act as a defense of southern traditions or as a response to northern encroachment. The Citizens' Councils denounced the killing, Bryant and Milam were unable to find legal representation, and even Sullens's *Jackson Daily News* condemned the murder as "a brutal, senseless crime and[,] just incidentally, one which merits not one iota of sympathy for the killers."[94] As Houck and Grindy summarize, "The first several days of newspaper coverage reveal a sympathetic treatment of Emmett Till."[95]

By the time of the trial, however, spurred by incendiary comments from the NAACP, things had changed. Roy Wilkins called the murder a "lynching" and laid the blame on the entire state of Mississippi: "The State of Mississippi has decided to maintain white supremacy by murdering children."[96] Moreover, the NAACP's *Crisis* used the murder of Emmett Till to attack "the state of Jungle fury" in Mississippi and argued (falsely) that no "highly-placed Mississippian denounces the crime."[97] These comments were quoted—and misquoted—throughout the southern white press.[98] In the already embattled Delta, the sense that the NAACP was encroaching on their way of life struck a well-prepared nerve. The white *Greenwood Commonwealth* denounced in the strongest terms the "unwarranted, libelous and slanderous attack by the National Association for the Advancement of Colored People."[99] And when the Till trial became a referendum on the autonomy of the Delta, the southern establishment changed course. The same lawyers who once refused to defend Milam and Bryant now did so pro bono.[100] The same councils that had once denounced the murder now visited every juror to assure an acquittal.[101] Whitfield writes, "Local pride and self-sufficiency were imperiled, and the capacity of Mississippi whites to govern themselves . . . came to be the central issue in the Till case. The primacy of states' rights became so urgent, the feelings of defensiveness so raw and exposed, that the murder of an adolescent declined in moral magnitude."[102] Houck and Grindy agree; after the incendiary comments by Wilkins and the NAACP, the Till affair was no longer about the murder of a black boy: "The Till case quickly grew to encompass North–South relations; the role of Citizens' Councils and pro-civil-rights groups after *Brown v. Board of Education*; federalism versus localism." Southern segregationists fought this larger war, as it were, by proxy. They turned northern calls for justice into "an attack on the state, its people, and its segregated way of life."[103] Jackson, Mississippi's white *Clarion Ledger* went so far as to classify the Till murder as the "offspring" of "segregation issue."[104] And Mississippi Governor-Elect J. P. Coleman even blamed the interference of the NAACP for the Till acquittal.[105]

Milam's and Bryant's lawyer J. J. Breland certainly understood the Till trial as a referendum on southern autonomy. Upon the conclusion of the trial, Breland—the sixty-seven-year-old "ringleader" of the defense team—wrote two thank-you notes to professional colleagues who supported his defense of Milam and Bryant.[106] Both letters expressed similar sentiments: "It is unfortunate for us that we had to be the place where the NAACP selected in Mississippi to try to drive in an entering wedge in furtherance of their scheme for integration and equalization in the State of Mississippi, but we did not hesitate to assume our full responsibility and stopped them cold."[107] One month later, Breland penned a congratulatory note to Frederick Sullens of Jackson's *Daily News*. He thanked him for his coverage of the Till trial and on being "the first southern paper who has made a serious attempt to combat the NAACP propaganda against the South, and Mississippi in particular."[108] Breland's correspondence dramatically confirms Whitfield's and Houck and Grindy's analysis: by the time of the trial, the Till case was a referendum on Delta autonomy. It was, as Whitfield put it, "the outrage that was heard from 'up No'f' [that] was driving Delta whites to rally'round in defense of two of their own."[109]

It was precisely this "rally" that made the "Shocking Story" possible. When Huie first broached the topic of writing Till's story with Breland and Whitten, Breland responded by framing the murder trial in the larger context of northern intervention. According to Huie, Breland told him the following: "We don't need the niggers no more. And there ain't gonna be no integration. Their ain't gonna be no nigger votin'. *And the sooner everybody in the country realizes it the better.* Any more pressure is put on us, the Tallahatchie River won't hold all the niggers that'll be thrown into it." In Huie's estimate, "a man like Breland honestly believes that they can force the Supreme Court to reverse itself."[110] Huie capitalized (literally) on Breland's racism; he convinced the lawyers that his writing of the Till story would be to their own, segregationist interest. Huie promised, in other words, that he could make Delta violence serve Delta politics. He made this explicit in his letter to Basil Walters. Therein Huie explained why the law firm of Breland & Whitten complied with his request for exclusive access to the killers. In addition to the protections of double jeopardy and the enticement of money, Huie argued that the "most important reason" Breland & Whitten complied is that their Delta politics stood to gain thereby: "Publication of this story, with all its revolting details, is exactly what Breland's group in Mississippi *wants*. They want to 'put the North and the NAACP and the niggers *on notice*.' My proposal strikes them as being a 'good propaganda move.' They think of me as a 'rough writer' who ain't no nigger-lover and who'll 'lay it on the line.'"[111] One year later, preparing a follow-up story on the Till murder, Huie expressed the same sentiments. In an October 1956 letter, he assured John Whitten that his new book on Till would be "a bitter dose for the NAACP and the 'liberals.'" He then asked Whitten to pass a message on to his partner: "Tell Mr. Breland I'll send him the [damning U.S. Army] file on [Emmett's father] Pvt. Louis Till when I'm finished with it, and he can send it around and have it read aloud at all the meetings of the Citizens' Councils."[112] Huie, in other words, suggested to Breland and Whitten that his own work should be considered part and parcel of their fight to preserve Delta autonomy in the "free state of Tallahatchie." He even offered them materials with which to stoke the anger of the Citizens' Councils.

Although Breland and Whitten would not have been surprised by the contents of the "Shocking Story"—the contracts signed in their office, recall, dictated the content of the article—they could not have been more pleased when the "Shocking Story" hit the newsstands in January 1956. The story framed the murder of Emmett Till in the xenophobic terms of local autonomy and outside encroachment. At the climax of the "Shocking Story," it almost seems as if Breland has taken over the telling. Immediately before Till is killed, Huie provided what is purportedly a paragraph-long quotation from J. W. Milam. It is, of course, impossible to know whether Milam, Breland, or anybody else actually uttered these words, but it is certain that the words Huie put into Milam's voice bear a strong and marked resemblance to the words, quoted above, of J. J. Breland. Here is the explanation of the murder, written by Huie, ostensibly from Milam himself:

> Well, what else could we do? He was hopeless. I'm no bully; I never hurt a nigger in my life. I like niggers—in their place—I know how to work 'em. But I just decided it was time a few people got put on notice. As long as I live and can do anything about it, niggers are gonna stay in their place. Niggers ain't gonna vote where I live. If they did, they'd control the government. They ain't gonna go to school with my kids. And when a nigger even gets close to mentioning sex with a white woman, he's tired o' livin'. I'm likely to kill him. Me and my folks fought for this country, and we've got some rights. I stood there in that

shed and listened to that nigger throw that poison at me, and I just made up my mind. "Chicago boy," I said, "I'm tired of 'em sending your kind down here to stir up trouble. Goddamn you, I'm going to make an example of you—just so everybody can know how me and my folks stand."[113]

In Houck and Grindy's estimate, these were not the words of J. W. Milam. In their view, the fact that Huie has Milam "wax[ing] sociopolitical" is simply untenable; they suggest that Milam simply could not—or would not—have "waxed" with such polish: "Careful readers might have also been skeptical of Milam's ostensible rhetorical talents. It would take a degree of intellectual abstraction to situate and articulate what he was about to do in the context of a post-*Brown* world—to say nothing of doing it with a loaded pistol, while under the influence, and with a rapidly rising summer sun. By all accounts, Big Milam was not one for abstraction or careful rationalization; no, his talents, by his own admission, were in killing and in working negroes."[114]

If these words were not Milam's, to whom did they belong? Although a definitive answer to this question is impossible, the evidence points the ringleader of the southern defense, J. J. Breland. In the quotation, "Milam" is intensely local: "Niggers ain't gonna vote where I live." He is devoted to his "folks." He labels Till an outsider ("Chicago boy"). And he suggests that he was sent down, presumably by the NAACP, to "stir up trouble." All this, down to the level of word choice, resembles nothing so much as Breland's rant against integration and his desire to put the North "on notice." It is no wonder that Breland accepted Huie's proposal; when he saw the murderers initial the pages of Huie's draft, he must have believed that Huie was doing the work of the Citizens' Councils. Huie was going to tell J. J. Breland's version of the story and, to ensure that it was accepted, he was going to put it into the voice of J. W. Milam.

If Mich required "Consent and Release" forms before he would print the story, Breland required that the existence of these forms be forever secret. Thus the last clause of the contract was this: "This Consent and Release is also given upon the express condition that the existence of this instrument and the fact of my cooperation with Mr. Huie in writing the work will not be revealed publicly unless I, my wife, Juanita, or other member of my family, and/or Roy Bryant, his wife Carolyn, or other member of Mr. Bryant's family and/or anyone acting on my, our, or their behalf, should institute legal action against Mr. Huie."[115] The contracts, in other words, served a double purpose. They guaranteed that the "Shocking Story" could not be legally construed as a confession, but they also ensured that this guarantee was kept secret. This latter function was of the utmost importance to Breland. It ensured that the "Shocking Story" could be mistaken for a confession, a mistake that would, Breland must have suspected, done nothing but help his Delta politics.

This is how segregationist politics intersected with confessional politics in the fall of 1955. Huie convinced Breland and Whitten that he could turn the embarrassment of Till's violent murder into "propaganda" for Delta politics. It is no wonder that Breland and Whitten not only cooperated, but went out of their way to ensure that Huie's telling would be as powerful as possible by arranging whiskey-stocked "secret sessions" so that Huie could tell his story with direct quotations that would be mistaken for a confession.

Conclusion: Confessional Collusion and Public Memory

It must remain one of the great ironies of the Till tragedy that segregationists and civil rights activists both fought to authenticate the same version of Till's story. Breland and Whitten arranged the secret meetings and signed off on every page of the story, only to see their allies at the *Jackson Clarion Ledger* attribute the article to the NAACP and their chief antagonist, Roy Wilkins, champion the same rendering of Till's death.[116] While Wilkins and Whitten had drastically different motives, the effects of their unintended collusion were dramatic: with both sides proclaiming the authenticity of the "Shocking Story," the competing versions of Till's narrative had little chance of surviving. As I have written elsewhere, the "Shocking Story" dominated the twentieth-century public memory of Emmett Till.[117] To the extent that Emmett Till lived on in the twentieth-century imagination, he did so largely in the disguise given him by William Bradford Huie.

To be clear, not everyone championed the "Shocking Story." Till's mother, Mamie Bradley, for example, claimed that *Look* "lied" about her son, and Olive Arnold Adams also accused Huie of telling a partisan story.[118] But these lonely voices of dissent stood no chance against the combined resources of Breland, Whitten, and the NAACP. Consider: The story of Emmett Till has been a constant staple of the American imagination. Although Houck and Grindy demonstrate fluctuations in the attention given to Emmett Till, hardly a year has passed without at least someone attempting to cement further the memory of the murder. In the fifty-six year period between 1955 and 2011, only eight years have passed without the story appearing in the

New York Times.[119] Moreover, there has been an enduring and widespread effort to ensure that the story of Emmett Till circulated not only in elite newspapers, but also in a wide variety of media. James Baldwin put the story on the American stage, Audre Lorde lodged the story in American poetry, Bob Dylan assured the story a place in American rock and roll, and United Artists even tried to put the story on Hollywood's big screen.[120] The latest effort to ensure the circulation of Till's story is Keith Beauchamp's celebrated documentary *The Untold Story of Emmett Louis Till*, which toured the country to critical acclaim and was instrumental in the Justice Department's May 10, 2004, decision to reopen the case.[121]

Yet, despite the staggering number of remembrances, and despite the sheer variety of forms these remembrances took, the assumptions of the "Shocking Story" have been ingredient in almost every retelling. The fact that the "Shocking Story" was a partisan document calibrated to ensure that the perpetrators of the crime would not face further legal action has been completely forgotten. Its reification as a confession has obscured a fact otherwise so basic that even the famously illiterate J. W. Milam had no difficulty articulating it: namely, the "Shocking Story" was "written from a Mississippi viewpoint."[122] Milam knew this, as did Mamie Bradley and Olive Arnold Adams. But American racial politics proved more powerful than these three individuals. In fact, American racial politics proved powerful enough to consign Milam's public disavowals of the "Shocking Story" to relative oblivion. The fact remains that, in the 1950s, both segregation and civil rights had a vested interest in authenticating the "Shocking Story" by labeling it a confession. Huie's story served powerful interests, and these interests returned the favor by turning Huie's text into the definitive account of Till's murder. The historians David T. Beito and Linda Royster Beito conclude that Huie's story so "thoroughly dominated the discourse" surrounding the death of Emmett Till that it effectively "pushed aside" all competing accounts "for decades to come."[123] Sharon Monteith agrees: "Huie's version assumed the status of the primary 'account' of Till's murder for a very long time."[124]

Why did the "Shocking Story" exert such a powerful influence? It did so precisely because it circulated as a confession. And just as important, it circulated as a confession only because its constitution as such served powerful interests in powerful ways. The "Shocking Story" is thus a tragic example of the power of confession in the field of public memory. There is perhaps no better way to authenticate a partisan version of the past than by packaging it with all the accoutrements of confession.

The power of the "Shocking Story" over American memory has been staunchly challenged in the twenty-first century. Beauchamp's 2005 documentary did a remarkable job recovering versions of Till's story that were silenced by the "Shocking Story." It sought to challenge the hegemony of the "Mississippi viewpoint," and because it did so—and because it did so with grace and power—it is no surprise that the film was instrumental in the FBI's reopening of the Till case. Moreover, the FBI's 2006 "Prosecutive Report" went out of its way to document the falsity of Huie's tale. It provided meteorological data on the precise time of the sunrise in the 1955 Delta and concluded, among other things, that Milam could not have physically driven 164 miles after abducting Till and then depose of his body by dawn—all of which he claimed to do in the "Shocking Story." The cover of darkness on August 28, 1955, the FBI concluded, was sixty-two minutes too short to make Milam's story feasible.[125] In the wake of Beauchamp's documentary and the FBI's report, it has become clear that the "Shocking Story" had no right to dominate the memory of Emmett Till. This is Houck and Grindy: "Increasingly do we now realize that Huie had been bamboozled and *Look* hoodwinked. Thanks largely to the investigative work of filmmaker Keith Beauchamp and the FBI, the half-brothers' heroized confessional and impromptu defense of the southern way of life was pure hooey, so to speak."[126] Absolutely. But the very fact that it was "hooey" underscores a fundamental argument of this book. When a text becomes a confession, its constitution as such reveals more about the politics of the critic than about the content of the text. Put in stronger terms, given the right political environment *any* text can become a confession—even a text so full of "hooey" as Huie's "Shocking Story."

4

CONFESSION AND VIOLENCE: WILLIAM STYRON'S NAT TURNER

Twelve years after the death of Emmett Till, the question of confession was once again at the center of American racial politics. On October 9, 1967, accompanied by fanfare unprecedented in the world of American literature, William Styron published *The Confessions of Nat Turner*, a historical novel based on Nat Turner's 1831 insurrection. As he retold the story, Styron drew liberally from "The Confessions of Nat Turner," the 1831 pamphlet that made Thomas Gray's fortune when he sold it to a curious country as a transcription of Turner's jailhouse confession.[1] More than matters of fact, however, what Styron borrowed from Gray was a literary conceit: like Gray before him, Styron told the story in the first person. In the words of one sympathetic reviewer, "Styron became Nat and told Nat's story as if he were Nat, in one long astonishing re-creation of the way it must have felt to be a slave in 1831."[2] Styron was not shy about his literary ambitions. In order to provide a slave's perspective on a slave uprising, the white Anglo-Saxon southern Protestant William Styron claimed to "leap into a black man's consciousness" and thereby write the story as a confession.[3] The resulting novel, conceit and all, took the country and its Pulitzer Prize board by storm. When *Harper's* paid Styron an unprecedented $7,500 to print a fifty-page excerpt of his novel, and when the New American Library paid Styron a $100,000 advance for the paperback rights, and when the Book-of-the-Month Club added $150,000 to the author's take, William Styron became the second white man to make his fortune peddling the confessions of Nat Turner.[4]

One hundred and thirty six years before Styron made his fortune, Nat Turner led a slave rebellion. Under the cover of a dark August night, he headed a small band of insurgent slaves who proceeded systematically through the streets and homes of Southampton, Virginia, slaughtering all they found. Thus Richmond's *Constitutional Whig*: "Whole families, father, mother, daughters, sons, sucking babes, and school children, butchered, thrown into heaps, and left to be devoured by hogs and dogs, or to putrefy on the spot."[5] As Scot French's *Rebellious Slave* so powerfully demonstrates, no other uprising has had such a lasting influence on American cultural politics. Turner, French claims, "stands alone in American thought as the epitome of the rebellious slave, a black messiah whose words and deeds challenged the slaveholding South and awakened a slumbering nation. A maker of history in his own day, Turner has been made to serve the most pressing needs of every generation since."[6]

In the 1960s, these needs were acutely felt. Just three months before Styron's novel was published, racially charged riots in Newark and Detroit claimed sixty-nine lives. Stoked by what Peniel Joseph has called the "violent, angry, and punitive rhetoric of the Black Power Movement," anxieties over black violence were palpable.[7] In fact, Elliot Rudwick and August Meier argue that the second half of the 1960s saw anxieties over "Negro Revolt" raised to their highest pitch since the race riots that rocked several midwestern cities in 1919.[8] In such a context, Herbert Aptheker explains, historical "evidences of Negro militancy" were of "obvious" relevance.[9] Thus it is hardly surprising that in July 1965, well before the publication of Styron's novel, the *Negro Digest* republished Thomas Gray's "Confessions of Nat Turner," arguing that black Americans needed to be reminded that black militancy had a long, distinguished history.[10] In the very same issue, the *Negro Digest* reprinted Jean-Paul Sartre's "moving preface" to Frantz Fanon's *Wretched of the Earth*, a text that Homi K. Bhabha has called the "locus classicus of political resistance and the rhetoric of retributive violence."[11] That Turner's 1831 "Confession" and Fanon's 1961 call to violence were, in 1965, joined on the cover of the *Negro Digest* marks a convenient way to remember an all-important point: among the challenges faced by advocates of a militant Black Power was the need for a militant black history.[12] The "concept" of Black Power, John Oliver Killens explained, "calls upon us to write our own history, create our own myths and legends. Washington and Jefferson do not belong to our black children. They are not the founding fathers of black Americans. . . . No amount of falsification of history can disguise this fact. Our legendary heroes are Nat Turner, Frederick Douglass, Denmark Vesey, Harriet Tubman, Sojourner

Truth, white John Brown, and red Sitting Bull."[13] For Killens, as for the editors of the *Negro Digest*, the need for a militant black history pushed Nat Turner to the top of the list of black American heroes. For this reason, *Black Power* coauthor Charles V. Hamilton argued, "Black people today must not permit themselves to be divested of their historical revolutionary leaders."[14] Nat Turner was just such a leader: "Nat was our secret weapon, our ace in the hole, our private consciousness of manhood kept strictly between us. Our sacred promise to ourselves that someday . . . somehow . . . we would all rise up, black and beautiful, and throw off our Tomish ways, and stand up against the white man like men, even if it cost us our lives."[15] In sum, in the late 1960s the violence of Turner's rebellion provided Black Power with a much-needed, hero-studded history. As one of Nat Turner's biggest 1960s advocates wrote, "History's potency is mighty. The oppressed need it for identity and inspiration; oppressors for justification, rationalization and legitimacy."[16]

William Styron, for his part, had no such need for Nat Turner. Far from an "ace in the hole" or a "historical revolutionary leader," Styron confided to his father that Turner was "pretty much a bastard through and through."[17] Beyond this uncharitable estimation of his protagonist, Styron seemed unaware that the current anxieties over racial violence had made Turner a timely topic. He naïvely suggested that what he derisively called his "nigger book" single-handedly "put Nat Turner on the map": "Before my book appeared, there was no general knowledge among either the black or white community in America about a person named Nat Turner."[18] Styron, unimpressed by Nat Turner, unmoved by the need for a black militant history, and unaware of Turner's 1960s cachet, produced what Mary Strine has called a "dramatic counterstatement" to the Turner produced by and for Black Power.[19] Unlike the militant Turner of the *Negro Digest*, Styron's novel portrayed Turner as a befuddled religious fanatic who could not control the violence he set in motion.[20] This is Styron: any "honest reading of Nat Turner's confession" demonstrates that Turner himself "was almost unable to grapple with violence, to carry it out successfully."[21]

From the perspective of Black Power, Styron's novel thus constituted a "deliberate attempt to steal the meaning of a man's life."[22] Stokely Carmichael and H. Rap Brown issued a joint statement: "*The Confessions of Nat Turner* is a joke to us black people. . . . Nat Turner is a black hero who belongs to our people, and hunkies such as William Styron do not have the right or authority from black people to speak for us or interpret our heroes."[23] Founding member of the Harlem Writers Guild Loyle Hairston put it this way: Styron's novel constituted "thinly veiled slander, a malicious attempt to revoke [Turner's] credentials as an authentic hero in mankind's struggle against tyranny."[24] Finally, Charles Hamilton wrote, "Black youth . . . can never and should never accept the portrayal (or is the word 'betrayal'?) of Nat Turner as set forth by Styron." He promised that "black people today" will "not permit Styron to picture unchallenged Nat Turner."[25] Indeed they did not. The Black Power movement sparked a debate over Styron and his version of Turner so intense that, as the literary historian Albert Stone recalls, "ordinary readers, college students and teachers, and others inside and beyond the academy felt the unexpected force of a concentrated assault on basic white values and assumptions."[26]

It is in the context of this debate over the meaning of Nat Turner that the genre of confession once more entered public debate, for what better way to establish the meaning of a man's life than his own confession? The key question in this confessional crisis was that of violence. It could hardly have been otherwise. Rudwick and Meier note that by 1969 the question of violence had "moved closer to the center of the race relations stage."[27] Moreover, the violence of Turner's rebellion, the violence of Newark and Detroit, and the violent rhetoric of the Black Power movement ensured that Styron and his novel could hardly be talked about in any terms save the language of violence. If the focus on violence is predictable, the focus on confession is less so. Yet, with remarkable consistency and startling energy, both sides of the debate tied their claims about Styron, Turner, and violence to a more fundamental argument about the genre of Styron's novel. Styron's white critics argued it was a confession; his black critics argued it was not; both parties, however, tethered their readings of violence and its place in American history to William Styron's decision to write his novel as a confession.[28]

If black and white critics alike focused on the generic classification of the novel, this is because both sides recognized confessional hermeneutics—the activity of distinguishing what is and is not a confession—as an ideological resource of the first order. To take a position on the genre of the novel was, simultaneously, to take a position on two hotly contested, racially coded debates: First, a historiographical debate over the relative brutality of slavery and the "personality" of slaves. Were slaves generally docile? Did they accommodate themselves to white rule? Was Nat Turner an aberration in an otherwise contented demographic? Or was resistance the norm, violence an established tactic, and Turner's rebellion simply an exaggerated moment in an otherwise routinized, retributive violence? Thanks to the recent work of

Cedric J. Robinson and Steven Hahn, it is now clear that violent forms of resistance to white rule were ingredient in the American experience from the very introduction of slavery.[29] My point is not that these were open questions in the 1960s (though they were), but that the classification of Styron's novel as a confession was compatible only with the view that slaves were docile, masters kind, and violence exceptional.

To take a position on the genre of Styron's novel was also to take a position on a second debate, a proto-postcolonial debate over the capacities of rhetoric to bridge the experiences of black and white Americans. If, in the first debate, the history of violence was at issue, here the continued necessity of violence was at stake. According to Frantz Fanon, social justice required violence because the oppressed shared absolutely nothing in common with the oppressor. No common beliefs, assumptions, or values could ground deliberation.[30] Styron's claim to "leap" into the consciousness of a black slave, so far as it was successful, seemed to prove that there was at least common ground enough for a white author to give voice to the inner motivations of a black rebel. And if this was the case, perhaps violence was not as indispensable as Fanon suggested.

It was in the context of these two debates that the genre of confession became a focal point in the larger 1960s debates over violence. By labeling Styron's text a confession, white liberals were able to suggest that racial violence was historically exceptional and currently unneeded. Conversely, by refusing the designation, Styron's black critics emphasized the productive history of racial violence and its current necessity.

Styron, Southern Historiography, and Slave "Personality"

A year and a half after the publication of *The Confessions of Nat Turner*, William Styron recalled the first "mauling" his book received from a hostile critic.[31] The review came at the hands of the Marxist historian Herbert Aptheker, who, writing in *The Nation*, argued that Styron's novel was based on "an utter misapprehension of the nature of American slavery."[32] This certainly could not have surprised Styron, who, six years earlier, on March 9, 1961, had written Aptheker, author of the 1943 *American Negro Slave Revolts*, to ask for assistance with a "new novel I am writing, based on Nat Turner's revolt."[33] Aptheker was happy to help, and sent Styron his manuscript for what would become, five years later, a book titled *Nat Turner's Slave Rebellion*. Although Styron was momentarily taken by Aptheker's work, the enchantment soon faded.

In a letter to his father, Styron derided Aptheker as a "stupid, vicious jackass of a Communist."[34] In 1963, upon the reissue of *American Negro Slave Revolts*, Styron challenged the most basic assumptions of Aptheker's thesis. Writing for the *New York Review of Books*, Styron argued that Aptheker's work was an unjustified overreaction to the long delegitimized conclusions of the southern apologist Ulrich B. Phillips.[35]

From its release in 1918 until its first substantive challenge in 1944, Phillips's *American Negro Slavery* dominated the historical field.[36] Yet, as Styron noted in his review of Aptheker, *American Negro Slavery* was "befogged by Southern pride and often by frank racism."[37] Chief among Phillips's racist conclusions were his beliefs that chattel slavery effected a "general improvement in negro character," that the mastership of the white race was "benevolent in intent and on the whole beneficial in effect," that the "training" provided by slavery was "just what the bulk of the negros [sic] most needed," that the "American regime" was "mild" and "picturesque," and above all, that many slaves were so content in slavery that they "made their master's interests thoroughly their own."[38] As the historian Stanley Elkins put it, Phillips placed his stress on the "genial side of the regime, on cheerfulness and contentment, on the profoundly human relationships between the paternal master and his faithful and childlike blacks."[39]

Aptheker would have none of it. As Styron wrote in the *New York Review of Books*, Aptheker's *American Negro Slave Revolts* was written as a direct "repudiation" of Phillips's thesis that the slaves were so "content with their lot and in any case so docile by nature as to be incapable of rebellion."[40] It had tremendous influence; John H. Bracey wrote, "From personal experience, I can testify that [Aptheker's] *American Negro Slave Revolts* made a tremendous impact on those of us in the civil rights and Black liberation movements. It was the single most effective antidote to the poisonous ideas that Blacks had not a history of struggle, or that such struggle always took the forms of legal action and non-violent protest. It provided Black youth with that link to our past that few even thought existed or were willing to help us find."[41] To Aptheker's mind, *American Negro Slave Revolts*—which was a virtual compendium of slave unrest—demanded a revision of the "generally accepted notion" that the slave responded to his bondage with "passivity and docility." He concluded, "The evidence . . . points to the conclusion that discontent and rebelliousness were not only exceedingly common, but, indeed, characteristic of American Negro slaves."[42]

Styron found this conclusion wanting. If Phillips, "befogged" by racism, erred by emphasizing the "genial side of the regime," Styron argued that

Aptheker made the opposite mistake. "One does not have to be a white supremacist," Styron argued, to agree with some of Phillips's conclusions. Styron suggested, just as Phillips had, that slaves were, taken as a whole, docile and predisposed against rebellion: "The character (not characterization) of 'Sambo,' shiftless, wallowing happily in the dust, was no cruel figment of the imagination, Southern or Northern, but did in truth exist." "The plantation slaves," he continued, "*were* often observably docile, *were* childish, *were* irresponsible and incapable of real resistance."[43] Yet there was one crucial difference that separated Phillips's conclusions from Styron's: While both insisted on the docility of slaves, only Phillips grounded this docility in an "innate and inherited racial inferiority."[44] Styron, by contrast, followed the "brilliant analysis" of Stanley M. Elkins's 1959 volume *Slavery: A Problem in American Institutional and Intellectual Life*.[45]

It is important to pause on the work of Elkins, for without it *The Confessions of Nat Turner* would have taken a drastically different form. Looking back on the novel, Styron claimed that he had been attempting "with little success" to write about Nat Turner since 1950. Part of the problem, he explained, was that "the work required a sound understanding of slavery." That understanding came in 1959: "Elkins was my breakthrough."[46] In this Styron was not alone; Elkins's *Slavery* was massively influential. The historian Eugene Genovese called *Slavery* "one of the most influential historical essays of our generation."[47]

In *Slavery*, Elkins aimed to step outside the moralistic din that he argued had characterized the historiographical debate over slavery theretofore. Even with the dramatic shift from Phillips's racist vindication of slavery, to Kenneth M. Stampp's 1956 *Peculiar Institution*, which marked the high-water mark of anti-Phillips historiography, and Aptheker's reclamation of a militaristic bondman, "it was not the debate itself that changed; it was just that a reverse moral tone was making its way back into historical thinking." And this, Elkins claimed, was the "rhythm" of southern historiography, the endless to-and-fro of moral exoneration and moral censure.[48] To escape this rhythm, Elkins abandoned the categories that had long structured the academic inquiry into slavery: "food, shelter, police, medical care, etc."[49] In their place he substituted a comparative method: how did slavery in the United States differ from slavery in South America and elsewhere? When seen in this light, the immense, unchecked brutality of American slavery struck Elkins—and his many readers—with new force.

Elkins captured the character and immensity of this brutality by describing American slavery as a "closed" institution. Only in the United States,

Elkins found, was the slave totally cut off from forms of social life that might check the dehumanizing process of chattel slavery. In Latin America, for example, "the very tension and balance among three kinds of organizational concerns—church, crown, and plantation agriculture—prevented slavery from being carried by the planting class to its ultimate logic." In Latin America, in other words, the slave had access to social norms not defined by the institution of slavery itself. In the United States, by contrast, slavery was "virtually unchecked by institutions having anything like the power of their Latin counterparts." For this reason, North American slaves had access only to the norms of the slaveholding regime, their "contacts with free society could occur only on the most narrowly circumscribed terms," and thus "all avenues of recourse for the slave, all lines of communication to society at large, originated and ended with the master."[50]

Elkins postulated that the sheer totality of the system—its ability to eliminate all recourse beyond itself—was bound to have effects on the "personality" of slaves. Thus he resurrected—and secured with new, purportedly scientific grounds—the old figure of "Sambo." This is Elkins: "The typical plantation slave was docile but irresponsible, loyal but lazy, humble but chronically given to lying and stealing; his behavior was full of infantile silliness and his talk inflated with childish exaggeration. His relationship with his master was one of utter dependence and childlike attachment."[51] Unlike Phillips, Elkins was careful to insist that the "Sambo" could not be accounted for with recourse to "'race' or 'inborn nature.'" And unlike Aptheker, Elkins argued that "Sambo" cannot be dismissed as a figment of the ruling imagination. For Elkins, "Sambo" was real enough: "Too much folk-knowledge, too much plantation literature, too much of the Negro's own lore, have gone into its making to entitle one in good conscience to condemn it as 'conspiracy.'"[52]

We can now understand on what grounds Styron could argue that "one does not have to be a white supremacist to note that Aptheker fails almost completely in his attempt to prove the universality of slave rebellions." This, to Styron, was the precise importance of Elkins; Elkins made the "Sambo" stereotype available outside the confines of racism. While Phillips had derived him from the geniality of the system, Elkins had derived him from its sheer brutality. Thus Styron suggested that Aptheker, with his assertions of a militant bondman, had underestimated the awesome terror of a system that had "swiftly managed to cow and humble an entire people with a ruthless efficiency, unparalleled in human history." Styron thus challenged Aptheker's dearest conclusions. Where Aptheker had found "rebelliousness and discontent" to be "exceedingly common," Styron countered that "save for two enthusiastic but localized conspiracies . . . there was only one sustained, effective revolt in the entire annals of slavery: the cataclysmic uprising of Nat Turner."[53]

This Elkins-inspired reading of southern history not only grounded Styron's response to Aptheker, it also—as Styron himself confided to the *Boston Globe* years later—informed the writing of *The Confessions of Nat Turner*. Thus we can now understand Aptheker's "mauling" of Styron in *The Nation*. In that article, recall, Aptheker argued that Styron's novel was based on "an utter misapprehension of the nature of American slavery." This misapprehension, in turn, could be laid at the feet of Stanley Elkins and the well-known author of *Slave and Citizen*, Frank Tannenbaum, from whom Elkins got the idea of a comparative study: "[Styron's] novel reflects the author's belief that the views of slavery in the United States associated with the names of Frank Tannenbaum and Stanley Elkins—which, *in substance*, are those of U. B. Phillips, the classical apologist for plantation slavery—are valid." Aptheker then used the remainder of his review of Styron's novel to reinstate the conclusions he had advanced in *American Negro Slave Revolts*. Empirical historical data, he argued, render the nuance between Phillips and Elkins immaterial: "Whether 'Sambo' is seen as the creature of racism [Phillips] or the creation of a latter-day socio-psychological environmentalism [Elkins], the fact is that 'Sambo' is a caricature and not a reality." In contrast to Phillips, Elkins, and Styron, Aptheker insisted that "Nat Turner . . . was real; perhaps a novelist will yet come along to do justice to him."[54]

In sum, was the American slave a "Sambo," a happy-go-lucky, bumbling fool, given to petty thievery but fundamentally docile? Or was the slave a seething embodiment of resentment, incensed by the brutality of the ruling class and prone to rebellion? In the 1960s, both positions had support from the highest reaches of the academy, and both positions saw in Styron's Nat Turner grist for their own ideological mills. Critics of Styron's novel did not need a *Boston Globe* interview to tell them of Styron's affinities for Stanley Elkins. Dozens of critics—black and white—made the association well before the interview. When Martin Duberman wrote his review for the *Village Voice*, for example, he felt compelled to first review the long academic debate that had lately come to a head with the publication of *Slavery*. He concluded that Styron's Nat Turner was a "resistant, heroic Negro" who owed more to the work of Kenneth M. Stampp's *Peculiar Institution* than to Elkins's *Slavery*. Only the minor characters in the novel, he concluded, "readily fit Elkins's psychograph of the brain-washed, infantilized slave."[55] Similarly,

Ebony editor Lerone Bennett, Jr., argued that Styron was "playing the 'new history' game." Yet Bennett reached different conclusions: "[Styron] is trying to prove that U.B. Phillips, the classic apologist for slavery, and Stanley Elkins, the sophisticated modern apologist, were right when they projected Sambo—the bootlicking, head-scratching child–man—as the dominant plantation type." Bennett argued that Styron "manipulated" the evidence in order to create a Nat Turner that would confirm the "Elkins-Phillips-Styron dream" of a "harmless, dull, [and] malleable" slave.[56]

Whether Styron's Turner registers in the histories of Stampp or Elkins is an open question. One thing is certain: in the wake of Styron's novel, it was precisely this debate over slavery and violence that determined the form and function of confession. Was *The Confessions of Nat Turner* really a confession? The answer to this question turned, of course, on what exactly a confession was. And the answer to this question, in turn, was figured with recourse to the competing visions of Elkins and Aptheker. Before turning directly to confession, consider the second debate about violence that informed the reception of Styron's novel.

Confession, Postcolonialism, and "Negro Writing"

William Styron's *Confessions of Nat Turner* was a controversial novel well before its release in October 1967. Two and a half years earlier, Styron used a "Special Supplement" to the April 1965 edition of *Harper's* to publicly announce his novel on Nat Turner and his ambition to write it in the first person. Titled "This Quiet Dust," Styron's *Harper's* article explained his decision to assume the "inner vantage point" of Nat Turner as a product of lessons learned growing up in southeastern Virginia, only miles from the site of the 1831 rebellion.

Reflecting on his childhood, Styron argued that southern segregation was "devastatingly effective in accomplishing something that it was only peripherally designed to do: it prevents the awareness even of the existence of another race." Consequently, "an unremarked paradox of Southern life is that its racial animosity is really grounded not upon friction and propinquity, but upon an almost complete lack of contact." Thus there is absolutely no truth, Styron claimed, to the myth that the southerner "'knows' the Negro.'" As evidence, Styron pointed to the novels of one of the premier southern writers of the twentieth century, a writer to whom Styron was often compared, and in whose shadow he explicitly worked: William Faulkner.[57] Even *The*

Sound and the Fury, that great experiment in the limits of first-person narration, abandoned the conceit when, in section 4, it came time to tell the story from Dilsey's black perspective. To Styron's mind, this was evidence that not even Faulkner could "think Negro," for unlike his own Nat Turner, Faulkner's Dilsey was not "created from a sense of withinness." For Styron, Faulkner's shortcomings were evidence of a broader racial problem: "White Southerners have grown up as free of knowledge of the Negro character and soul as a person whose background is rural Wisconsin or Maine." To Styron's liberal mind, this was intolerable: "The Negro may feel that it is too late to be known, and that the desire to know him reeks of outrageous condescension. But to break down the old law, to come to *know* the Negro, has become the moral imperative of every white Southerner." Or at least that was Styron's imperative. In "This Quiet Dust," he confessed that *The Confessions of Nat Turner* should be understood as "at least a partial fulfillment of this mandate."[58] With this novel, he claimed, he would get "within" the Negro, write from an "inner vantage point," and in so doing satisfy the moral imperative of the white southerner.

One year later, in an interview with *Per/Se*, Styron reiterated the importance of his first-person conceit. He admitted that he considered telling the story from an "omniscient" or "reactive" point of view. Yet these literary modes, Styron confessed, "didn't seem right." To use the language of the "This Quiet Dust," the omniscient or reactive conceits could not, for Styron, provide the decisive "sense of withinness" that the "inner vantage point" achieved. Given these limitations, Styron "realized that the only way to do it was from Nat's point of view": "I realized that inevitably one of the profoundly difficult things I would have to set up for myself would be the telling of this story from the point of view of Nat himself—a first person narrative which would somehow allow you to enter into the consciousness of a Negro in the early decades of the 19th century." While he admitted that entering into a slave's consciousness would be "difficult," he always insisted it was possible. When his interviewers expressed skepticism that Turner's story could be adequately told within the confines of his own "restricted vocabulary," Styron responded, "I don't think this at all turned out to be difficult, because I know recent backwoods speech, and it is quite similar to backwoods speech of 130 years ago." As it turned out, Styron's "backwoods speech" turned out to be virtually indistinguishable from elevated Victorian prose.[59] To those who doubted that such a style befit a nineteenth-century slave, Styron responded by suggesting that such doubts were themselves condescending and racist; they "implied that Negroes don't think like the rest of us." Moreover, Turner was particularly well educated, and thus "it seems to me perfectly plausible . . . that he thought in the way that I'm describing things—that is, in a regular literary fashion." Thus, to Styron's mind, whether he endowed Turner with a "restricted," "backwoods" dialect or a Victorian, "literary fashion," was of little importance. Either idiom, he insisted, supported his central conceit. His own familiarity with "backwoods speech" and Turner's exceptional education meant that, rhetorically speaking, nothing separated Styron from Turner: because both thought in the same idiom, Styron implied that achieving the "inner vantage point" was not "difficult" after all.[60]

Styron's confidence in his ability to write from the perspective of Nat Turner might be measured by the frequency with which he returned to the topic. In a *New York Times* interview with George Plimpton, for example, Styron suggested that the only difficulty of writing the novel in the first person was a result of the fact that nothing "of the sort has been done by a white American writer—to assume the persona of a Negro and make it convincing." But, Styron told Plimpton, he did not believe that the feelings of the "dispossessed, whatever their color," are really "all that different."[61] In an interview with *Yale Alumni Magazine*, Styron claimed that he wrote the novel because "I wanted also to explore in some kind of depth this whole area of American life and history, to take on the lineaments as well as I could of a slave and, using that persona, walk myself through a time and place in a manner of self-discovery. I was learning all along as I wrote about Nat what it must have been like to be a slave." When the Yale historian C. Vann Woodward commented on the boldness of the strategy, Styron responded by emphasizing "what an important factor it was for me to try to turn myself into a unique slave."[62] When *Yale Literary Magazine* questioned his audacity a year later, Styron vigorously defended his novel: "I think it's a denial of humanity, our mutual humanity, to assume that it is pretentious and arrogant and wrong for a white man to attempt to get into a black man's skin." Moreover, he explained that he wrote in the first person because "I wanted to risk leaping into a black man's consciousness." And this, Styron boasted, was the originality of *The Confessions of Nat Turner*: "If I did do anything original in Nat Turner it was to, for the first time so far as I know, plunge a white consciousness into a black incarnation."[63]

Thus, well before the novel was released, in "This Quiet Dust" and in a wide variety of interviews Styron was remarkably, and perhaps naïvely, open about the extent of his literary ambitions. He did not simply want to tell the story of Nat Turner; he wanted to write *The Confessions of Nat Turner*. And he took his title seriously. With all the earnestness of a moral imperative, Styron insisted on writing a first-person account of a black slave's rebellion. Indeed, given how much he talked about it, it is not too much to say he was obsessed with the confessional genre of his novel. It is important to be clear here: for Styron, confession signaled neither the disclosure of sinfulness nor a discourse of authenticity. Rather, it was a genre uniquely suited to give voice to the "mutual humanity" of black and white. If Styron was ever to "plunge a white consciousness into a black incarnation" and thereby "*know* the Negro," he needed to write the *confessions* of Nat Turner. For his capacity to tell Turner's story in the first person functioned—at least to his own satisfaction—as evidence that WASP and dispossessed rebel were really not "all that different." And after reading portions of his forthcoming novel to a friendly audience at Wesleyan University, he concluded that he had succeeded in doing so: "I can only say that I've tried this out on enough people to feel that I'm right. No one has yet really had any major reservations about this form of narrative."[64]

On this last point, however, Styron was simply wrong. In the context of the 1960s, there were massive and widespread reservations about precisely "this form of narrative." Frantz Fanon's *Wretched of the Earth* (1961), *The Autobiography of Malcolm X* (1964), and Eldridge Cleaver's *Soul on Ice* (1968) each posed fundamental challenges to Styron's literary conceit.[65] These challenges were nowhere more concisely articulated than in a series of three articles Richard Gilman penned for the *New Republic*. Titled "Negro Writing," the series began in March 1968 and culminated seven issues later with a critique of Styron's novel. Each article advocates for what academics would later refer to as "postcolonialism"—a project dedicated to the irreducibility of subaltern styles and the inability of the powerful to access or understand the idioms of the oppressed.

In the first article in the series, Gilman agued that Cleaver's *Soul on Ice* stands at "the exact resonant center" of a heretofore unrecognized genre: "Negro Writing." Gilman's review focused far more on the characteristics of this genre, and the problems it poses for white critics, than it did on Cleaver's memoir. "Negro Writing," Gilman wrote in March 1968, is defined by "its way of looking at the world, its formulation of experience is not the potential possession—even by imaginative appropriation—of us all; hard, local, intransigent, alien, it remains in some sense inassimilable for those of us who aren't black."[66] This, of course, is a direct refutation of Styron's project, for Styron sought, by a means of "imaginative appropriation," to "*know* the Negro." Styron, for his part, recognized clearly the threat Gilman posed to his project. In a letter to his friend Philip Roth, Styron derisively—and inexcusably—dismissed Gilman as an "urban, Jewish critic" who "could barely write grammatical English." Beyond the offensive ad hominem, Styron suggested that Gilman's thesis that "whites could not understand or evaluate black life and letters" was "poisonous."[67]

"Negro writing," Gilman argued, stands outside the "great flawless arc of the Graeco-Roman and Judeo-Christian traditions" and is thus impervious to their categories of judgment. For this reason, Gilman concluded that Cleaver's autobiography must remain "in some profound sense not subject to correction or emendation or, most centrally, approval or rejection by those of us who are not black." The critical assessment of "Negro Writing" in terms of traditional categories amounts to a "very contemporary form of injustice, that of sanctioning Negro thought from the standpoint of white criteria." As a white critic, Gilman argued, "it isn't my right to draw him [Cleaver] into the Western academy and subject his findings to the scrutiny of the tradition."[68]

Gilman carefully delimited the boundaries of "Negro Writing." As a category, it was not coextensive with the writings of a black author. "I will go on judging and elucidating novels and plays and poetry by Negros," Gilman concluded, "but the kind of Negro writing I have been talking about, the act of creation of the self in the face of that self's historic denial by our society, seems to me to be at this point beyond my right to intrude on."[69] It is for this reason that Gilman chose Cleaver and Malcolm X as his examples par excellence. For these are not just books by black authors—they fit more precisely into the intimate categories of memoir, autobiography, or confession. For Gilman, the force of these books, like the force of Styron's Nat Turner, rested ultimately in their quest to describe a self that cannot be reduced to the circumambient society. As he put it a month later, Negro Writing is "an act of creation and definition of the self on the part of a Negro who . . . lived now across an abyss not bridgeable by simple good-will or by independent, 'disinterested' intellectual criteria."[70] It is not difficult to read this as a "major reservation" regarding Styron's literary ambitions. By writing the rebellion in the first person, by offering the "confessions" of Nat Turner, Styron suggested that there was nothing irreducible or fundamental about the black creation of the self. As he suggested in "This Quiet Dust" and his *Per/Se* interview, his southern background and his knowledge of "backwoods speech" was sufficient for writing the confessions of Nat Turner. To Styron's mind, there was no unbridgeable abyss separating him from his subject. There was only a dialect, and with enough time spent in the backwoods, he could master that with as much facility as his ancestors had mastered the black population of southeastern Virginia.

It is thus not surprising that when Gilman finally turned his attention to *The Confessions of Nat Turner*, he called out Styron for attempting to bridge the abyss. Styron's ambition, he wrote, was an attempt "to try to imagine yourself into an alien phenomenon, into a new tradition." And because this constituted nothing less than a "miraculous transposition" of realms, his ambition was fated to fail. Gilman put it kindly, writing that Styron's "ambitions always exceed his gifts." For no matter how gifted his imaginative prowess, as a matter of principle "we can't know the truth of Nat Turner through the imagination."[71]

Given this intellectual milieu, Styron's comment that "no one has yet really had any major reservations about this form of narrative" is deeply misleading. A friendly audience at Wesleyan may well have encouraged Styron's stubborn faith in the capacity of his literary (and liberal) imagination to bridge the abyss between himself and Nat Turner. But such faith in the literary imagination was, at the time, hotly contested. Indeed, Gilman claimed that there was a widespread "anxiety" over the capacity of critical standards—long considered universal, now considered white—to account for the black experience.[72] For this reason, when Styron publicized his forthcoming novel by celebrating his purported capacity to write from inside a black consciousness, he was hitting a well-prepared cultural nerve. This, I suspect, explains why Gilman argued that *The Confessions of Nat Turner* had "a life laid out for it in advance."[73] How could the novel not incite controversy, when its central conceit challenged the fundamental premises of the then-emerging postcolonial theory? What Gilman could not have known is that the controversy that followed the publication of *The Confessions of Nat Turner* would take this proto-postcolonial debate and imbricate it with a debate over the violence of slaves and the boundaries of confession.

Confession and an Inexplicable Violence

If Styron's conceit meant that his novel had a life of controversy laid out for it in advance, it is important to note that this controversy was not immediate. In the immediate wake of its October publication, Styron's novel enjoyed a brief period of favorable reviews from black and white critics alike. James Baldwin, John Hope Franklin, and Saunders Redding joined a host of white critics in praising the novel.[74] Despite the fact that this period was short-lived, it was not simply a honeymoon phase marked by obligatory words of kindness. Rather, the initial, favorable reviews possess an intellectual rigor all their own, and by examining them closely, we can gain important insight into the politics of confession.

Without doubt, the most conspicuous and widely shared characteristic of these early white reviews was their repeated insistence that *The Confessions of Nat Turner* provided an answer to a theretofore irresolvable mystery: what could have prompted someone to lead a rebellion so violent? The sheer violence of Turner's rebellion was so distressing to Styron's white critics that, almost to a person, they declared Turner's motivations unfathomable, incomprehensible, and fundamentally mysterious. From the perspective of Styron's white critics, it was precisely the mysteriousness of the rebellion that sanctioned Styron's decision to write the novel as a confession, for only a confession—an insider's account—could possibly redress so profound a mystery. The confession offered, in its very form, the opportunity to comprehend the rebellion from the inside and render legible that which had long defied comprehension. As we shall see, white critic after white critic intertwined the inexplicability of Turner's rebellion and the necessity of a confession. Why did they do so? It allowed them to condemn violence categorically. It allowed them, first, to affirm Elkin's reading of the Old South, in which violence was exceptional and destructive rather than a strategic means of pursuing freedom. And it also allowed them to deny the chasm Gilman placed between the races and which functioned for Fanon as a justification for retributive violence.

There was wide agreement among Styron's white critics that the historical record of Nat Turner was threadbare at best. Styron himself often commented on the paucity of the historical record as justification for the vast artistic license with which he proceeded. In an interview with *Per/Se*, for example, Styron claimed that, aside from Gray's "Confessions" and "a few little newspaper articles," the historical record "wasn't anything to speak of."[75] This was standard Styron fare. In "This Quiet Dust" he argued that "very little can be known" of Nat Turner. He told the *Boston Globe* that, unlike John Brown, Nat Turner was not "buried with tons of stultifying testimony and documentary credentials." And he used an interview with *Yale Alumni Magazine* to explain why: The news of John Brown was carried by telegraph and railroad across the nation. Because no such infrastructure existed in 1831, the story of Nat Turner was, within the year, "forgotten all over the country."[76] For the moment, it is important to take William Styron at his word and bracket, if only momentarily, Henry Tragle's valid insight that

Styron's insistence on the poverty of the historical record demonstrates only the poverty of Styron's capacity for historical research.[77] So bracketed, it becomes clear that Styron needed the historical record to be impoverished, as this served him in basic ways. After rehearsing his standard lines about how little can be known of Nat Turner, Styron wrote in *Harper's*, "This is not disadvantageous to a novelist, since it allows him to speculate—with a freedom not accorded the historian—upon all the intermingled miseries, ambitions, frustrations, hopes, rages, and desires which caused this extraordinary black man to rise up out of those early mists of our history and strike down his oppressors with a fury of retribution unequaled before or since."[78] More than artistic license hangs in the balance here. The impoverishment of the historical record—real or imagined—is deployed to support two ideologically charged positions: the exotic, exceptional character of Turner and the concomitant necessity of explication.

Styron's white critics would rehearse this logic incessantly. They, too, spoke constantly of a threadbare history, and they too used it to render Turner exotic, his rebellion inexplicable, and, by extension, Styron's conceit requisite. Chief among Styron's supporters was his "life-long friend" C. Vann Woodward.[79] Reviewing *The Confessions of Nat Turner* in the *New Republic*, Woodward introduced Styron's novel by faithfully rehearsing the paucity of the historical record. Comparing Turner once more to John Brown, Woodward concluded, "Scholarly as well as creative writing about [Nat Turner] are minuscule." Aside from a "pedestrian monograph or two," our entire knowledge of Turner's rebellion—the "only slave rebellion of consequence in the 19th-century world"—rests on the "stilted prose" of Gray's "Confessions." Beyond simply providing a "free hand for the novelist," the pedestrian state of the scholarship functioned politically for Woodward as it did for Styron: the lack of historical materials proved the inexplicability of the rebellion.[80] The two positions—one a matter of historical documentation, the other a matter of interpretation, emphasis, and politics—were for Styron and Woodward inseparable. Because neither "pedestrian monographs" nor "stilted prose" were adequate guides to historical truth, Woodward reasoned, the entire rebellion remains wrapped in mystery: "No one has more than an ill-informed guess about why the greatest slave republic in the New World had by far the fewest rebellions; why smaller and allegedly more benevolent slave societies bred vast insurrections. . . . And most of all, what explains the terrible enigma of Nat Turner, the other-worldly young carpenter of obscure origins and apocalyptic visions who at the age of thirty-one took the road to Jerusalem, Va., martyrdom, and immortality." The "terrible enigma" of

Nat Turner needed to be explained, and for this task, nothing but a confession would do. "Nat's story would have to be seen from behind the black mask," Woodward wrote. "That was the boldest decision William Styron made." Unlike Melville's dark-skinned rebel Benito Cereno, who is "viewed entirely through the eyes of the white man" and for that reason cannot speak to the "enigma" of slave rebellions, Styron's novel explains "what is was like to *be* slaves."[81] In the capable hands of Woodward, Styron's literary conceit is the only possible response to the mystery of Nat Turner.

Or consider Shaun O'Connell's review for *The Nation*. Like Woodward, he emphasized the fact that only one book theretofore had been written on Nat Turner and, for this reason, Styron was obliged to expand on the "scant notes" that existed in the historical record. This appalling state of the scholarship suggested, for O'Connell, as it had for both Woodward and Styron, the inexplicability of the rebellion and the exceptionality of Turner: "Who was he? Why did only he, in the long history of American slavery, lead an uprising? Why, when about sixty whites were slaughtered, did he personally kill only one? . . . Why did the thrust of Nat's rebellion flinch after this murder?" For O'Connell these questions are further exasperated by Turner's comparatively light servitude. Drawing on Styron's account, O'Connell reminds us that Turner was "favored," that he was lucky enough to be owned by an enlightened master, and that he was "pampered" by whites and "ate well." All this, of course, is an Elkins-inspired reading of the Old South (a "pampered," "lucky" slave), and it thereby renders the rebellion that much more problematic: "The need to slaughter those who are most compassionate is, [Styron's] Nat says, 'the central madness of nigger existence.'"

For O'Connell, this madness was intolerable. It demanded an explanation, if for no other reason than this: the very fact of offering an explanation served as a down payment on the moral "imperative" to "*know* the Negro." That is to say, for O'Connell, the fundamental lesson of the novel is the capacity of the confessional form to satisfy the unresolved anxieties of Turner's rebellion and render legible the "central madness" of Nat Turner: "Styron chances a daring, imaginative leap into a tormented, black psyche to better understand himself and his country." This "leap" may well be daring, and it will certainly "raise some resentment," but without it the lasting questions could never be answered: "To argue that this is arrogant and futile is to resign oneself to fragmentation, alienation, violence."[82] For O'Connell, too, the mysteriousness of the rebellion serves him in basic ways: it legitimates Styron's literary conceit, which in turn confirms Elkin's view of history and disconfirms any rationale for violence that posits two irreducible races.

Or consider the review Raymond A. Sokolov wrote for *Newsweek*, which put Styron on its October 16, 1967, cover. In Sokolov's telling, Styron "combed the skimpy records" and "sparse traces" of Turner's insurrection for twenty years. In the end, Styron concluded that the historical records were so rare that "any C+ history student can master the official sources in several days." With "every physical trace misplaced, destroyed, or forgotten," Sokolov wrote, "the imagination is the only possible source." But it was a golden source. Unconstrained by historical facts, "Styron slowly thought himself into the mind of Nat Turner," and in so doing addressed the perpetual anxiety that Sokolov (like Styron, Woodward, and O'Connell) believed still haunted the "skimpy" record: "What made him kill?" The central conceit of Styron's novel, the fact that it was written as a confession, was again justified by the inexplicability of the rebellion, and it again proved the "mutual humanity" of black and white. On Sokolov's reading, the conceit was perfect. The "psychic integration" between Styron and Nat Turner "worked so well," Sokolov wrote, that Styron "took a step as unique in American letters as the revolt is in its history": "Styron became Nat and told Nat's story as if he were Nat, in one long astonishing re-creation of what it must have felt like to be a slave in 1831." For Sokolov, everything else in the novel paled when compared to the shining fact that Styron wrote the novel as a confession. It was this fact alone that made *The Confessions* a unique step in American letters, for not even Melville's celebrated story of a slave rebellion managed to tell it "from the Negro viewpoint." Yet "Styron has gambled everything on doing just that, writing the autobiography Nat had no time for." This, Sokolov continued, was Styron's "big gamble." Had it failed, the novel would have been a "disaster, a melodrama clotted with pretension." But "it works," Sokolov announced ecstatically: "Pure literary convention hooked up to a great ear. It works."[83]

The well-known literary critic Alfred Kazin was no exception to the pattern. Writing the cover story for the October 8, 1967, *Chicago Tribune Book World*, Kazin too framed *The Confessions of Nat Turner* as a response to the mysteriousness of the rebellion. To the literary mind, Kazin writes, "violence is always awesome." In its awesomeness, it challenges the capacities of comprehension. And "this," Kazin agues, "is why William Styron was drawn to make an imaginative narrative of his own out of Nat Turner's leadership of the 1831 slave revolt." In order to make sense of the violence and "dispel the strangeness" of Nat Turner, someone Styron "wants and needs to understand," Styron wrote the story in the first person: "Entering into his mind and his life as intimately as we do, we recognize that what our contemporary, William Styron, wants most to do is to become a Negro mind, to get past the everlasting barrier, to make human and clear what makes us afraid in the shadows we now occupy." Kazin thus assumes his place: for him, too, Styron's literary conceit was justified by the need to comprehend the inexplicable and overstep the chasm (or "everlasting barrier") that Gilman posited between the white author and his black subject.

Styron, Woodward, O'Connell, Sokolov, Kazin. Their sheer consistency is shocking. For each of these critics, the poverty of historical scholarship, the inexplicability of the rebellion, the necessity of confession, and the shared humanity of Styron and Turner were woven into a single cloth. It is because these critics interpreted the limitations of historical scholarship as evidence of lingering uncertainty, and because they interpreted uncertainty as unacceptable, that they repeatedly applauded Styron's novel and his choice to write it as a confession. For each of these critics, the confession, before it was anything else, was the rhetorical form par excellence for redressing uncertainty by bridging the chasm that ran the length of the color line.

What I wish to stress is that the sheer act of calling Styron's confession a novel was, for the white critics reviewed here, an intervention into the politics of violence. First, mysterious rebellions fit only in Elkin's inspired view of the Old South. From the perspective of Aptheker and Black Power, there was nothing mysterious about the violence of slavery. By insisting on the inexplicability of Turner's rebellion, Styron's critics were affirming the view that violence had no methodological role in the gradual emancipation of slaves. Far from a strategic technique of achieving freedom pursued by black revolutionary leaders, violence was rather a destructive force stumbled upon by random misfits such as Turner. Second, as a confession, the very form of Styron's novel challenged the Gilman–Fanon thesis that an "everlasting barrier" separated the races. By overstepping that "barrier," Styron's novel undermined Fanon's rationale for violence, which posited violence as the only means of communicating across the divide.

Legible Violence

The black response to *The Confessions of Nat Turner* was as widespread as it was harsh.[84] The unquestionable centerpiece of black resistance, however, quickly became John Henrik Clarke's edited volume *William Styron's Nat Turner: Ten*

Black Writers Respond. Published seven months after Styron's novel, Clarke recruited an impressive array of black public intellectuals—many of whom had already published critiques of Styron in other venues—and collected in one volume what Styron would later refer to as a "collective *cri de coeur* of throbbing pain and rage."[85] Although the text repeated points made elsewhere and was criticized on scholarly grounds, the collective voice of the ten black writers and the sheer pathos of their outcry, French writes, turned the volume into "the political and cultural manifesto for the grass-roots movement" against Styron, his story, and, above all, his Turner.[86]

The primary complaints of *William Styron's Nat Turner* have been widely noted: the arrogance of a white aristocrat claiming to speak for a black slave, the casting of slavery as a genial institution, and Styron's frequent historical miscues.[87] Yet, with as much frequency as the ten black writers returned these well-worn topics, they also returned to the question of confession. Indeed, it is not too much to say that they—like Kazin and Woodward—were preoccupied with the genre of Styron's novel. According to John Oliver Killens, Styron's decision to write the novel as a confession was a more significant blunder than the historical miscues or even the Elkins-inspired picture of the Old South. Second only to his decision to write at all, Killens reasoned, Styron's biggest mistake "was to pretend to tell the story from the point of view of Turner, and it was a colossal error, one that required tremendous arrogance. And naiveté."[88]

The black writers saw the contestation of the generic classification of the novel as a shorthand mode of advancing their politics. By retrofitting the genre of confession in such a way that Styron's novel could not possibly qualify, the black writers were able to weigh in on the pressing questions of violence, its history, and its current necessity. Simply by denying Styron's text the classification he claimed for it, they challenged Elkins's historiography and maintained Fanon's rationale for violence.

Historical Violence

No issue was more offensive to the black writers than Styron's domestication of Nat Turner. Although *William Styron's Nat Turner* can be read as a virtual compendium of historical flaws—the absence of Turner's wife, his homoerotic experiment, the role of his mother, the complicity of slaves in the suppression of the rebellion, and Turner's penchant for white sex—no flaw was quite as important as Styron's Elkins-inspired rendering of violence. Thus Aptheker writing in *The Nation*: "The discrepancies between the realities of the Turner rebellion and Mr. Styron's rendition thereof are numerous, often quite serious, and form, I believe a pattern amounting to consequential distortion": a "personality" distortion. "The Turner rebellion cannot be understood," Aptheker argued, "unless it is seen as the culminating blow of a particular period of rising slave unrest."[89] Clarke agreed: "The Turner revolt cannot be understood out of context with the atmosphere of revolt that prevailed throughout the first half of the nineteenth century." There were "hundreds of uprisings," Clarke continued, and revolts "all over the South."[90] John Oliver Killens put it this way: "Dear old Dixieland was in a constant state of insurrection. Thousands of rapturous slaves killed their mistresses and their masters, put spiders in the Big House soup, broke their farming implements accidentally-on-purpose, set fire to the cotton patches, and, all in all, demonstrated their contentedness in most peculiar ways."[91] For Killens and the black writers more generally, their primary objection was that Styron had robbed Turner (and Dixieland) of this "rapturous" tendency to revolt. Speaking for the whole, Clarke argued that the ten black writers "collectively maintain" that Styron's distortions turned Turner into an "uncle tom" and the South into a scene drawn by Stanley Elkins.[92] Robert Sussman summarized the black complaint. From the perspective of the black critics, he wrote, none of Styron's historical falsifications raised as much ire as his fundamental taming of Nat Turner, his "reducing the stature of Nat's authentic black heroism."[93]

Once the violence of Turner was placed in its proper context—in which it was a strategic and routine part of slave resistance—there was no longer anything mysterious about Turner's rebellion. Indeed, one of the most conspicuous differences between Styron's white and black critics concerned the legibility of violence. While Woodward, Kazin, and O'Connell failed to comprehend a rebellion so violent, Styron's black critics found no difficulty explaining the violence of the rebellion. Indeed, in the late 1960s the inexplicability of Nat Turner's rebellion was a partisan position; the violence he wreaked posed serious questions only for white critics. For Styron's black critics, the violence of Turner's rebellion was perfectly legible. "What's the big mystery about Nat's motivation?" John Oliver Killens wrote. Turner "was a slave, PERIOD," he continued, and "every slave is a potential revolutionary."[94] For Killens and his ilk, Turner's rebellion was a simple matter of physics: every action produces an equal and opposite reaction. "It should not now be necessary to search for the motives, personal and otherwise, for the Nat Turner revolt," John Henrik Clarke wrote. Lloyd Tom Delany put it this way: despite "great effort," Styron missed "the obvious, that men treated as they were under slavery will hate, and that they will hate in unmitigated fashion." And given the extent of this hatred, the rebellion is stripped of its mystery: "Nat Turner saw a way for slaves to obtain their freedom. Then they struck. It was as simple and complex as that."[95] Similarly, Vincent Harding argued that the "obscurity" of Nat Turner was a function only of the "blindness of the white observer–experts."[96]

Thus, with as much persistence as Styron's white critics insisted on the paucity of the historical record and the concomitant inexplicability of Nat Turner's rebellion, his black critics focused on Styron's historical blindness and the concomitant obviousness of the rebellion. And an obvious rebellion served the black critics in basic and interrelated ways: it affirmed Aptheker over Elkins, and proved that Styron's novel could not be a confession.

On this last point, the black writers were explicit. Styron's failure to understand Dear Old Dixie, they argued, functioned as proof positive that Styron's novel held no claim to be Turner's confession. Given its reliance on Stanley Elkins, Lloyd Tom Delany cried, *The Confessions of Nat Turner* was "a white man's view of a black man's mind."[97] And if this was the case, then Styron had clearly not "leap[ed] into a black man's consciousness" and his novel was certainly not Nat Turner's confession. Again, John Oliver Killens: "The title of this novel should have been *The Confessions of Willie Styron*, because that is precisely what this novel is all about. It reveals more about the psyche of the 'southern liberal' Styron, direct descendant of ol' Massa, than it even begins to reveal about the heart and soul and mind of black revolutionary Nat Turner." To ensure his audience did not miss this point, Killens repeated it nearly verbatim: "I repeat: What we have in this new novel, is not the confessions of Nat Turner, but rather the confessions (unintentional to be sure) of Master William Styron, White Anglo-Saxon Southern Protestant. Moreover, they are confessions which reveal that Styron has progressed but a very short distance from the attitudes of his grandfather."[98]

Killens's repetition should not suggest that he was making a unique argument that, if not stressed, might be lost amid the din. Rather, in these two quotations, powerful as they are, Killens was simply repeating the single most rehearsed critique of Styron's novel: it could not be Turner's confession because the Turner that appeared therein had been robbed him of his revolutionary stature. Quoting Lloyd Delany, John Henrik Clarke summarized the central point of *William Styron's Nat Turner* as follows: "'These are the confessions of Styron, not Nat Turner, for there exist significant historical discrepancies. . . .' The book's implications about human motivations, he continues, 'contain not only serious error, but subtly support certain stereotype views of the most ardent racists.'"[99] John A. Williams put it this way: Styron injected "Whitey Serum" into black history, and thus the novel would be better titled the "faked confessions" of Nat Turner.[100] In sum, over and again Styron's claim to write the confessions of Nat Turner is undermined by his failure to properly understand the violence of Dixieland.

Consider the complaint of the celebrated black journalist Lerone Bennett, Jr. Like so many of his colleagues, Bennett decried Styron's "distortion of the facts." He claimed that Styron "ignores evidence," "contradicts the facts," was "oblivious" to historical truth, and evaded any historical documentation that "clashes with [his] purposes." The "real Nat Turner," Bennett claimed, was a "virile, commanding, courageous figure," a "defiant black rebel" who was "obsessed with black liberation." "*This* Nat Turner," Bennett complained, "is displaced in the book by the white man in blackface." As the reference to minstrel suggests, Bennett's complaint was, above all, that in the place of the virile figure of Nat Turner was placed a caricature of the "Big Black Sambo"— the "bootlicking, head-scratching child–man," the docile "plantation type" who "went beyond the call of the whip in accommodating himself to slavery." For Bennett, Styron substituted "an impotent, cowardly, irresolute creature of his own imagination for the real black man who killed."[101]

Bennett, for his part, was not about to allow Styron uncontested claim to the meaning of Turner and his mission. The work of reclaiming Turner for the purposes of Black Power required first that Bennett contest the genre of the novel. Given the fact that Styron's novel replaced the "real" Nat Turner with a black-faced figment of the white imagination, Bennett concluded that the novel must not be read as Turner's confession: "Nat Turner does not speak in William Styron's *Confessions*. The voice in this confession is the voice of William Styron. The images are images of William Styron. The confession is the confession of William Styron."[102] Thus, like Killens, Clarke, Delany, and Williams, Bennett, too, connected the question of Turner's violence to the question of Styron's genre. For these thinkers, violence and confession were inextricably linked: Styron's failure to appreciate the violence of the old regime signaled his failure to write the confessions of Nat Turner.

Consider finally the contribution of Loyle Hairston. Hairston laments the fate of Nat Turner in the hands of a novelist "who still subscribes to the fantasy–history of an *Idyllic South*" and reads history within "the narrow confines of regional loyalty to the so-called southern tradition." Within this tradition, the slave registered as a "happy darky" and the meaning of rebellion could register only on criminal scales.[103] Given an Elkins-inspired idyllic

South, the only possible explanation for Turner was as a "rogue-nigger": an "emasculated," "anguished," savage interrupting civilization itself.[104] In truth, Hairston countered, the southern tradition is little more than "a euphemism for institutional white supremacy."[105] Unfortunately, Styron's commitment to the southern tradition means that the reader "never really feels the mind of a man turned insurrectionist by the repulsive circumstances of his existence."[106] And if the reader never really feels the mind of Turner, it follows that Styron's title is as false as the southern tradition itself. The purported "'confession' is—to put it bluntly—a blatant forgery," for Turner "is not allowed to speak his own piece, to give expression to sentiments and passions which are born of the slave's tragic experience."[107] The "first-person narrative," Hairston concludes, "destroys whatever plausibility [Styron's] Nat Turner might have had," "for [Turner's] concerns are clearly not his own, but those of William Styron's rather medieval conceptions of what the inner life of a 'Negro,' a black slave, was like."[108] Thus for Hairston, like so many others, questions of historical agency and rhetorical form were deeply intertwined. Styron's novel could not possibly lay claim to the confessional form because it gave voice to the fantasies of the southern tradition (read: Elkins) rather than the facts of slavery's horror (read: Aptheker). Thus did the black contestation of the genre of Styron's novel advance a partisan reading of the historical violence of slavery.

Present Violence

Contesting the genre of Styron's novel advanced the interests of Black Power in one other way: it allowed for the affirmation of Fanon's rationale for retributive violence. Fanon argued that violence was needed because racism had produced a "Manichaean" world, in which black and white were two totally different "species." Famously, Fanon added that the societal superstructure was just as divided as the infrastructure. For this reason, the black and white races shared no values, no common assumptions, no religious traditions, and no common norms of discourse. Styron's black critics agreed, and they did so by contesting the genre of Styron's novel. If Styron's novel was a confession, then Fanon's two-species theory had much to answer to, for the very fact that Styron could write the confessions of Nat Turner indicated a substantial shared reservoir of common values.

This was nowhere more clear than in the work of John Oliver Killens and Mike Thelwell. Both men addressed themselves to the central implication of classifying Styron's novel as a confession. Thelwell, the founding chair of the important University of Massachusetts Afro-American Studies Department, posed the question this way: is it possible "for a white southern gentleman to tune in on the impulses, beliefs, emotions, and thought-patterns of a black slave?"[109] Robert F. Durden has argued that this was the most "crucial" question raised by the ten black writers.[110] The answer was a resounding no. Like Fanon, both Killens and Thelwell argued that there were two "irreconcilable moralities," the master's morality and the slave's.[111] Styron's inability to see the brutality of slavery and resultant militancy of every slave clearly indicated which morality he inhabited. His attempt to write the confessions of Nat Turner was, then, bound to fail, for Styron was, as Killens put it, unable to "transcend his southern-peckerwood background."[112] In Thelwell's words, because the "gentleman and the slave lack common language or experience," Styron's conceit would have required a "miracle of empathy." Thelwell had no faith in miracles, and neither did Killens. It is for this reason that, as I noted above, Killens believed that Styron's fundamental mistake was "to pretend to tell the story from the point of view of Turner, and it was a colossal error, one that required tremendous arrogance. And naiveté." It was arrogant because it assumed that the differences that separated him from slavery might be bridged by his literary prowess; and it was naïve because it required ignorance of the extent to which his own understanding of history was informed by a "master's morality."[113]

For these reasons, there was a virtual consensus among the black writers that only a black person could tell Nat Turner's story. Killens argued, "Only the black brethren can really understand the deepest meaning of the 'Long Hot Summers.'"[114] As Addison Gayle, Jr., put it two years later, "Those who condemn Styron for his portrait [of Turner], who demand that he portray Nat Turner with some semblance of reality, demand the impossible. To demand a realistic portrayal of Blacks by whites is to demand the impossible; for whites are neither mentally nor culturally equipped for the task."[115] Finally, Vincent Harding felt compelled to take James Baldwin to task over this very issue. Whereas Baldwin had praised *The Confessions of Nat Turner* as a "common history" of black and white, Harding countered that "it is nothing of the kind." Riffing on the Langston Hughes line "You've taken my blues and gone," Harding argued, "No one else can speak out of the bittersweet bowels of our blackness." William Styron tried to do just that, as if "entrance into the black skin is achieved as easily as Styron-Turner's penetration of invisible white flesh." The result? "You've taken my Nat and gone."[116]

For Killens, Thelwell, Gayle, and Harding, Styron had embarked on an impossible project. Each of these critics agreed with Gilman's "Negro

Writing" thesis, and each of them agreed with Fanon that blacks and whites were different species, separated by an unbridgeable chasm. Thus Styron's was an "impossible" task, and as a matter of course he could not transcend his "master's morality" or his cultural background. When these critics refused Styron's novel the status of a confession, they were driven by their Fanon-inspired convictions about the irreducibility of the black experience. And in the context of the 1960s, Fanon's two-species argument was not simply a theory of racial organization; it was also a rationale for violence. Thus, by contesting the genre of Styron's novel, the ten black writers both legitimated a history of violent resistance and left intact a widely circulating rationale for violence in the present.

Conclusion: Confession and Violence

I conclude this chapter with reflections on confession and violence. First, confession. Over the years, scholars have come up with different sets of criteria for defining what is and what is not a confession. At the moment, the criteria set forth by Foucault in the mid-1970s still dominate the scholarly conversation on confession. Foucault may be smart, and his definition of confession may tie the practice directly to practices of power, but like so many others, he still begins with a substantive definition of confession and then searches for examples. Working from Foucault—or for that matter, from Augustine or Rousseau or Freud—we would be blind to a great deal of confessional politics simply by starting with an arbitrary, stipulated definition. Styron's novel would never register as a confession by anyone's definition. Yet, despite this fact, it was made a confession by people who needed it to be one. This is an important reminder that, unlike other genres, the confession simply cannot be defined by recurrent formal characteristics; the only way to study the politics of confession in twentieth-century America is to study what people call a confession, no matter how unlikely a candidate it seems. In this sense, confession may be a wholly performative genre: a confession is that which is called a confession.

Second, violence. There is a long literature that suggests that it is in the very nature of violence to demand an explanation. Karen Halttunen, for example, has argued that the disorder of violence must be met with the order-giving powers of rhetoric: "The [violent] act rends the community in which it takes place, calling all relationships into question . . . and posing troubling questions about the moral nature of humankind. Murder thus demands that a community come to terms with the crime—confront what has happened and endeavor to explain it, in an effort to restore order to the world."[117] Along similar lines, Foucault has argued, "The injury that a crime inflicts upon the social body is the disorder that it introduces into it." Like Halttunen, Foucault emphasizes that the disorder of violence must be answered by a punishment that restores order to the community. Finally, and most relevantly, Stephen H. Browne has argued that the sheer violence of Turner's rebellion "poses serious questions as to how violence on this scale gets represented."[118]

As we have seen, these questions plagued Styron's white critics and organized their response to his novel. It is important to insist, however, that Halttunen, Foucault, and Browne have overstated the powers of violence. Despite their eloquent testimony, nothing in the nature of violence demands an explanation. Rather, the relative obscurity of violence is itself a differential variable. To take a stand on the obscurity or clarity of Turner's violence was, in the 1960s, to align oneself with a particular political position. Only liberal white critics were stymied by the violence of Southampton. Writing in *Freedomways*, Loyle Hairston captured nicely the ways that the legibility of violence was organized along racial and political lines: "Why then does a slave revolt? The answer to that question would seem simple enough—unless of course the slave in question happened to have been black and his revolt against *American* slavery. Then—lo and behold—the question takes on such an extraordinary complexity."[119] The relative inexplicability of Turner's rebellion, in other words, functioned for Hairston as an index to political commitments. The existence of violence was "simple enough" until it was placed into political context. In that context, it became inexplicable for white liberals but remained perfectly legible to Black Power. This is a poignant reminder that there is nothing mysterious in the nature of violence. Violence does not demand its own explanation. The next time someone tells you to please explain what could possibly motivate a violent action, you should ask what he or she is selling. The inexplicability of violence has more to do with the politics of the dumbfounded than it does with the nature of violence. Or put another way, to be mystified by violence is a political position. It can be read as a will to ignorance, the politics of which tends to be masked by ideology, in this case the illusion that violence always requires an explanation.

5

CONFESSION AND RELIGION: JIMMY SWAGGART'S SECULAR CONFESSION

On February 21, 1988, Jimmy Swaggart publicly confessed to the more than eight thousand people crowded into his Baton Rouge Family Worship Center. The confession was, by all accounts, quite a spectacle. The *Houston Chronicle* reports that Swaggart wept throughout the entirety of his nearly thirty-minute confession, during which he was interrupted ten times for standing ovations.[1] Between ovations, Swaggart's confession apparently mesmerized the thousands of onlookers. The *Washington Post* recorded that a "hush fell over the sanctuary as stunned onlookers, some speaking in tongues, wept and then shouted support. Men bowed their heads and cried, and women dabbed at running mascara with tissues from boxes thoughtfully scattered about."[2] When it was over, Swaggart's wife, Frances, members of his board, and hundreds of congregants gathered on the stage in what the *San Francisco Chronicle* termed a "giant huddle of hugging."[3] Long after Swaggart was gone and the huggers dispersed, many congregants remained, kneeling at their pews praying, or lying prostrate on the floor, crying.[4]

Time magazine called it "without question, the most dramatic sermon ever aired on television."[5] The rhetorician Quentin J. Schultze labeled it "one of the most masterful programs of all time, perhaps even the single most effective televisual performance of any American evangelist."[6] Likewise, Michael J. Giuliano argued that the confession was instrumental in Swaggart's unprecedented return to power. Reversing the precedents of Jim Bakker and Marvin Gorman, televangelists whose recent scandals had led to their defrocking, Swaggart emerged from the scandal relatively unscathed.

And, Giuliano concludes, until three years later when a California police officer pulled Swaggart over only to find him accompanied by a local prostitute and volumes of pornography, Swaggart was "clearly headed back to the top of the religious television ratings."[7]

As effective as the speech may have been, the eight thousand teary-eyed worshippers could not possibly have known the particular events that brought Swaggart to his Baton Rouge stage that February morning. He had certainly broken the tenets of the creed he professed, but it was not contrition that motivated his confession. Swaggart was being blackmailed by the across-town pastor Marvin Gorman. Two years earlier, Swaggart had humiliated Gorman by publicizing his infidelities and orchestrating his termination. Now Gorman was getting his revenge. Armed with pictures of an escorted Swaggart entering and leaving a pay-by-the-hour motel, Gorman demanded that Swaggart speak openly of his sexual addiction. After Gorman rejected Swaggart's counteroffer of church jobs for his family, Swaggart agreed to Gorman's terms: he would publicly confess his sexual addiction. But he did not keep his promise. After four months of inactivity, Gorman expedited Swaggart's confession by flying the incriminating photos to the Springfield, Missouri, Assemblies of God headquarters. The following Sunday, Swaggart delivered the now-famous "Apology" sermon, in which he claimed that although his "sin was done in secret," the Lord desired that it be revealed before the "whole world."[8]

Although the Lord (and Gorman) may well have desired disclosure, the Assemblies of God preferred discretion. As I will demonstrate, the Assemblies of God and Jimmy Swaggart Ministries combined in the execution of what the *Boston Globe* would later refer to as a protracted "silence campaign."[9] It seems that the entire denomination—at local, state, and national levels—was determined to conceal the details of Swaggart's secret pleasures. Although it is impossible to know precisely why the denomination was so committed to protecting Swaggart's secrets, it is not difficult to speculate. Swaggart was an essential part of the church's financial viability. He single-handedly raised more money than any other televangelist of the time and, without this fund-raising, it is unclear whether Jimmy Swaggart Ministries would have remained solvent. Finally, from the perspective of the church, because Jimmy Swaggart Ministries brought Christianity to five hundred million viewers worldwide, every financial loss was also a spiritual loss.[10] As the Swaggart hagiographers Charles and Lynda Fontaine put it, as a result of Swaggart's financial losses, "thousands of lost people around the world are not hearing the gospel even once and are going to hell."[11]

Swaggart was thus in a fix. On the one hand, he faced the photo-armed Marvin Gorman, who was demanding a public confession. On the other hand, the disclosures involved in a traditional, Christian confession threatened the economic stability of his ministry and, by extension, the spiritual vitality of numberless souls. The situation demanded a rhetorical performance of a particular kind, one that would publicly register *as a Christian confession* even if Swaggart defaulted on the genre's most basic obligation: the disclosure of sinfulness. He needed, in other words, a performance that could be labeled a confession despite its substantive content, rather than because of it.

His speech of February 21 was just this. It was completely silent on the subject of Swaggart's misdeeds *and* widely received as a confession. Consider first its silence. Despite the fact that Swaggart began his confession with a promise to face issues "head-on," and despite his further insistence that he has never "sidestepped or skirted unpleasantries," Swaggart never disclosed the particular "unpleasantry" that had him confessing in the first place.[12] To be sure, stories circulated in the media about a meticulous, detailed, ten-hour *private* confession delivered earlier in the week to the governing board (the Executive Presbytery) of the Assemblies of God. Moreover, the content of this private confession was eventually leaked, and the media had no problem constructing a detailed ledger of Swaggart's moral debts.[13] But despite his promised candor, Swaggart never said a thing about the illicit rendezvous that had him crying in front of millions.

Swaggart's widely noted silence, however, did not disqualify the speech as a confession. Those close to Swaggart insisted that the speech was a confession, even if it meant blatantly ignoring Swaggart's silence. Consider the comments of Dr. Thomas Miller of the Jimmy Swaggart Bible College: "There couldn't have been a more frank and open confession of failure." Likewise the church official Forrest Hall: "I've never seen a man come completely clean and have the humility to do this."[14] Or as Swaggart's "copastor" Jim Rentz put it, Jimmy Swaggart "confessed to the world."[15] These statements push the bounds of credulity. Miller's suggestion that there could not possibly have been a "more frank" confession and Hall's suggestion that Swaggart came "completely clean" are simply not true. As nearly every media pundit noticed—and as Swaggart himself later acknowledged—he did not in fact come clean.[16] This insistence that the speech was a "frank confession" can only be ideologically driven. For Miller, Hall, and Rentz, I suspect that the sermon was a confession only because it needed to be one. As I have stressed in every chapter of this book, when it comes to determining what texts count as confessions, politics trumps traditional considerations of rhetorical form and content. The case is no different here: Gorman's strong-arm tactics required a confession, and so the church declared Swaggart's performance a confession.

What separates Swaggart's speech from the texts considered in previous chapters is that, in this case, those with no political connections to the church nonetheless classified Swaggart's speech as a confession. The *Houston Chronicle, Chicago Tribune, Washington Post, New York Times, San Francisco Chronicle,* and *London Financial Times* all labeled the performance a confession. More startling still, well-qualified academics have confirmed the media consensus. The University of Southern California's Leonard K. Firestone Professor of Religion Donald Earl Miller praised Swaggart for, of all things, "candor." Swaggart, Miller wrote, "came before 7,000 worshipers in his church last Sunday with candor; there was no pretense, no cover-up, no self-serving excuses, no scapegoating."[17] That there was also no admission of wrongdoing went without comment. Miller may sound the most like a church official, but there is nothing unique in his assessment. Indeed, scholars have praised Swaggart's sermon as an exemplary model of Christian confession. This is the respected evangelical scholar Quentin Schultze: "Swaggart's televised confession in 1988 was one of the most emotionally moving religious broadcasts of all time. With an agonized look on his face, and tears streaming down his cheeks, Swaggart conveyed genuine repentance. His repentance seemed real, even to many skeptics of televangelism."[18] No one, however, was as excited by Swaggart's sermon as Susan Wise Bauer. Because Swaggart unequivocally accepted blame, and because he reassured his audience that he was a common sinner like them, Bauer makes of Swaggart's speech a standard against which the confessive attempts of Jim Bakker, President Bill Clinton, and Cardinal Bernard Law were tried and found wanting.[19]

The fact that Swaggart's February 21 sermon was so widely received as a Christian confession, and the fact that it was so classified by people with so little to gain from it, requires an explanation. How could a speech that so blatantly ignored the first requirement of the Christian confession—the admission of wrongdoing—register so consistently as a Christian confession? How, we might ask, was *this* text turned into a confession? In this chapter, I suggest that we can answer this question by focusing on the two competing traditions of confession within which the meaning of Swaggart's performance may be discerned. The first tradition is Augustinian, Christian, and, in an important sense, classical; the second is modern and secular, with roots in the *Confessions* of Jean-Jacques Rousseau. Peter Brooks agues that the American "confessional imagination"—what Americans think about when they consider confession—comprises elements from both traditions, awkwardly and inconsistently cobbled together. He suggests that the Christian tradition of confession informs even the most secular accounts of confession, and conversely, that the work of Rousseau is "decisive for the modern confessional tradition."[20] Swaggart, I argue, capitalized on the composite nature of the American confessional imagination. Because his February 21 sermon fit perfectly within a secular tradition of confession, his speech was widely recognized as a confession; because it was nonetheless fairly littered with a religious vocabulary and biblical quotations, it was mistaken for a Christian confession.

Rhetorically speaking, the two traditions of confession are fundamentally at odds with each other. In the Christian tradition, the public confession is, above all, the disclosure of sinfulness.[21] It is, I argue, a deeply classical tradition of public confession in the sense that it celebrates the art of rhetoric—and the art of disclosure in particular—as an essential condition for political flourishing. In the modern tradition, by contrast, public confession is understood as self-disclosure rather than the admission of sinfulness. Despite the common topos of disclosure, however, the modern tradition of public confession must be understood as a rejection of the classical emphasis within the Christian tradition. The modern tradition of public confession suggests that the arts of rhetoric and disclosure stand at odds with each other. From the perspective of this tradition, speech may be necessary for a public confession, but it is woefully inadequate; the depths of the self are too personal and too real to be adequately disclosed through the conventions of speech. This insistence that the arts of rhetoric are inadequate for self-disclosure is hardly innocent; Jay Fliegelman describes it as a means of "scripting silence."[22] To the extent that the modern public confession posits a fundamental opposition between the art of rhetoric and the art of disclosure, and to the extent that Swaggart operates within this tradition, it is possible to understand how Swaggart could not disclose a thing *and* have his speech celebrated as an exemplary confession.

I argue that the modern, secular tradition of public confession best explains the formal features of Swaggart's confession and the unlikely political work it accomplished. To be sure, Swaggart is a preacher and a self-proclaimed Christian, and there are, accordingly, references to the Christian tradition of confession. But we must not be deceived by the pervasive religious language, the constant references to sin and forgiveness, the speaking in tongues, or the much talked about consequences of the Swaggart scandal on the future of televangelism. Swaggart's confession is, in fact, deeply indebted to a profoundly secular rhetorical tradition, and it is precisely this tradition that renders his confession capable of accomplishing the political work of the Assemblies of God: a widely enforced silence campaign.

In order to explain the secular tradition of public confession, its differences from the Christian tradition, and its political capacities, I isolate three features of Swaggart's rhetoric: his insistence on the inadequacy of speech, his disregard for syntactical and grammatical conventions, and his repeated emphasis on his own humanity. I argue that each of these features has its "primitive source" in a modern, secular tradition of confession.[23] In the case of Jimmy Swaggart it is particularly important to insist that he is operating within an established tradition. For without this insistence, it is too easy to dismiss his devaluations of speech as simply the rhetorical trope of *adynaton*, by which a speaker emphasizes a point by insisting on the impossibility of sufficient emphasis. Likewise, without insisting on Swaggart's placement within a tradition it is too easy to dismiss his ramblings as sheer incoherence, or as a failure to achieve basic levels of rhetorical proficiency. And finally, without insisting on tradition, it is too easy to dismiss Swaggart's emphasis on his own humanity as an innocent communitarian impulse. By locating each of these features within a specific tradition of confession, I seek to foreground the ways each of them contributed to the political work of the Assemblies of God.

In explaining the rhetorical and political capacities of a particular tradition of public confession, I address two areas of common concern in confessional studies. First, by demonstrating the historical variation of the public confession, I hope to provide yet another counterpoint to the scholar whose name is, unfailingly, associated with the study of confession, Michel Foucault.[24] While I have already highlighted what I take to be Foucault's most serious liability—the fact that he begins from a predetermined definition of confession—this chapter foregrounds a second liability: the fact that he does not recognize fundamental differences between traditions of confession. Instead, Foucault posits a "line going straight" from the Catholic confessional to the anonymous *My Secret Life*—an eighteenth-century sex text that bears little resemblance to Christian penance—and from the thirteenth-century sacrament of penance to our own confessional culture.[25] This chapter suggests, pace Foucault, that the critique of public confession cannot proceed pro forma; as I have suggested in every chapter, the rhetorical function of a confession is determined more by the political needs of the confessant than by the formal features of the text.

The second area of common concern addressed in this chapter is the critical evaluation of religious rhetoric. Swaggart challenges the ease with which we distinguish religious discourse from its secular counterpart. Is Jimmy Swaggart's confession an example of religious discourse because it is a sermon, because it is given in a church, because he quotes the Bible? This analysis suggests that we must also ask questions about the rhetorical tradition in which a discourse operates. In this instance, I argue that despite the conspicuous religiosity of Swaggart's confession—it was in fact a Bible-quoting sermon given in a church—its rhetorical form and political function can best be accounted for with recourse to a definitively secular tradition of public confession.

Does this mean that Swaggart's confession is not religious? This an important question, not because it treats "the classification of discourse as an end in itself," but because, at least in the case of religious rhetoric, questions of classification have determined critical practice.[26] To take only the most relevant example, the idiosyncrasies of American fundamentalist rhetoric have long been explained with recourse to an insular religious community. Giuliano argues that the success of Swaggart's confession depended on an audience that shared the same basic theological assumptions.[27] Martin J. Medhurst likewise suggests that understanding Pentecostal enthymemes demands understanding their biblical premises.[28] Finally, Susan Friend Harding argues that fundamentalists use a "language of faith" in which logical contradictions and other "infelicities" are harmonized in accordance with insular "interpretive conventions."[29] To the extent that my analysis holds, however, fundamentalist rhetoric cannot be accounted for with recourse only to the interpretive conventions of religious groups or their distinctive theological assumptions. To do so would be to miss the indebtedness of religious discourses to widely shared rhetorical traditions. In sum, the example of Jimmy Swaggart, properly read, provides insight into both the historical evolution of the public confession and the manifold resources of contemporary religious rhetoric.

Historical Contexts: Feuding Televangelists and Covert Operations

The second half of the 1980s was a particularly rough period for Evangelical televangelists. From Oral Roberts's controversial assertion that God would "call him home" unless his (mostly elderly) viewership donated $4.5 million, to Jim and Tammy Faye Bakker's adultery/hush-money/extortion scandal, evangelical televangelists suffered so many high-profile scandals that a year before the Swaggart scandal broke, *Time* magazine had already labeled televangelists "TV's Unholy Row."³⁰ The televangelists' problems were aggravated by severe infighting. Bakker accused Swaggart of designing a "diabolical plot" to take over his church, his cable network, and his theme park, Heritage USA. Swaggart, in turn, responded by calling Bakker a "cancer that need[s] to be excised from the body of Christ" and ensuring that Bakker's tryst with his secretary Jessica Hahn was widely publicized.³¹ After Swaggart ensured Bakker's demise, Bakker arranged that the Moral Majority's founder Jerry Falwell—and not Swaggart—would assume control of his empire when he was forced to resign. This arrangement, however, was not long to Bakker's liking. He later claimed that "the Virginia Fundamentalist [Falwell] had duped him in order to grab his empire."³² In sum, the only high-profile evangelicals to emerge from 1987 unscathed by scandal were Billy Graham and Robert Schuller.

At the most concrete level, it was precisely Swaggart's penchant for feuding with fellow televangelists that led to his 1988 confession. Throughout the early 1980s, Jimmy Swaggart Ministries competed with the Reverend Marvin Gorman's First Assembly Church of God for New Orleans parishioners and their pocketbooks. Located on the outskirts of New Orleans, the First Assembly Church of God was drawing five thousand worshippers each week, operating on a budget of $4.5 million a year, and producing a five-day-a-week TV show that aired in all fifty states—all under the dynamic leadership of the rising televangelist star Marvin Gorman. In July 1986, however, when Swaggart got news of Gorman's illicit habits, he orchestrated not only the resignation of Gorman, but also the dismantling of the entire ministry of the First Assembly Church of God. Following Swaggart's accusations, Gorman resigned his pulpit. This was not enough for Swaggart, however, who helped to write a lengthy statement accusing Gorman of "numerous adulterous and illicit affairs," to be read in front of Gorman's five-thousand-member congregation. Three weeks after this letter was read, Swaggart personally wrote Louisiana District Superintendent Cecil Janway and demanded that Gorman not be given special treatment because of his large operating budget or TV show. In the letter Swaggart made his position clear: "I want it to be clearly understood that I will take whatever steps I feel are necessary to see that this situation is not covered up and that Marvin is not treated differently than any other minister."³³ Immediately following Janway's receipt of this letter, Gorman was permanently dismissed from the denomination.

It was a little over a year later that a private investigator, hired by Gorman, took several pictures of Jimmy Swaggart entering and leaving a hotel room on the seedy Airline Highway not far from Gorman's now-defunct church. After capturing Swaggart on film, the investigator called Gorman and then—to give Gorman time—let the air out of the right front tire of Swaggart's Town Car. When Gorman arrived, the two preachers sat in Gorman's car and talked for two hours. The *Washington Post* reports that during this conversation Swaggart wept throughout, confessed an enduring penchant for prostitutes, and begged Gorman to show mercy. In fact, if Gorman is to be believed, Swaggart did more than beg. According to Gorman, Swaggart offered him and his family jobs with Jimmy Swaggart Ministries if Gorman would agree to forget the incident.[34] Swaggart, in other words, attempted to bribe Gorman and thereby buy the silence of the televangelist whom he had so forcibly silenced just a year earlier. Gorman refused. He demanded that Swaggart confess and speak openly about his sexual addiction to ecclesiastical authorities. Swaggart agreed, but it was not until Gorman flew the incriminating photos to the Executive Presbytery of the Assemblies of God some four months later that Swaggart took to the stage and assured his congregation that he never sidestepped unpleasantries.

Historically speaking, Swaggart's claim to face issues head-on was simply not true. As I noted in the introduction, the Assemblies of God went to great lengths to protect Swaggart's privacy. Consider, for example, the five-minute introduction of Jimmy Swaggart given by Forest Hall immediately preceding Swaggart's confession. Hall, the secretary–treasurer of the Louisiana District of Assemblies of God, explained that Swaggart had given a "detailed" but private confession of "specific incidents of moral failure" to the Executive Presbyters of the Assemblies of God. Hall emphasized that Swaggart had shown true humility in his willingness to speak privately of his sins, but that the congregation should not expect to hear him speak publicly about transgressive details: "No spiritual purpose would be served by answering questions about details. There has been a detailed confession to those wronged and to established church authority. . . . No doubt much speculation will naturally find its way into the secular media. But for the church, the body of Christ, such speculation and rumor has no place."[35] Hall thus prefigured the public confession with an introduction that provided ecclesiastical justifications for silence. Those who would seek to know the details, he suggested, are not fit for membership in the "body of Christ," wherein such speculation, rumor, and detailed speech have no place. This functioned as an argument that Swaggart's public confession could be successful even if he did not disclose the details of his moral debts—indeed, the confession could be marked successful precisely because Swaggart did not succumb to the temptation to fuel rumors with the description of specific moral failures.

Despite the inevitability of speculation in the "secular media," Hall emphasized that the church would do its best to stop it there as well. He said that he was urging Swaggart to "resist the urgings of those outside the church to respond to questions." It quickly became the official policy of the Louisiana Assemblies of God that there was "no need for any details to be released."[36]

Hall's introduction mirrored a statement by the Louisiana District of the Assemblies of God, which announced that there would be no public disclosure of the detailed confession and, accordingly, urged church members to "refrain from speculation and imagination about this matter."[37] The *New York Times* reported that parishioners were not simply instructed to avoid imagination and speculation, but also were "admonished not to discuss the matter."[38] Speculation and speech regarding Swaggart's unapproved sex was thus constructed as a moral infraction, silence was turned into evidence of spiritual superiority, and the old category of sinner was applied with as much vigor to the talkative parishioner as to the illicit pastor.

The church followed these prescriptions of silence resolutely. The following day, Cecil Janway announced that Swaggart would not talk to the secular media and refused to answer any questions about the developing story.[39] Church members, too, apparently took the silence campaign quite seriously. William Treeby, Swaggart's attorney, parishioner, and friend, and a member of the Louisiana District of the Assemblies of God, refused to talk to reporters, claiming that "the Louisiana District has asked us not to say anything." Likewise, a "Swaggart confidant," said this: "You'd love to let people know the real story, but I have to abide by church orders not to comment."[40] Even students at Swaggart's Bible College abided by the mandate. *People Weekly* reported that "no comment" was the standard and expected response of students to reporters.[41] After a few days of the "no comment" response, students and faculty at the Bible College took an even harsher stance, asking journalists to leave the premises.[42] Finally, even the informant and accuser himself, Marvin Gorman, refused to break the silence: the *New York Times* reported that Gorman would make no comments about the specific details of Swaggart's mistakes.[43]

It is in the context of a silence campaign pursued at several levels and instituted across a variety of social sites that we must understand Swaggart's rhetorical response to the scandal. The best way to reconcile the fact of the confessions with the vigor of the silence campaign is to focus on the competing traditions of public confession that inform Swaggart's work.

Theoretical Contexts: Competing Traditions of Confession

Swaggart concluded his "Apology Sermon" by borrowing words from what is perhaps the most storied public confession in the Christian tradition, that of the Psalmist David. The particular words Swaggart borrowed—"For I acknowledge my transgressions"—are important.[44] Hundreds of years after David wrote these words, Augustine would make the acknowledgment of transgression central to the Christian confession. The fact that Swaggart did not in fact "acknowledge his transgressions" is the first clue that, the quotation of Psalm 51 and the pervasive religious language notwithstanding, Swaggart's own confession is not explicable in the Christian tradition. Indeed, with the exception of the borrowed words appended to his own, Swaggart's confession is wholly remandable to the thoroughly secular and philosophically modern tradition of confession inaugurated by Jean-Jacques Rousseau. While I will make good on this claim below, what I wish to underscore in this section is the political implications of the two traditions of confession informing Swaggart's performance.

A Christian Tradition of Confession

It is well-known that public confession in the Augustinian tradition is a response to the Christian category of sinfulness. What is less well-known, but in this context far more important, is that Augustine's political understanding of sin entailed a political understanding of confession. Sin was, for Augustine, always the result of a deep-seated self-love constitutive of the natural human condition. Indeed, all the particulars that fill Augustine's *Confessions*—the pear stealing, the sexual trysts, the attachment to heretical beliefs—were simply so many surface effects of a natural but prideful independence that Augustine located at the root of transgression.[45] This natural independence, Augustine insists, is not simply a turning away from God, but also a turning away from the "common good." In a crucial passage that reveals the influence of classical thought at the heart of Augustine's theology, he argues that pride, the very essence of sinfulness, is "the attitude by which a person desires more than what is due by reason of his excellence, and a certain love of one's own interest, his private interest, to which the Latin word *privatus* was wisely given, a term which obviously expresses loss rather than gain. For every privation diminishes. Where pride, then, seeks to excel . . . [it turns] from the pursuit of the common good to one's own individual good out of a destructive self-love."[46] Charles Mathewes summarizes: "Human sin is 'privation' in a way that is not merely etymologically related to privacy: it is solitude, isolation, what Robert Markus calls 'man's liability to close in on himself . . . at bottom, sin [is] retreat into privacy.'"[47] As Markus himself puts it, pride is "the basic disorder in the human self and the basic force disruptive in society: it isolates the self from the community with its fellows." Sinfulness, then, is politically "disruptive" because it is a form of "self-enclosure," a means of "living according to oneself" at the expense of the community.[48]

And this is the importance of the Augustinian confession. Confession is a means of reversing the political currents of pridefulness. If sinfulness is a form of self-enclosure, the acknowledgment of transgression is a means of submitting the self and its deeds to the judgment of the wider community. To disclose transgression is to rob it of its self-enclosing force, to turn away from "private interest" and back toward the "common good." The Augustinian confession, in other words, is consonant with the classical assumption that political flourishing does not just happen, but needs to be fought for and maintained in the teeth of a natural propensity to "retreat into privacy."[49]

A Secular Tradition of Confession

While Swaggart closed his "Apology Sermon" with the borrowed words of David, he began with the assurance that his confession itself was not borrowed: "Everything that I will attempt to say to you this morning will be from my heart. I will not speak from a prepared script."[50] It is important here to note that the distinction between scripted speech and heart speech, and the insistence that only the latter is suitable for the confessive form, does not sound on an Augustinian register. Swaggart is here working within a thoroughly secular and philosophically modern understanding of confession. An appreciation of this tradition can help us understand how it is that Swaggart's heart speech was both widely recognized as a confession and yet managed to fit so snugly within the Assemblies of God's "silence campaign."

Although Rousseau was reading Augustine's *Confessions* immediately before the composition of his own, it is important to remember that the two confessants were working with radically different assumptions regarding the relationship between speech and politics. Pace Augustine, Rousseau believed that political flourishing was a *natural* human capacity that has been obscured by the conventions of society: "Man is born free, and everywhere he is in chains."[51] The political theorist Patrick J. Deneen sees in these famous words the "radical premise of democracy": that it requires for its achievement only "the realization of [humanity's] inherent decency."[52] This is the fundamental disjunction between Augustine and Rousseau: Augustine understood the human condition as one of flawed self-enclosure rather than basic decency, and he deployed the confession in the name of the common good. Rousseau, to the contrary, proclaimed the "inherent decency" of the human condition, and the public confession thereby assumed an entirely new function.

To Rousseau's mind, the confession was a means of accessing this buried decency. "A man who can delve into himself," as Jean Starobinski puts it, "can rediscover the resplendent face of god."[53] In less grandiloquent terms, Charles Taylor explains the logic: once the good is located in the depths of the self, access to the good is earned via self-disclosure.[54] It is not incidental that Rousseau shifts the form and function of the confession. Once about the disclosure of things done wrong, for Rousseau it is now about the disclosure of the self: "The particular object of my confessions is to make known my inner self."[55] Yet this was no easy task, for Rousseau believed that the conventions of language were too blunt an instrument to disclose the recesses of the inner self. In fact, Rousseau was so critical of the arts of speech, Starobinski reports, that he believed "man has practically lost the ability to communicate what matters."[56] Confronted on one hand with the necessity of accessing the "inherent decency" of the inner self and, on the other hand, with the paucity of language, Rousseau concluded that "to say what I have to say would require me to invent a language as new as my project."[57] And thus the modern, secular confession was born: philosophically modern because it is motivated by the "dream of shared interiorities," secular because it is premised on the conviction that the natural human condition is sufficient for human flourishing.[58]

The language Rousseau invented, and which he deployed in his *Confessions*, is developed theoretically in the now-famous "Essay on the Origin of Languages." It is worth attending to the "Essay" in some detail because understanding the theoretical investments that guided Rousseau's "invention" will help us understand the logic of Swaggart's confession. In the "Essay," Rousseau tried to isolate the particular characteristics of speech that enabled it to disclose the passions, which functioned for Rousseau as the site of the truest self. To isolate these characteristics, he created a fictional story regarding the origins of speech. He claimed that it originated in grunt-like sounds (which he called the "voice"), evolved into speech proper, and finally terminated in writing.

The decisive characteristic of the voice is its *naturalness*; the voice signifies those "simple sounds" that instinctively and unintentionally issue forth from the "naturally . . . open" human mouth and glottis—the vocative organs.[59] Cries, groans, sounds, and especially accents, these are the rich and "natural" resources of the voice.[60] Rich, because the myriad ways these resources can be combined almost renders the further development of language unnecessary; natural, because they are involuntary, unwilled, and reflexive.[61] The decisive point is this: it is the *accents* of the voice—the sonorous distinctions and tonal variations by which the voice *sounds*—that render it capable of self-disclosure. As John T. Scott explains, "The accents of the voice pass all the way to the soul, for they are the natural expression of the passions."[62]

Immediately following the development of the "voice" is articulation. Like all "developments" in Rousseau's scheme, the emergence of articulation marks a degeneration of language. Articulation is conventional rather than natural; it is "mechanical," in that it requires technique, practice, and attention, and is learned only with difficulty.[63] Whereas the voice is understood as the natural and spontaneous emission of sound, articulation is the mechanical modification of that sound; it is the technique of the lips modifying and thereby muting the natural and euphonic sounds of the voice. When articulation is carried to its logical end, it eventuates in the silence of writing. Jacques Derrida, one of the most famous readers of the "Essay," explains, "The more a language is articulated, the more articulation extends its domain, and thus gains in rigor and in vigor, the more it yields to writing, the more it calls forth writing."[64] Writing, for Rousseau, marks the perfect antithesis to voice; it is analytical, it "substitutes precision for expression," and most important, it cannot communicate the inner self: "In proportion as needs increase, as affairs become entangled, as enlightenment extends, language changes character; it becomes more precise and less passionate; it substitutes ideas for feelings, it no longer speaks to the heart but to reason. As a result, accent is extinguished, *articulation extends*, language becomes more exact and clearer, but more drawn out, *more muted*, and colder."[65] In the sharpest possible contrast to the accented "euphony" of the voice, articulation moves steadily toward silence and, when the degeneration of language eventuates in writing, this articulation in extremis is quite literally silent.[66] The euphonic voice of nature is eclipsed by silent conventions: as Derrida put it, "Writing is always atonal."[67] As it is the "beauty of sounds" that accounts for the capacity of the voice to disclose the self, Rousseau believes that the progress of articulation also marks the progressive inability of language to disclose the self.

It is only after Rousseau has considered the degeneration of the voice into writing that he returns to consider speech (*parole*). Speech occupies for Rousseau a midpoint between the sounding of the voice and the muted silence of writing. Because speech is the speaking of words it requires articulation, and thus speech is complicit in that degenerative process that eventuates in writing. On the other hand, speech sounds; even the most articulate turns of phrase are modified by a particular tone of voice.[68] Speech is situated between the competing extremes of the voice and writing. Derrida explains, "A speech without consonantic principle, what for Rousseau would be a speech sheltered from all writing, would not be speech; it would hold itself at the fictive limit of the inarticulate and purely natural cry. Conversely, a speech of pure consonants and pure articulation would become pure writing, algebra, or dead language."[69] And as Rousseau continues to chart the degeneration of language, the capacities of speech to disclose the self will be determined by its position relative to these two poles. The closer speech remains to the *voix*—to the unreflective, unarticulated sounding of the self—the more capacity it harbors for disclosure. And it is precisely this insistence—that confession becomes possible to the extent that speech bears the "mark of its father," that it retains its ties to the sounding of the voice—that is decisive for understanding Swaggart's confessions.[70]

To bear "the mark of its father" and retain the power of self-disclosure, the public confession must minimize the conspicuously artificial: tropes, figures of speech, "polite turns of phrase," complex chains of reasoning, logical arguments, and precise calculations. Inversely, it must maximize simplicity, instinctiveness, and reflexivity. In short, the confession must minimize anything that might suggest that it is the product of *techné* or conventional training, and maximize anything that might suggest it is simply an expression of nature's inarticulate cries. Rousseau thus praises simple and unreflective speech, for the simplicity of speech suggests that it is a natural expression or an effusion of the heart—those properties by which it resists the encroachment of writing and retains its confessive power. In *Emile* Rousseau argues that "simple phrases" that "speak from heart" are far superior to the "delicate phrases and expressions by persons of politeness." The delicate phrases of polite society are self-evidently the product of convention and thus threaten the communicative power of simple phrases. Rousseau thus praises "the language of plainspoken goodness" and denounces "fine speeches carefully prepared."[71]

This ideal of speech as a simple effusion of the self is found throughout the *Confessions*; two prominent examples are the speech of Mme de Luxembourg and Rousseau's own speech in the presence Mme de Warens.

In both instances, Rousseau equates the confessive power of speech with its unadorned simplicity and unreflective expressiveness. Consider first the speech of Mme de Luxembourg. Her speech "does not sparkle," is not "witty," has no "subtlety" about it, and is, above all, "simply expressed." To Rousseau's mind, the simplicity of her speech indicates its purity; it is the unadulterated expression of her heart: "Her flatteries are the more intoxicating for being simply expressed; *it is as though they have escaped her lips without her having given them any thought and from a heart that pours itself out* for no other reason than that it is full to overflowing."[72]

This unreflective simplicity also characterizes Rousseau's relationship with Mme de Warens. What is important to Rousseau about his relationship is the intimacy and immediacy of their communion: "my heart lay open before her as before God," and there was a "sympathy between [our] souls." This communion was achieved through simple and unreflective speech: "No sooner had [a] thought struck me than I expressed it; for when I was with her to think and to speak were one and the same thing."[73] There is no reflective pause between thought and expression that could detract from the power of speech. This is the sonorous ideal of the voice: speech understood as the uninhibited and spontaneous effusion of the heart.

This simplicity of confessive speech finds its antithesis in the carefully measured, ornate speech that bespeaks an artistic or technical training. The speech of Rousseau's antagonist Friedrich Melchior baron von Grimm provides a case in point. In book 9 of the *Confessions* Rousseau approaches Grimm in order to apologize for his own mistaken assumptions. When he arrived at Grimm's residence, Rousseau used a "few words" to apologize and was then subjected to "a long harangue which [Grimm] had prepared in advance." As Rousseau reports it, this lengthy rant was simply Grimm's cataloging of his own virtues, namely, his ability to preserve friendships over great lengths of time: "He returned to this point so often and so ostentatiously that it occurred to me that, if he were *simply speaking from the heart*, he would insist less on this principle, and that he was turning it into an *art* that could be useful to him in his plans to succeed."[74] In the person of Grimm speech has turned from the *simple* expression of the heart into an *artistic* rendering of the self, from an effusion of nature's voice into a calculated contrivance. The language of confession now stands opposed to the traditional rhetorical category of *techné*.

In sum, the modern tradition of public confession, which finds its most concise expression in the work of Rousseau, denies articulateness and descriptiveness in order to approximate the speechless ideal of the *voix*—it minimizes everything that might suggest the language of confession is, after all, a language. Starobinski explains:

> The humble posture, the embrace, the sobs tell the whole story without the aid of words. Not that words never play a part. But they are always superfluous, never needed to translate into clear language what first appeared outside language. Everything is said through emotion itself, of which words are never more than an uncertain echo. That is why Rousseau's language, in describing such moments, is so unhinged: exclamatory, syntactically disorganized, uncoordinated. His words no longer need to be organized as discourse because they no longer play the role of intermediary; language has ceased to be an indispensable means of communication. Recall the "disorienting rapture" of the Third Letter to Malesherbes, in which Rousseau can only cry out: "O Great Being!" Remember, too, the prayer of the poor old woman who can only say: "Oh!"[75]

Rousseau's language of confession, in other words, is "unhinged, exclamatory, syntactically disorganized, [and] uncoordinated" precisely because the power of confession depends on its ability to deny that it is a language. The unhinged and the exclamatory, in direct opposition to words "organized as discourse," bespeak the uninhibited effusion of the heart.

All this is absurd, and it has been recognized as such. To the extent that Rousseau's "Essay" now registers in the academy, it does so largely as the example par excellence of the excesses of eighteenth-century thought. The philosopher Newton Garver has argued that the "Essay" "is probably the most outrageous thing [Rousseau] ever wrote, and one of the least plausible of the numerous general treatises on language in the history of western thought."[76] Far more influentially, Derrida has made the "Essay" the centerpiece of his *Of Grammatology* and therefore an iconic text in the Western logocentric tradition.[77] In the wake of Derrida's critique it is easy to miss the fact that the "Essay" describes a rhetorical ideal that is still profoundly influential. Theoretically speaking, Derrida is right to insist on the primacy of writing; practically speaking, this insight has done nothing to temper the emulation of Rousseau's (anti)rhetorical ideal. For evidence, we need look no further than Swaggart himself, for there can hardly be a better description of his prose than that Starobinski used to describe Rousseau's *Confessions*: "unhinged, exclamatory, syntactically disorganized, [and] uncoordinated." But to see in such a description only a failure to meet standards imported from a classical tradition of rhetoric is to miss both the tradition that authorizes syntactical disorganization and the political work such disorganization is capable of achieving.

Swaggart's Rhetorical Campaign

Despite the fact that he concluded his confession with an extended quotation from the Old Testament, Swaggart's "Apology Sermon" and his "Comeback Sermon" fit far more comfortably in the modern, secular tradition of confession described above. Within this tradition, Swaggart's sermon can be a confession without the explicit admission of misdeeds, and it can thereby satisfy the demands of both Gorman and the Assemblies of God. In what follows, I provide a careful reading of Swaggart's rhetorical campaign to return to the pulpit. I focus on two consecutive Swaggart sermons, his "Apology Sermon" sermon and his "Comeback Sermon." Although only the first of these is generally recognized as Swaggart's "confession," Giuliano has astutely noted that they function together within Swaggart's campaign to regain the pulpit.[78] In these sermons, I foreground three stylistic tokens by which Swaggart forcibly situated his own confessions within a modern, secular tradition: his emphasis on the inadequacy of speech, his devaluation of grammatical sensibilities and logical coherence, and his emphasis on his humanity.

First, consider Swaggart's preoccupation with the inadequacies of speech, which is evident from the first words of his apology sermon: "Everything that I will attempt to say to you this morning will be from my heart. I will not speak from a prepared script." This immediate dismissal of scripted speech in favor of speaking from his heart is not exceptional. Time and again he declared that he would disclose the recesses of his self, not via the spoken word but despite it: "I am positive that all that I want to say I will not be able to articulate as I would desire. But I pray you would somehow feel the anguish, the pain, and the love of my heart."[79] Note the logic: despite the poverty of articulation (which functions similarly for both Rousseau and Swaggart), Swaggart hopes that his audience will nonetheless "feel" his heart. Swaggart is delimiting the form of the public confession by providing the essential criterion: if confession is to be successful, it must be understood as simple effusion, an uncontrollable overflow of the passions. Scripted or articulate speech indicates the manipulation of the inner self or its strategic deployment. In either case, the confession is compromised by the appearance of the arts of speech.

Rousseau is certainly not the only source for the devaluation of articulate speech. Such devaluations are a part of the much larger eighteenth-century anxieties over textuality. Kames's *Elements of Criticism*, Sheridan's *Lecture's on Elocution*, and Blair's *Lectures on Rhetoric* all share these anxieties to a certain extent.[80] I choose Rousseau to explain Swaggart's rhetorical choices not because Rousseau was unique, but because in him the anxieties over textuality are made ingredient to the genre of confession.

In his "Comeback Sermon," three months after his February 21 "confession," Swaggart was still talking about the incapacities of speech. Swaggart began, "It is so good to see you today. And *I don't have to tell you* how happy I am to be here."[81] Again, such a beginning could be ascribed to the conventions of introductions, but given what we know of Swaggart, it seems plausible that he really believed he didn't have to "tell" his congregants anything, particularly things related to his "happiness" or his feelings more generally. His previous sermon, after all, had established that feelings could not be articulated, but rather that they must be "somehow felt" by the audience.

Swaggart then thanked those friends and family who had helped him through the last three months. His gratitude is worth quoting at length because it nicely captures Swaggart's distrust of the arts of speech:

> I could say an awful lot and I want to about so many of the people who have helped us and stood with us and the pastors of this church and the ministers in the ministry itself. But I would invariably leave out someone if I were to do that and that would be someone I would not want to leave out; so I will let discretion be the better part of valor on that. But I will ask Frances and Donnie and Debbie to step out here. And you can't know the load and the burden that these have had to bear the past months and I have leaned on them second only to the Lord. And to say that I love them would be the classic understatement of my life. They mean more to me than words could ever begin to say.[82]

Swaggart is so consistent in his denunciations of the arts of speech that the conventions of public address cannot exhaust the significance of the criticisms. To Swaggart's mind, even the most powerful expressions of speech—proclamations of love—can only ever be "understatements." That Swaggart loves his family more than "words could ever begin to say" has as much to do with the limitations of *saying words* as it does with Swaggart's estimation of his family.

In the two sermons immediately following the exposure of Swaggart's trysts, these denunciations of the arts of speech proliferate endlessly.[83] I will cite only one more example. Explaining the pain of the ordeal, Swaggart said, "You will never know, you will never know the pain. The hurt. Words could never describe it and I am saying God, how can I forget?"[84]

This is standard Swaggart fare. I suggest that the sheer accumulation of examples in which Swaggart disclaims the power of speech suggests that expressions such as these are not simply rhetorical devices used to convey magnitude. To the contrary, they signal the rhetorical premises from which Swaggart's rhetoric operates. As Derrida wrote of Rousseau, it "is the *inadequation of the designation* . . . which *properly expresses* the passion."[85] In other words, within the tradition of the modern public confession, the inadequacy of speech is not to be construed as a rhetorical failure; rather, it is integral to the very form of the confession. When Swaggart claims that words could never describe the pain he has experienced, this is not only a comment on the magnitude of the pain, but also a signal of the confessive tradition in which he operates, a tradition in which the capacity to disclose the self hinges on the inadequacy of the words deployed. Thus it is that the much-proclaimed silence of Swaggart's sermon is not a defect, but the perfect deployment of a long-standing rhetorical—indeed, confessional—tradition.

What I wish to emphasize here is that the inadequacy of speech required by the modern public confession fit perfectly the politics of a "silence campaign." For within the confines of this tradition, Swaggart's insistence on the inadequacy of speech functioned as a justification for not using speech to disclose his misdeeds. The only thing his tradition of confession demanded of him was that the effusions of the voice not be wholly eclipsed. Thus the meaning of his confession was to be determined not by words adequate to their object, but by tones, sounds, and gestures. This is Rousseau: "He who speaks varies the meanings by the tone of his voice, he determines them as he pleases."[86] And one need only recall the extremes of Swaggart's stage antics—the dancing, crying, crawling, and groaning—or the nasal, tear-choked tone of his confession, to see the contemporary resonance of Rousseau's confessive language. Just as the "poor old woman" of Rousseau's prayer can say only "Oh," so Swaggart, it seems, could only cry. And both these provide examples of speech on the model of the *voix*. The counterfactual ideal of pure effusion had as its tangible effect Swaggart's repeated insistence on the poverty of language and the compensatory exaggeration of tone and delivery. It is no wonder that Fliegelman refers to the insistence on the inadequacy of speech as a way of scripting silence, and it is no wonder that a public confession on this model could accomplish the political work of the Assemblies of God. The oblivion of Swaggart's misdeeds is effected by a tradition in which meaning is wholly remanded to the inarticulate.

I turn now to consider the second of Swaggart's tokens: the devaluation of grammatical sensibilities and logical coherence. The logic, to be sure, is not Rousseau's alone. The eighteenth century, Fliegelman reminds us, witnessed a large-scale movement away from "the conventions of grammar."[87] Yet in Rousseau this tendency is applied to the genre of confession: "My narrative can no longer proceed except haphazardly and according to whatever ideas return to my mind."[88] Because Rousseau's words are legitimized only insofar as they are the product of emotional intoxications, he cannot be held accountable to such standards as order, logic, and arrangement. If speech is simply the outpouring or effusing of the heart, such speech cannot be subjected to social conventions.

Swaggart's rhetorical campaign is, perhaps even more than Rousseau's *Confessions*, marked by a devaluation of logic, arrangement, and order. Consider, for example, this representative but nonsensical exposition of some verses in the New Testament:

> When we pertain to the past [Paul] said, first of all in the 13th verse, "Brethren, I count not myself to have apprehended" and then he said, "but this one thing I do" the scripture related to us singleness of heart. Paul writes to us, or it is Luke? Paul does, I think, and then the Master related singleness of eye. This one thing I do. I don't know in reading this of Paul's struggles. I have no idea. Paul to me is a giant of giants. I do not know when he wrote this, if he wrote it from his own experience, or he wrote it guided by the Holy Spirit. Either way, of course, for all of mankind that would name the name of Jesus.[89]

Notice all the things that are explicitly unimportant to Swaggart. Questions of who wrote the passage, how and when it was written, and even what it means in its context are unimportant. The most fundamental principles of hermeneutics, in other words, have no impact on Swaggart's reading of the text. Perhaps more important, notice what is *implicitly* not important to Swaggart: sentence structure and logical coherence. Consider the jumbled first sentence in which the subject of the sentence changes, unannounced, from Paul to "the scripture." Consider also the inexplicable "I don't know in reading this of Paul's struggles." Consider finally that when Swaggart claims to "have no idea," he never explains what idea escapes him. But, and this is the point, within the confines of modern tradition of public confession, this failure to achieve coherence is not a failure at all. The modern public confession precisely reverses the classical operating premises of speech and turns Swaggart's very inarticulateness into first-order evidence of authenticity.

The connection between inarticulateness and authenticity reaches its apex near the end of Swaggart's "Comeback Sermon," when he begins speaking in tongues. Glossolalia, Medhurst explains, is a form of personal prayer that uses a language "unknown to anyone on earth." It functions as a sign of "complete surrender to the will of God and [it is] a language of praise and adoration."[90] While sympathetic to these devotional functions of glossolalia, Giuliano invites us to interrogate it from a strictly rhetorical perspective: he explains glossolalia as a "form of nondiscursive prayer in an unintelligible language, which from a linguistic viewpoint, is meaningless but phonologically structured."[91] There could hardly be a more apt description of the Rousseauian confession: it depends for its force on unintelligible sounds. Without denigrating whatever else it might be on a spiritual plane, "from a linguistic viewpoint," Giuliano suggests, glossolalia is the pure expression of the voix unhindered by articulation. Thus glossolalia serves Swaggart on two registers. Given his audience and their religious tradition, glossolalia clearly functioned as evidence of divine blessing.[92] It also, and this is the point on which I focus, guaranteed the authenticity of his confession in a tradition that distrusts techniques of speech. Articulation would suggest manipulation or the strategic presentation of his self, both of which are inappropriate within the modern tradition of public confession. Within the confines of this confession, formal structure and authenticity stand opposed. As Swaggart himself put it, "I don't have any technique. The only thing I'm trying to do is lead you to Jesus and he'll handle it."[93]

If Swaggart's insistence on the inadequacy of speech justified his silence and thus furthered the politics of the Assemblies of God, his devaluation of syntax and the corresponding valuation of spontaneous talk harbor a broader political threat. Perhaps the best evidence of this threat is the fact that scholars as diverse as Michael Schudson and Daniel Bell agree that democracy requires syntax. Schudson argues that "an emphasis on the spontaneous draws attention away from the contrivances necessary for democracy." To Schudson's mind, a democratic style is rule-governed rather than spontaneous precisely because the rigor of rules ensures that the "slow of speech" have equal access to decision-making procedures. Schudson admits that rule-governed "democratic talk" is not good for the disclosure of the self, but it is, he argues, essential for democracy.[94] Schudson's critique cuts to the heart of the modern confession, suggesting that speech on the model of the voix—the sine qua non of confessive speech—is a hindrance to the practical functioning of democracy.

Daniel Bell, for his part, suggests that the advent and "debasement" of modernity can both be attributed to Rousseau's *Confessions*. He argues that Rousseau is the source of a distinctly modern aesthetic in which "thought should not mediate spontaneity," and in which "acting out of impulse, rather than the reflective discipline of the imagination becomes the touchstone of satisfaction." Without a distinction between impulsive action and reflective discipline, Bell argues, the very possibility of culture is undermined. And, in a phrase that foregrounds the connections between Rousseau and Swaggart, Bell argues that culture cannot be preserved by "speaking in tongues."[95] Thus Daniel Bell, whom Habermas has called the "most brilliant of the American neoconservatives," and the liberal "genius" Michael Schudson come together in their insistence that political flourishing—democracy for Schudson, culture for Bell—requires the primacy of syntax over the spontaneity of speaking in tongues.[96]

Consider finally the third of Swaggart's stylistic tokens: the emphasis on his own humanity, which is couched in the theological language of sin. It would be easy to see in Swaggart's constant talk of sin evidence that he in fact operated in a Christian tradition of confession. I believe this would be a mistake. While Augustine surely took the notion of sin quite seriously, and while he certainly believed "all have sinned," the role of "sin" in the Augustinian tradition of confession is quite different from the role it plays in Swaggart's confession. For Swaggart, the notion of sin functioned as an indicator of his humanity—it departicularized his actions by folding them into the general category of sin, from which no one is exempt. By contrast, for Augustine the notion of sin performed an opposite function. Rather than folding him into the general category of humanity in which no one appears worse than anyone else, for Augustine it led him to recount his particular misdeeds and the things that set him apart from other sinners.[97] Although both Augustine and Swaggart confess their sins, this sin functions quite differently in each case. Because for Swaggart sin functions only to remind him of his common humanity, it is not inconsistent with the secular tradition of public confession in which he operates.

Less than two minutes into his "Apology Sermon," Swaggart offered the most quoted lines of the confession: "I do not plan in any way to whitewash my sin. I do not call it a mistake, a mendacity; I call it sin."[98] Swaggart was insistent on this; he referred to his deeds fourteen times in the sermon, each time with a cognate of the word "sin," and Giuliano notes that in the three months following the confession, neither Swaggart nor the Assemblies of God ever referred to the events in question as anything but sin.[99] It is important here to note that the decisive difference between "mistakes" and "mendacities" on the one hand, and "sin" on the other hand, is this: while "mistakes" and "mendacities" are political acts because they are committed by and against particular people, "sin"—at least in the Pentecostal tradition— is a *natural* or *human* condition because it afflicts everyone indiscriminately. Giuliano explains that Swaggart's audience "was convinced that sin was a universal experience" that does not admit of degrees.[100] In other words, sin is a part of the human condition, and it is equally deplorable regardless of whether it manifests itself in the sexual forays of Jimmy Swaggart or the less visible but equally inevitable sins of Swaggart's congregation. Thus, Giuliano concludes, "in this simple act of naming his deed a sin, Swaggart was invoking an entire systematized approach to wrongdoing that could only help him in his attempt at restoration."[101] It helped him by subsuming the particularity of his tryst into the general category of sin. Within this category, the particularities of Swaggart's tryst are of absolutely no relevance. It is no wonder he did not mention them.

It is this understanding of sin that renders Swaggart's deployment of the term consonant with the secular tradition of public confession. Because sin is defined as a natural rather than a political condition, its expression does not require the resources of articulation. In other words, Swaggart could not call his misdeeds "mistakes" or "mendacities" for the simple reason that the modern, Rousseauian confession, with its emphasis on the inadequacy of speech and its devaluation of syntax, is best suited to communicate the natural. Without the resources of articulation, Swaggart's glossolalia could communicate nothing more than his common humanity. The labeling of misdeeds as "sin" naturalizes the misdeeds and renders them fit for confession.

Referring to his past in terms of sin, however, elides the fact that Swaggart's misdeeds *were* "mistakes" and they *were* "mendacities." The modern confession necessarily elides the political aspects of Swaggart's choices by suggesting that his tryst with a prostitute in a pay-by-the-hour motel was simply an expression of his human nature. According to this logic, Swaggart's auditors would have seen in the self-proclaimed sinful Swaggart nothing more than exposed, and possibly magnified, versions of their own sinful selves.

It is perhaps not surprising that Swaggart explicitly connected his sinfulness to his humanity. Near the end of his sermon he addressed the question of why he sinned. His answer: "I have asked myself that 10,000 times through 10,000 tears. Maybe Jimmy Swaggart has tried to live his entire life as though he were not human."[102] His sexual failures function here as a reminder of his humanity—and humanity, in its sheer indiscriminateness, is not a political category. Swaggart's son, Donny, made this logic explicit soon after his father's public confession: "If there's no forgiveness for Jimmy Swaggart, there's no forgiveness for you either."[103]

Swaggart ended his confession with the lengthy recitation of Psalm 51, which reaffirms that sin is simply a natural expression of humanity. "Behold I was shapen in iniquity," Swaggart claimed. "In sin did my mother conceive me." Swaggart's sin is literally in his blood; he is a sinner by virtue of being born; and he suffers not from guiltiness, but from "bloodguiltiness."[104] Sin here is not the province of the evildoing monster, but rather part and parcel of the human condition—one is sinful on account of being born. According to this sinful logic, the tryst proved only that Swaggart was, like his would-be accusers, human. And—this is the point I want to emphasize—it's as if the more *human* Swaggart became, the less *politically accountable* he remained.[105] If Swaggart called his deeds "mistakes," they could have reminded him that he was unfaithful and had hurt other people; if he called his deeds "mendacities," they could have reminded him that he was duplicitous and deceptive; as "sins," however, his deeds meant only that he, like everyone else, was simply human. This is the political insidiousness of the modern confession: folding his misdeeds into a natural category, so that they are fit for expression within the terms of the voix, precludes the sorts of discriminations needed for political judgment.

Conclusion: The Relevance of Jimmy Swaggart

It is tempting to ignore Jimmy Swaggart. His virulently anti-intellectual and financially lucrative version of Christianity that preys on the pocketbooks of an elderly and uniformed viewership is, to say the least, distasteful. Unlike so many in American religious traditions, his sermons and writings do not reward careful criticism. His work has few carefully nuanced arguments, little thoughtful engagement with culture, and no careful replies to his critics. His sermons are, in many ways, simply an enumeration of non sequiturs disguised by the magnitude of his performance. As the *Chicago Tribune* put it, Swaggart is simply a "disguised game-show host," enacting a "sweaty performance art" consisting of a "prowling, growling manipulation of the stage and camera."[106] Perhaps these are among the legitimate reasons that he has received little attention from rhetorical critics.

Yet I've been trying to suggest that Swaggart's rhetorical style, although it eschews thoughtfulness and syntax, is nonetheless understandable as the product of a tradition I have called the modern confession. We should not, in other words, see in Swaggart's ramblings a failure to conform to the "norms of rhetorical culture," but rather the rigorous enactment of rhetorical norms drawn from a competing tradition.[107] And, at least in the case at hand, this tradition provided the resources with which Swaggart could satisfy the demand for a confession while still executing a silence campaign.

The fact that the modern confession was complicit in the execution of a silence campaign suggests something of its political character. As I argued above, the modern public confession entails a form of rhetoric that is incompatible with "democratic talk" and the sorts of discriminations necessary for political work. This suggests that a "rhetoric against rhetoric," to borrow Bryan Garsten's phrase for a rhetorical style that insists on the inadequacy of speech, is also a rhetoric against politics.[108] For the particular topoi of Swaggart's rhetoric I have highlighted—the emphasis on the inadequacy of speech, the devaluation of syntax, and the emphasis on humanity—all functioned in the service of a silence campaign. Indeed, Garsten writes that a "rhetoric against rhetoric" seeks to "minimize the space for persuasion in politics" and "obscure the work of ruling."[109]

It would, however, be unfair to extend this criticism to the genre of confession tout court. I have been at pains to suggest that the adverse political consequences of Swaggart's confession were the product of a particular tradition of confession. And I briefly reviewed an alternative tradition to emphasize my point that the political consequences of confession cannot be determined without considering the various forms that confession may take. At least in the case of Jimmy Swaggart, the fact of his confession is less politically relevant than the tradition in which that confession stands. Traditions of public confession are not interchangeable and their divergent forms cannot be ignored, for there is, with apologies to Foucault, no "line going straight" between the Christian confession and its secular appropriation. It is incumbent on those of us invested in public discourse to understand the confession, not as a stable, ahistorical form, but as a practice informed by competing traditions.

As this chapter has made plain, the competing traditions of confession are a critical resource in confessional crises. Precisely because confession has, historically speaking, meant different things to different people, and because these meanings have coalesced in the confessional imagination, a wide variety of texts are eligible to be deployed as confessions. In this regard, Swaggart's "Apology Sermon" must be example number one. Although his rhetoric was rambling and at times incoherent, and although he never admitted his sexual liaison, the imbrication of confessional traditions in the American imagination made it possible for a wide variety of people to see his "Apology Sermon" as a Christian confession.

Finally, the fact that Swaggart was able to sell a secular confession as a religious practice suggests something about his continued relevance for students of rhetoric and American culture. Rhetorically speaking, we cannot dismiss him as a religious fanatic. He may be a card-carrying member of the radical right, and for this reason tempting to dismiss, but his rhetorical choices cannot be explained as a "language of faith" or as the result of an isolated ideological community. As I have shown, the fact that his sermon counted as a confession had very little, if anything, to do with the theological beliefs of his particular brand of Christianity. Swaggart's performance may have been dressed up with religious terms and surrounded by Bible verses, but historically speaking, his performance was grounded in a deeply secular—even liberal—intellectual tradition. This is difficult news. Indeed, perhaps one of the most disconcerting aspects of Jimmy Swaggart's rhetoric is the fact that his virulent fundamentalist style draws so deeply on a cherished liberal tradition—the same thinker who gave us the social contract also "invented" the modern confession.

6

CONFESSION AND DEMOCRACY: CLINTON, STARR, AND THE WITCH-HUNT TRADITION OF AMERICAN CONFESSION

On April 25, 1998, three months into the Monica Lewinsky scandal, President William Jefferson Clinton finally confessed. Theretofore, despite public calls for public confessions, the Clinton administration had responded to the scandal with a strategy described by the political journalist Howard Kurtz as an "all-out stonewall."[1] As Walter Shapiro put it, "Clinton has implicitly rejected any possible strategy of throwing himself on the mercy of the American people with a tearful, lip-biting apology."[2] In fact, Clinton had *explicitly* rejected such a strategy. On January 21, the very day on which the *Washington Post*, the *Los Angeles Times*, and ABC News broke the Lewinsky story, Clinton asked his former consultant Dick Morris about the political viability of a public confession. Morris concocted a snap poll and by the end of the day determined that such a course was too risky. Accordingly, on January 26 Clinton took a break from practicing his State of the Union speech to stare angrily into a White House camera, wag his index finger, and deny the charges: "I did not have sexual relations with that woman."[3]

By April, however, Clinton seemed keenly aware that a public confession was much on the public mind. He thus began his Correspondents' Dinner address with a "moment of cleansing": "Ladies and gentleman, I regret so much—I regret our long neglect of the Planet Pluto. It took until 1930—1930—to welcome Pluto into the community of planets, and that was wrong. And I am so sorry about disco."[4] Clinton proceeded to apologize for leisure suits, lava lamps, Susan B. Anthony dollars, and pineapple pizza. This much may have been in jest, but it illustrates a fundamental point: the Clinton–Lewinsky scandal incited a confessional crisis. As the *USA Today* put it, the "silver lining" of the presidential sex scandal was that the practice of confession was "getting headlines like never before."[5] Although this is an overstatement—confession had been getting headlines throughout the twentieth century—it is certainly true that the Lewinsky scandal created an anxiety about confession palpable enough to render Clinton's Correspondents' Dinner jokes funny.

Clinton's twin strategy of denial and joking almost worked. It likely would have worked if Independent Counsel Kenneth Starr had his way on July 17. On that day, a young prosecutor from the Office of Independent Counsel (OIC) named Robert Bittman convinced a reluctant Starr to subpoena Bill Clinton. Starr, for his part, advocated ending the Lewinsky investigation immediately by turning over the findings of the OIC to Congress. Had he prevailed, Clinton never would have appeared before a grand jury, never would have been forced to admit an improper relationship to the American people, and a long string of public confessions may well have been averted. As it happened, however, Bittman prevailed upon his boss: "The only way to beat the president," he argued, "was to haul Clinton's rear end in front of the grand jury and pin him down under oath."[6] Starr conceded; Bittman subpoenaed Clinton; and Clinton, now "pinned down under oath," abandoned his strategy of denial and joking. On August 17, as a direct result of the subpoena, Clinton offered the first of what would become a long list of public confessions.

By September 1998, the list of confessions had grown so long that the news media began listing them catalogue-style. The *National Journal* and the *New York Times* both counted five; *Newsweek* counted six; and *People Weekly* counted more than eight attempts at public confession.[7] The listing of confessions, however, is never an innocent exercise. As I have demonstrated in the preceding chapters, classifying a text as a confession or denying the same is always a political action. The fall of 1998 is no exception; from August 1998 through January 1999, the debate over the guilt or innocence of Bill Clinton was remarkably entangled with a rhetorical debate over which texts counted as confessions.

All were agreed that Clinton's brief statements in Massachusetts, Moscow, Dublin, and Orlando counted as confessions, but these received little critical commentary and even less popular coverage. Beyond these, all parties were also agreed that two major speeches were confessions. The first was the "Map Room speech," Clinton's short, nationally televised speech on the evening of August 17, 1998. The second came three weeks later, on the morning of September 11, 1998. On that day, Clinton confessed to 130 American clergy assembled for the president's annual Prayer Breakfast. Unlike the minor statements listed above, these latter two texts were the source of endless reflection by media pundits and academic critics alike on the form and function of confession.

For most critics, these two speeches were the only major texts that counted as confessions.[8] With the field so demarcated, a particular understanding of confession emerged. Noting that the August 17 speech was defiant and poorly received while the September 11 confession was religious, contrite, and well received, scholars have been quick to conclude that the best confessions are those cast in religious terms. For these critics, a confession is a statement of contrition, an admission of wrongdoing, and an unqualified abdication of rights. To confess is to yield the entirety of one's self-defense to an accuser. The rhetorical critics Ronald Lee and Matthew H. Barton put it most succinctly. By contrasting Clinton's August 17 and September 11 speeches, they concluded, "Public confession and legal defense are rhetorically disconsonant."[9] This understanding of confession was, of course, a convenient one for Kenneth Starr and the OIC. Like Lee and Barton, Starr himself understood confession and legal argument as competing rhetorical styles. Years after the scandal, Starr expressed disappointment that Clinton never ceased his legal maneuvers long enough to simply say, "I recognize that I have made some pretty serious mistakes."[10]

Not surprisingly, neither Clinton nor his administration agreed with such a definition of confession. Accordingly, his legal team, headed by his personal attorney David Kendall and White House Counsel Charles Ruff, and his communications team, headed by Mike McCurry, joined forces to redefine the very genre of confession. They did so by expanding the list of texts that counted as confessions. To the standard list enumerated above, they added two: Clinton's August 17 grand jury testimony, which immediately preceded his televised address, and the Starr Report, the public release of which immediately followed Clinton's September 11 Prayer Breakfast. To be sure, both these texts lacked all the formal and substantive markers of a confession—the first was an argument between hostile interlocutors, and the second was a narrative written by a third party. Neither of them contained *any* of the traditional characteristics by which texts are recognized as confessions. However, both of them *were talked about* in confessional terms. Consistently. Kenneth Starr was compared to Torquemada, Joseph McCarthy, and Dostoevsky's "Grand Inquisitor"; Clinton was compared to Hawthorne's Hester Prynne, Kafka's Josef K., and the protagonist of Arthur Koestler's

Darkness at Noon. Perhaps most telling, Arthur Miller, author of the Salem Witch Trial play *The Crucible*, was called upon to explain the Starr investigation to the readers of the *New York Times*—apparently only such an expert in the abuse of public confession was qualified to explain Starr's tactics. This is only a sampling, but I trust it makes the point: despite their composition, and despite all the formal characteristics to the contrary, Clinton's grand jury testimony and the Starr Report were constituted as confessions. In the language I have been using, they *became* confessions because their constitution as such promised political advantage.

More precisely, Clinton's grand jury testimony and the Starr Report became confessions of a particular type. From Hawthorne to McCarthy, Miller to Kafka, each of the confessional referents used to describe these two texts figured confession vis-à-vis the witch-hunt tradition in American politics.[11] In this tradition, confession is figured as the speech act proper to a victim pursued by an overweening power. So defined, the very existence of confession signals the abuse of power, and, importantly, the primary offense lies with the confessor who demands a confession, rather than the confessant who provides it. In the Lewinsky-inspired debate over the definition of confession, it was the Clinton administration and the pro-Clinton press who assumed the role of Foucauldians. It was they who ensured that confession was joined once more with what Foucault has called its "dark twin": practices of inquisition and torture.[12] It was they who, like Foucault, understood confession as a response to an invasive surveillance. Finally it was they who, like Foucault, inverted traditional understandings of confession in order that guilt might be attached to the one who inquires and examines rather than the one who, like a prisoner in a backlit jail cell, is set on display for the world to see. In other words, the Clinton administration turned two further texts into confessions so that Clinton might appear the helpless victim of Kenneth Starr's invasive, overstepping inquiry.

Although scholars have paid scrupulous attention to the two texts that were conspicuously confessional (the Map Room speech and the Prayer Breakfast speech), the fact that Clinton's grand jury testimony and the Starr Report were also talked about in confessional terms has gone virtually unnoticed. In this chapter, I argue that understanding how and why the Clinton administration turned these latter texts into confessions provides for a radically different interpretation of the former texts. The Map Room speech and the Prayer Breakfast speech were, after all, separated by only hours from Clinton's grand jury testimony and the Starr Report, respectively—arguably the most flagrant excesses of the entire Starr investigation. For a speech act historically associated with practices of inquisition, this seems an important context. Acknowledging this context, there is simply no way to endorse the lesson that the vast majority of rhetorical critics have drawn: that public confessions should be marked by contrition and an abdication of legal maneuvering. When the Map Room speech and the Prayer Breakfast speech are situated in their immediate historical context (the excesses of the Starr investigation), rather than abstractly compared with each other, a rather different lesson emerges. So contextualized, these speeches suddenly look very similar. Both represent Clinton's attempt to reshape the genre of confession to meet particular political exigencies. More specifically, both confessions can be read as Clinton's attempt to fashion a distinctively public form of confession, one designed to protect the speaker from the abuses of the witch-hunt tradition and therefore suitable for a democracy. Given the conflicted legacy of confession, I suggest that Clinton's refashioning of the genre marks an important attempt to render the practice of confession compatible with the norms of democratic society. The premier marker of this new confessive form is its refusal to separate legal argument from an admission of wrongdoing.

Conventional Lessons

Abstracted from their historical contexts, Clinton's August 17 Map Room speech and his September 11 Prayer Breakfast speech are a study in contrasts. On August 17, the emphasis of the speech was on Clinton's legal innocence. Although he acknowledged an inappropriate relationship, this admission came only after he established that his earlier denials of such a relationship were "legally accurate." Moreover, after admitting improprieties he immediately qualified this admission: "But, I told the grand jury today, and I say to you now, at no time did I ask anyone to lie, to hide or destroy evidence, or to take any other unlawful action."[13] No one liked this speech. The Pulitzer Prize–winning journalist Mary McGrory called it "surpassingly stupid," and as J. Michael Hogan notes, academic critics joined journalists in a "virtually unanimous voice," decrying the speech as "perhaps the worst of Clinton's political life."[14] The legal analyst Jeffrey Toobin went even further, suggesting that it was one of the worst speeches "in the history of presidential oratory."[15]

On September 11, by contrast, the emphasis was on contrition. Clinton acknowledged that he had reached "rock bottom"; he explained that forgiveness requires "genuine repentance"; he announced that he was seeking pastoral support; and he assured his audience that neither the excesses of Kenneth Starr's investigation nor his own legal maneuvering should obscure the fact that "I still sinned."[16] As religious allusions displaced legal arguments, Hogan's "unanimous voices" of derision gave way to widespread praise. The *New York Times* editorial board, John F. Harris of the *Washington Post*, and Joanna Coles of *The Times* of London each claimed that this was the speech Clinton should have given on August 17. As the editorial board put it, "With its unmitigated confession, its declaration of repentance, its forthright apology to Ms. Lewinsky, this was a striking speech. But its most striking feature was its lateness. The same words delivered in January, when he lied, or on Aug. 17, when he equivocated and hurled blame, might have lifted Mr. Clinton on to a road of guaranteed survival. He has no such guarantee today."[17] On August 17, Clinton laced his confession with assertions of legal innocence and leveled a defiant attack on Kenneth Starr; it was a speech with no apologies, no contrition, and no remorse. On September 11, Clinton took the opposite tack, a "forthright apology" and an "unmitigated confession." The first confession was widely condemned; the second was widely praised.

What more could rhetorical critics ask for? We have two speeches, easily distinguished by their substantive characteristics, and matching these, two equally distinguishable public judgments. This is made-to-order rhetorical criticism. All the critic need do is note the respective characteristics of each confession, their differential reception, and draw conclusions about the form and function of confession. Indeed, this logic dominates the literature—both popular and academic—focused on Clinton's confessions. With remarkable consistency, pundits and scholars alike have focused on the sheer distance between the two speeches and the favorable reception of the second as a means of enshrining a religious tradition of confession and the preeminent importance of contrition. The unrivaled disdain for the August 17 speech seemingly proved the incompatibility of legal argument and public confession. Thus, for many critics, confession became an unqualified admission of guilt and an unchecked abdication of legal maneuvering.

This understanding of confession was further entrenched by Clinton's well-known penchant for hairsplitting legalisms. Forever memorialized by his attempt to parse the meanings of the word "is," Clinton's constant recourse to fine legal distinctions gave rise to a bipartisan condemnation of legal argument and, accordingly, made it that much easier to understand confession in opposition to legal defense. The conservative columnist George Will must have been surprised to hear Democratic Senators Tom Daschle and Dick Gephardt agree with his critique of Clinton's "evasive sophistries." As Daschle put it, "There is a basic understanding of the standard of truthfulness that the president failed to meet.... The president and his advisers must accept that continued legal jousting serves no constructive purpose." Or as his colleague Dick Gephardt argued, "The considered judgment of the American people is not going to rise or fall on the fine distinctions of a legal argument but on straight talk and the truth."[18] For Gephardt, "straight talk and the truth" prevailed only in the absence of legal jousting. His basic agreement with George Will is evidence of what the *New York Times* called the "backlash that has been building across the country against the use of legal fine points and distinctions."[19] Whatever the philosophers may say, in the fall of 1998 neither falsity, nor error, nor heresy constituted truth's great challenge. Rather, owing to Clinton's "propensity for shaving the English language as fine as a Tuscan truffle," the proper antagonists to "straight talk and the truth" were legal distinctions and lawyerly logic.[20]

From this point it was a very small step to define the genre of confession in terms of the abdication of legal argument. This step was made repeatedly by journalists and scholars seeking to find grounds for their dislike of Clinton's August 17 speech. Jeffrey Toobin condemned the address as a "heavily lawyered speech" and criticized Clinton for his failure to recognize that "this was a moment for contrition, not calumny."[21] Likewise, McGrory argued that "clinging to split hairs ... [is] the kind of dodge not permitted in true confession."[22] The scholarly community rallied just as quickly to the binary opposition of confession and legal argument. Herbert Simons, for example, argued in a well-known *Quarterly Journal of Speech* article that the "insufficient remorse" of the speech was "reinforced by Clinton's repeated retreat to legalisms."[23] Likewise, the academy's finest authority on scandal negotiation, William Benoit, argued with his student Joseph Blaney that Clinton's legal arguments threatened to "reduce the effectiveness of his professed contrition."[24] In sum, before it was anything else, in the fall of 1998 confession was a discourse that was truthful primarily because it was stripped of legal argument. Thus, said Lee and Barton, "public confession and legal defense are rhetorically disconsonant."

This disconsonance, of course, was not new in 1998. The antithesis between legal argument and confession has deep roots in various religious traditions of confession. From Augustine's *Confessions* to the 1994 *Catechism of the Catholic Church*, legal argument has never fit comfortably within religious practices of confession.²⁵ For this reason, Clinton's two conspicuous confessions have been read as a gradual approximation of a religious confession. As Teresa Watanabe wrote in the *Los Angeles Times*, with each confession Clinton moved closer to "satisfying the requirements of penitence upheld by Jewish and some Christian faiths."²⁶ Rhetorical critics—to a person—have interpreted this movement toward a religious ideal of confession as a movement toward better, more successful confessions. Susan Wise Bauer, Benoit and Blaney, Koesten and Rowland, Lee and Barton—for each of them, Clinton's confessions were more successful, more appropriate, more moving, and more powerful as they became more traditional, more contrite, and more religious. For each of them, moreover, the August 17 speech was a failure because it favored legal arguments over religious contrition; the August 28 Massachusetts speech, if mentioned, was better, but really only a "run-up" to the September 11 Prayer Breakfast speech, which alone constituted a successful (read: religious) confession. As per usual, no one put it more directly than Ronald Lee and Matthew H. Barton: "Each successive speech embraced more fully the generic demands of religious confession."²⁷

These then are the conventional lessons taken from the Lewinsky saga of 1998: to be called a confession, a text must be stripped of legal argument so that it may register in a religious tradition. As a means of setting up my own analysis, I want to stress that these readings depend on an assumption about the nature of generic criticism, the viability of which I question. The assumption is this: Each of the aforementioned critics assumed that the only relevant texts were those whose substantive characteristics matched a predetermined definition of confession. Thus for all these critics, rhetorical criticism was simply a matter of measuring the distance between a speech that said "I'm sorry" and an ideal form. As must be clear by this point, this assumption runs counter to a fundamental premise of this book: that if we are to understand the politics of confession, we must recognize above all the sheer plasticity of the form, its propensity to be stretched beyond recognition, and its capacity to exist in the absence of any particular substantive or formal characteristics. By beginning with particular ideas about what constitutes a confession, these critics were blind to the confessional crisis of late 1998. They could not see that, beyond the borders of their narrowly circumscribed form, raged a rhetorical battle—not about how well Clinton's performances matched Elysian standards, but over which standards should govern public confession. The crisis, in other words, was not about Clinton's proficiency at confession or his gradual approximation of the religious ideal. The crisis, rather, was a battle over what it means to confess in the first place.

The Two Confessions of August 17, 1998

A little after 6:30 p.m. on August 17, the president gathered his lawyers, advisers, friends, and family into the White House Solarium. He had just ascended from the Map Room, where, with closed-circuit cameras carrying his testimony to displaced grand jurors, he was interrogated by Kenneth Starr's prosecutors for four hours. Three and a half hours hence, he would descend once more to the Map Room and, with television cameras carrying his message live to sixty-seven million Americans, he would confess to an inappropriate relationship with Monica Lewinsky. This short, four-minute, 543-word speech has come to be known simply as the "Map Room speech." It began as follows: "Good evening. This afternoon in this room, from this chair, I testified before the Office of Independent Counsel and the grand jury. I answered their questions truthfully, including questions about my private life, questions no American citizen would ever want to answer."[28] Thus Clinton began his "Map Room speech" by reminding his audience that there were in fact two Map Room speeches on August 17. Both of them involved the first-person disclosure of private actions, and as Clinton's language suggests, he thought of both of them as confessions.

And yet the conventional wisdom treats the second Map Room speech as the only confession of the day. Instead of contextualizing this speech against the grand jury testimony, as Clinton's opening lines suggest it should be, scholars have contextualized it vis-à-vis later attempts at confession. From this perspective, the Map Room speech emerges as a failed confession because of its sheer distance from the religious ideal. I want to offer a counter-reading of this speech by taking Clinton's first lines seriously, reading the 10:02 p.m. Map Room speech in the context of the 1:03 p.m. Map Room speech. From this perspective, a completely different understanding of confession emerges. Rather than reading the evening address as a failed confession, overly lawyered and insufficiently contrite, I read it as an admirable attempt to protect the genre of confession from the abuses of the witch-hunt tradition. As I demonstrate, the grand jury testimony that immediately preceded it was, in essence, a debate over what sorts of texts count as confessions. The 10:02 p.m. speech, accordingly, was neither a failed Christian confession nor, as Toobin has suggested, a product of Clinton's anger getting the best of him.²⁹ Indeed, from Clinton's perspective, the speech was not a failure in any sense of the word. When Senior Advisor to the President for Policy and Strategy Rahm Emanuel told Clinton his speech was "getting panned" by the media, Clinton responded, "I said what I wanted to say, and I don't care what those people [the critics] say—and I don't care what happens now."³⁰ Why did Clinton, that master of spin, suddenly become so principled? On my reading, he did so because he just spent the afternoon arguing in front of a hostile audience for a particular form of confession. How could he now offer anything but a confession on his own terms? He "said what [he] wanted to say" because his 10:02 p.m. performance was an enactment of his 1:03 p.m. argument. It was his chance to demonstrate to the world what a confession could look like when it is adumbrated to the needs of a democratic nation.

In order to make this argument, I begin in 1992, six years before the grand jury testimony. That year, in the context of the Gennifer Flowers sex scandal, Clinton provided one of his most explicit definitions of confession. It was an understanding of confession that Clinton believed to be uniquely suited for public life, and which six years later he would deploy in the context of Monica Lewinsky scandal.

Gennifer Flowers and Public Confession

In the closing months of 1991, Arkansas Governor Bill Clinton was competing with Paul Tsongas for the Democratic presidential nomination. In January 1992, heading into the crucial New Hampshire primary, Clinton saw his sixteen-point lead over Tsongas evaporate, due in part to allegations of an affair with the nightclub singer turned television personality Gennifer Flowers. On January 26, immediately following Super Bowl XXVI, Hillary Clinton joined her spouse to address the allegations jointly in an exclusive, much-publicized *60 Minutes* interview. When Governor Clinton acknowledged "causing pain in [his] marriage," *60 Minutes* host Steve Kroft pushed him for details. What precisely were these "problems" that plagued the Clinton marriage? Communication problems? Separation? Divorce? Adultery with Ms. Flowers? The governor refused to specify. Such details, he suggested, were appropriate only in a private conversation with one's spouse. When Kroft continued to push, Clinton pushed back, responding this time with neither a confession nor a denial, but rather a theory of confession and its place in public life: "Look, Steve, you go back and listen to what I've said. You know, I have acknowledged wrongdoing, I have acknowledged causing pain in my marriage. I have said things to you tonight and to the American people from the beginning that no American politician ever has. I think most Americans who are watching this tonight, they'll know what we're saying, they'll get it, and they'll feel that we have been more than candid. And I think what the press has to decide is: Are we going to engage in a game of gotcha?" From Clinton's perspective, he had "leveled" with the American people simply by acknowledging pain in his marriage. Moreover, Clinton was confident that Americans would "get it." They needed no details to understand what the Clintons were "saying." A vague admission of wrongdoing was all a public confession required. Kroft's insistence that Clinton detail this pain went far beyond the requirements of confession; it amounted to a dangerous, invasive game of "gotcha." Moments later, Mrs. Clinton made the same point: "There isn't a person watching this who would feel comfortable sitting on this couch detailing everything that ever went on in their life or their marriage. And I think it's real dangerous in this country if we don't have some zone of privacy for everybody. I mean, I think that is absolutely critical." Like her spouse, Mrs. Clinton understood the danger of unfettered public confession. "Detailing everything" would compromise the "critical" "zone of privacy" in a dangerous "game of gotcha." The only way to evade this game, the governor and Mrs. Clinton argued, was to acknowledge the proper limits of public confession: "The only way to put it behind us, I think, is for all of us to agree that this guy has told us about all we need to know. Anybody's who's listening gets the drift of it. And let's go on and get back to the real problems of this country."[31] According to this theory—a theory I have much sympathy for—if a confession is to be fit for public life, it must stop short of detailing everything and be content with the drift of things. Beyond this, the act of confession constitutes a dangerous game of gotcha and it compromises an essential zone of privacy.

Six years later, Clinton's view of public confession remained the same. But, as Joan Didion noted, when Monica Lewinsky replaced Gennifer Flowers, the reception of Clinton's view of confession suffered. In 1992, even the conservative A. M. Rosenthal applauded the *60 Minutes* interview.[32] In 1998, the conservative Kenneth Starr had zero tolerance. In fact, Clinton's view of what constitutes "candidness" became the storm center of the grand jury testimony. That is to say, while there was little disagreement between Clinton and the Office of the Independent Counsel over matters of fact or even matters of law, there was pervasive disagreement about what Clinton's oath obligated him to say and the level of detail he was obliged to disclose. Starr and his prosecutors took on the persona of Steve Kroft, arguing for the disclosure of intimate details. Clinton, for his part, insisted in 1998, as in 1992, that it was possible to be candid without sacrificing the all-important zone of privacy.

Competing Visions of Confession in the Grand Jury Testimony

Seven minutes into the interrogation, Deputy Independent Counsel Robert J. Bittman began as follows: "Mr. President, we are first going to turn to some of the details of your relationship with Monica Lewinsky." After warning the president that these questions would be uncomfortable, he asked, "Mr. President, were you physically intimate with Monica Lewinsky?"[33] Rather than answering the question, the president read a statement he had prepared in advance. This statement, marked as Grand Jury Exhibit WJC-1 and included in volume 3 of Kenneth Starr's Referral, is of the utmost importance for understanding Clinton's response to the Lewinsky scandal. It began as follows: "When I was alone with Ms. Lewinsky on certain occasions in early 1996 and once in early 1997, I engaged in conduct that was wrong. These encounters did not consist of sexual intercourse. They did not constitute sexual relations as I understood that term to be defined at my January 17th, 1998 deposition. But they did involve inappropriate intimate contact."[34] Clinton then acknowledged his "regret" and claimed "full responsibility" for his actions. Although this statement has been ignored in most analyses of Clinton's confessions, the acknowledgment of wrongdoing, the acceptance of responsibility, and the admission of inappropriate behavior all serve to locate it within a tradition of confession. Clinton's legal team certainly understood it this way. In the months leading up to the impeachment, nearly every statement prepared for President Clinton by David E. Kendall, his personal attorney, and Charles F. C. Ruff, White House Counsel, looked back on Clinton's grand jury statement as a confession. As Kendall would put it three weeks later, "On August 17, 1998, the President expressed regret to the grand jury and, later, to the country, that what began as a friendship came to include this conduct, and he took full responsibility. He has frequently, to different audiences, made similar expressions of regret and apology."[35] Or as Kendall put it in his December memo to the House Judiciary Committee, "No one who watched the videotape of this grand jury testimony had any doubt that the President was admitting to an improper physical relationship with Ms. Lewinsky."[36]

The Office of the Independent Council was hardly satisfied. According to Toobin, the OIC understood Clinton's statement as a "limited confession"—a strategy whereby Clinton admitted to unspecified mistakes but refused to provide the details the prosecution needed.[37] From the perspective of the OIC, the essential problem with a "limited confession" was that it allowed Clinton to *both* confess and insist on his legal innocence. After all, wedged between the president's acknowledgment that his "conduct" with Ms. Lewinsky was "wrong" and his admission that it involved "intimate contact," was a legal qualification: his conduct "did not constitute sexual relations as I understood that term to be defined at my January 17th, 1998 deposition."[38] For the OIC, Clinton's recourse to a technical definition of "sexual relations" undermined any claim that this was a true (unlimited) confession. As Republican Senator Orrin Hatch put it, "[Clinton] is being very badly served with this legal hairsplitting. Nobody believes that. Nobody wants to hear that. What they want to hear is a president who is truly contrite."[39]

Moreover, immediately following Clinton's admission of "intimate contact," he announced that he would provide no further details. "Because of privacy considerations affecting my family, myself, and others, and in an effort to preserve the dignity of the office I hold, this is all I will say about the specifics of these particular matters."[40] Thus every time OIC lawyers asked Clinton to enumerate the details of his relationship with Ms. Lewinsky, he simply referred back to his statement. When, for example, OIC prosecutor Sol Wisenberg asked the president if he touched Ms. Lewinsky's breasts, Clinton responded, "My recollection is that I did not have sexual relations with Ms. Lewinsky and I'm staying on my former statement about that."[41] It was precisely this refusal to provide details that became the central point of contestation between the OIC and Clinton. Throughout the remainder of the grand jury interrogation, whenever Clinton was asked about the details of what precisely he did with Ms. Lewinsky, he refused to answer. Instead, he sought recourse in his statement and the counterintuitive, court-stipulated definition of "sexual relations."

This is an important point. To Clinton's mind, there was no tension between a "candid" confession and a legal argument. Indeed, the two modes of discourse needed each other as correctives. Without legal argument, confession would lose its public value; it would criminalize private life and become so invasive that its only possible function could be, as Kendall put it, to "cause pain and damage for absolutely no legitimate reason."[42] Conversely, without confession, legal argument would obscure the moral realities of life and the deep importance of contrition. What the OIC derided as a "limited confession," Clinton heralded as a form of confession uniquely fit for public, democratic life. The marriage of contrition and legal defense ensured that the genre of confession would never compromise the essential zone of privacy. David Kendall thus prefaced the Clinton's "Submission to the Judiciary Committee" with this note:

> In addition to the factual, legal and Constitutional defenses we present in this document, the President has asked us to convey a personal note: What the President did was wrong. As the President himself has said, publicly and painfully, "there is no fancy way to say that I have sinned." The President has insisted that no legalities be allowed to obscure the simple moral truth that his behavior in this matter was wrong; that he misled his wife, his friends and our Nation about the nature of his relationship with Ms. Lewinsky. He did not want anyone to know about his personal wrongdoing. But he does want everyone—the Committee, the Congress and the country—to know that he is profoundly sorry for the wrongs he has committed and for the pain he has caused his family, his friends, and our nation. . . . And just as no fancy language can obscure the fact that what the President did was morally wrong, no amount of rhetoric can change the legal reality that the record before this Committee does not justify charges of criminal conduct or impeachable offenses.[43]

For President Clinton and his legal team, "fancy language" and "rhetoric" were both needed; confession and legal argument discounted the excesses of each other, and thereby rendered both styles publicly serviceable. According to National Public Radio, in his grand jury testimony Clinton was "at once repentant and defiant, legalistic and talking turkey."[44] NPR failed to note, however, that this was neither an inconsistency nor a shortcoming. To the contrary, it was a deliberate balance of competing rhetorical styles. Since at least 1992, Clinton insisted that repentance and defiance must be wed in order to discount the excesses of each and produce a publicly suitable form of confession. To Clinton's mind, there was simply no incompatibility between legalisms and talking turkey. Indeed, their combination was essential for a truly public confession.[45]

The OIC countered with their own understanding of confession, one best illustrated in an exchange between Clinton and the OIC's chief hawk, Sol Wisenberg. Wisenberg found Clinton's abridged answers intolerable. He claimed that full answers to his "delicate and unfortunate questions" were "absolutely required." He became so exasperated with Clinton's refusal to provide specific details that he threatened the president: "I need to inform you, Mr. President . . . that the grand jury will consider your not answering the questions more directly in their determination of whether or not they are going to issue another subpoena."[46] Wisenberg was not alone in his frustration. In the Trial Memorandum submitted by the House of Representatives to the Senate, the House managers complained that during Clinton's testimony, he "attempted to use the statement to foreclose questioning on an incriminating topic on nineteen separate occasions."[47] Although the statement has "the appearance of being candid," the House managers concluded, it is actually "false and misleading."[48] Far from being an ideal confession—combining legal defense with humble contrition—in the view of the OIC Clinton's statement was an instrument of shutting down conversation and evading the truth.

Despite Wisenberg's pleas, Clinton would not expand his "limited confession." When he refused to tell the grand jurors whether Ms. Lewinsky performed oral sex on him, Wisenberg replied, "I am not going to argue with you about it. I am just going to ask you again, in fact direct you to answer the question."[49] Wisenberg was not interested in arguments or explanations; he wanted only a detailed ledger of positions, places, and body parts. In his view, anything less than full disclosure violated Clinton's obligation to tell the truth.[50] Clinton, for his part, would have none of it; he accused Wisenberg and the Office of the Independent Counsel of playing "some sort of gotcha game."[51] In the context of Clinton's 1992 interview, we know precisely what a "gotcha game" is: It is a game in which there are no limits to what the public needs to know and no zone of privacy within which the confessional has no jurisdiction. It is a game in which legal argument has no place. It is a game of public confession unleashed, unmitigated, untempered. It is, finally, a game proper to the witch-hunt tradition of American confession.

Although Wisenberg and the other, more moderate OIC prosecutors surely would not have recognized themselves in a witch-hunt tradition, the American public had no such difficulties. When the video of Clinton's grand jury testimony was released on September 21, it was consistently described as a coerced confession. This, it seems, was just what the Clinton team wanted. Harry Thomason, a Hollywood filmmaker and longtime Clinton friend who provided Clinton with public relations help, insisted that if the OIC wanted to film the proceedings (itself an unusual practice), the camera must remain focused always and only on Bill Clinton: "None of the Starr prosecutors, [Thomason] said, should appear on the live feed at all. The viewers would see the president at all times and be forced to 'imagine' his disembodied interrogators as if they were invisible gremlins."[52]

Thomason's strategy worked brilliantly. If the public response can be trusted, the steady, mid-distance camera focused exclusively on Bill Clinton for four hours without a single shift in angle or zoom, emphasized (or perhaps created) the sense that the grand jury testimony was an inquisitorial extraction of truth rather than an adversarial exchange of ideas. It suggested, in other words, that the interrogation was best understood as the extraction of a confession. To this end, it is important to note that reading the transcript of the testimony is a radically different experience from seeing the video. In the transcript, the interrogation is organized as a debate. The prosecution's questions are clearly marked, as are Clinton's answers. As a matter of course, Clinton is not the only participant in the debate; Deputy Independent Counselors Jackie M. Bennett, Robert J. Bittman, and Solomon L. Wisenberg play major roles—especially Wisenberg, who, because of his condescending questions and his refusal to drop the matter of oral sex, emerged as Clinton's primary antagonist. The text of the August 17 grand jury debate is, conspicuously, an adversarial document.

The video of the grand jury testimony seen by some twenty-two million viewers on September 21 has none of this adversarial texture. Because the camera focused exclusively on Clinton, the interrogators who played such a commanding role in the transcript are reduced to softened off-screen voices. As the *Washington Post*'s John Harris put it, "The Starr lawyers were never seen. They were only heard as disembodied voices that were sometimes tinged with sarcasm. The effect was reminiscent of the droning teacher's voice in the 'Peanuts' animated cartoon specials."[53] And as the adversarial texture of the transcript was lost, the testimony resembled more and more a medieval inquisition designed to extract a confession. Thus Tom Shales of the *Washington Post*: "The fact that the camera remained stationary and glued to him and that no other participants could be seen—and that the questions came from the ominous, off-camera voices of creepy-sounding attorneys—made Clinton seem a bit like Josef K, persecuted hero of Franz Kafka's 'The Trial.'"[54]

Shales was hardly alone in making this connection. The Washington, D.C., independent theater critic Nelson Pressley found it eerily fitting that D.C.'s Gunston Arts Center's rendition of *The Crucible* opened only four days after Clinton's grand jury testimony. It is "impossible," he wrote, "for informed audiences not to hear certain lines without thinking of the present troubles." Pressley reminded his *Washington Times* readers that Arthur Miller's play was an objection to the puritan-styled inquisition led by Senator Joseph McCarthy in 1950s. Like McCarthy's so-called Communists, Miller's puritans were forced to make self-damning confessions. Pressley even referred to the confessions in *The Crucible* as "Clinton moments."[55] Geoffrey O'Brien of the *New York Times* put it this way: "The grand jury deposition puts us, aesthetically speaking, in the position of watching a police interrogation."[56] Lars-Erik Nelson of the *New York Review of Books* described it as an "inquisitional drama."[57] James Caryn of the *New York Times* argued that the "unedited nature and the static, mid-distance camera" gave an impression of realism more profound than even a documentary could provide.[58] Finally, *Newsweek*'s Howard Fineman described the testimony as "an oddly intimate mix of public-access sex chat and an interrogation scene from 'NYPD Blue.'"[59] Two weeks later, *Newsweek*'s editorial board made Fineman's judgment explicit, referring to the grand jury testimony as a "confessional."[60]

But it was more than simply a "confessional." As I hope has been made clear, it was also a referendum on what precisely constitutes a confessional. Clinton began with a "limited confession": a statement that perfectly exampled his lifelong belief that a public confession must hold in equipoise the competing needs of contrition and legal argument. The OIC countered that legal maneuvering compromised rather than complemented contrition. In their view, only an unlimited admission of guilt counted as a confession. Thus, the grand jury testimony represents, in microcosm, the confessional crisis that gripped the United States in the fall of 1998. It gave voice to anxieties over what precisely counted as a confession. In the balance hung the presidency of Bill Clinton. If his understanding of confession triumphed, then it followed as a matter of course that guilt should be attached to the witch-hunter. The public reception of the interrogation in terms borrowed from Kafka, Hawthorne, and Miller suggests that Wisenberg's ruthless pursuit of Clinton may have backfired. The public, it seems, had no problem recognizing the OIC's pursuit within the witch-hunt tradition of American confession. Walter Shapiro's response to Kenneth Starr in *USA Today* captures this perfectly: "Have you no decency, sir?"[61]

Rereading the (Second) Map Room Speech

For many, the most astonishing thing about Clinton's 1992 *60 Minutes* interview is that it seemed to work. The increasingly conservative *New York Times* columnist A. M. Rosenthal wrote two days later that the Clintons gave the American people "a gift" by treating them "as adults." Because of this gift, Rosenthal continued, "we can at least treasure the hope that Americans would be fed up with the slavering inquisition on politicians' sexual history and say to hell with that and the torturers."[62] In 1998, it seems, precious few were willing to say "to hell with that." The sheer success of William J. Bennett's

Lewinsky-inspired manifesto *The Death of Outrage*, in which he argued that a "seamless web of deceit... connects Bill Clinton's private and public life," is a sobering reminder that many Americans sided with Wisenberg and the OIC.[63] For these, a public confession required unabridged, unqualified detail. Clinton, however, was not about to cede the contest.

Thus, at 6:25 p.m., when the clock ran out on the OIC, Clinton retreated to the White House Solarium where, surrounded by lawyers, political advisers, and family, he rewrote the confession he was slotted to give in three and a half hours. Three days earlier, the speechwriter Robert Shrum had drafted a contrite speech in which Clinton emphasized the seriousness of his infractions, the depth of his remorse, and the full extent of the pain he caused in the lives of his family, Monica Lewinsky, his staff, and the country.[64] Even the devout Roman Catholic Paul Begala, a Clinton counselor who was "personally devastated" by the Lewinsky affair, immediately recognized that the Shrum draft was too apologetic.[65] With the help of Rahm Emanuel and Linda Bloodworth-Thomason, Begala retooled the Shrum draft, working to eradicate any sense of "groveling." Their adjustments did not satisfy Clinton, who, working without a speechwriter, rewrote the entire second half of the speech less than thirty minutes before delivering it.[66] In the place of Shrum's contrition, Clinton substituted an attack on Kenneth Starr and insisted that even presidents are entitled to a zone of privacy.

Clinton's substitutions have been widely reviled; because of them, the confessional status of the speech has been called into question. As Gormley put it, "When the whole nation was expecting an apology," Clinton's "lashing" of Starr "appeared petty, inappropriate and unrepentant."[67] What I wish to insist on, however, is that while Clinton's insertion of a legal defense and an attack on Starr may have cost him points with the critics, it was, from his point of view, the only moral option. Starr was playing "gotcha" and advocating a form of confession that compromised the zone of privacy that Clinton believed was essential for democratic politics. From his perspective, it would have been immoral *not* to insert to a legal defense into his confession. Thus Clinton defended his rewritten text: "Dammit, somebody has to say these things. I don't care if I'm impeached. It's the right thing to do."[68] The form of the confession was more important than the presidency itself. Knowing full well that it might lead to his impeachment, Clinton chose to do the "right thing." That is, he chose to blend contrition and legal argument and thereby insist on a form of confession fit for democratic politics.

Three and half hours after he left the Map Room, he returned once more to make a case not simply for his own innocence, but for a particular understanding of confession. He began by reminding his audience that he had just testified before the grand jury and answered questions that "no American citizen would ever want to answer." Thus, before he sounded a single confessional note, Clinton cast himself as the victim of an inquisition that reached deep into his private life. Yet this subject position in no way relieved Clinton of the obligation to make a confession. By his own account, he "still" needed to "take complete responsibility for all [his] actions."[69] This responsibility, however, must be discharged with sensitivity to *both* the inappropriateness of his own actions *and* the inappropriateness of Starr's invasive questions. A confession that only groveled would, if only implicitly, endorse the legitimacy of the OIC's invasive questions by answering them publicly. Clinton refused to do so. He gave a speech that, in Gormley's words, "was essentially a condensed version of his effective testimony earlier that day."[70] On both occasions (the grand jury testimony that afternoon and the speech that evening), Clinton offered a confession that admitted wrongdoing without compromising his privacy.

The very structure of the speech reflects Clinton's twin commitments. After two paragraphs of introductory material, Clinton began his confession in the third paragraph with words of contrition. Here, he admitted that he did have an inappropriate relationship with Monica Lewinsky. In the fourth paragraph, with a sentence David Kendall insisted on including, Clinton turned away from contrition and insisted on his legal innocence: "But I told the grand jury today, and I say to you now, that at no time did I ask anyone to lie, to hide or destroy evidence, or to take any other unlawful action." Immediately following this statement, however, Clinton returned to his contrite tone in paragraph 5: "I misled people, including even my wife. I deeply regret that."[71] In paragraph 6 he reverted to legal arguments, noting that the investigation that landed him in front of the grand jury was itself under investigation. In paragraph 7 the contrite tone returned, as Clinton claimed that nothing is more important to him than putting things right with his family.

Paragraph 8, the last paragraph before the conclusion, is the most important of the speech. It represents in condensed form Clinton's ideal of a public, democratic confession. It includes both a sentence of contrition and a defense of a zone of privacy. The contrite sentence is certainly understated—"I take my responsibility for my part in all of this"—but it is understated on principle. The principle bears directly on the illegitimacy of the invasive questions Clinton mentioned in paragraph 1: "It is time to stop the pursuit of personal destruction and the prying into private lives and get on with our national life."[72] From the perspective of the OIC, this was a "limited confession." From Clinton's perspective, it was a democratic confession that admitted shortcomings without compromising privacy.

Clinton's final public words of August 17, 1998, were these: "And so, tonight I ask you to turn away from the spectacle of the past seven months, to repair the fabric of our national discourse, and to return our attention to all the challenges and all the promise of the next American century. Thank you for watching and good night."[73] In light of the day's events, Clinton's request that Americans "repair the fabric of our national discourse" was something more than a rhetorical flourish. It was precisely public discourse that had been under attack that day. Clinton's Map Room speech was a reminder that our democracy requires not simply public discourse, but public styles of discourse. The confession is no exception; if it is to advance public life, it must find its own public style.

The Two Confessions of September 11, 1998

On September 11, 1998, at 9:40 in the morning, President Clinton confessed his "sin" to one hundred and six religious leaders gathered in the East Room of the White House. This time the emphasis was on contrition. He acknowledged that he had reached "rock bottom"; claimed that forgiveness required "genuine repentance" and a "broken spirit"; announced that he was seeking pastoral support; assured his audience that neither the excesses of Starr's investigation nor his own legal maneuvering should obscure the fact that he "still sinned"; affirmed the importance of integrity and his confidence that "God can change us and make us strong at broken places"; quoted liberally from Jewish liturgy; and alluded at several points to the Psalms as well as the New Testament.[74] In short, nearly every sentence of this brief speech announced that it was to be situated in a religious tradition of contrition.

Given this dramatic shift in emphasis from the evening of August 17, there was a sentiment widespread among journalists and academics alike that this was the speech Clinton should have given three weeks earlier. The *Washington Post*'s John F. Harris, for example, wrote that this was "the speech that many of his aides wished he had given eight months ago, when the scandal first broke, or at the very least after his Aug. 17 grand jury testimony." Emphasizing the difference between the two speeches, Harris noted that while Clinton had "once [on August 17] lashed out angrily at independent counsel Kenneth W. Starr for invading his privacy, the president [now] said the investigation into his extramarital affair may actually have been 'a blessing' because it forced him to confront his failings."⁷⁵ Across the country and across the Atlantic, the media sounded similar notes. From London, Joanna Cole wrote for *The Times* that this "was the speech [Clinton's] advisers had hoped he would give back in August." Cole told the story of how, three weeks earlier, Clinton had torn to pieces the contrite speech crafted for him by his speechwriting staff and composed instead his own angry tirade against Kenneth Starr. "Yesterday," by contrast, Clinton "was positively begging, even asking forgiveness from Monica Lewinsky, the very same person he had previously referred to in a finger-jabbing moment as 'that woman.'"⁷⁶ As I noted above, there was no shortage of scholarly backing for this thesis. Blaney and Benoit, Bauer, and Lee and Barton, all agreed that "Clinton's speech at the White House Prayer Breakfast was much more appropriate than his [August 17] address to the nation."⁷⁷

As I have been at pains to establish, such a conclusion requires contextualizing the Prayer Breakfast speech vis-à-vis the 10:02 p.m. Map Room speech of August 17. On September 11, 1998, however, there was a much more immediate context. As the *Washington Post*'s John F. Harris noted, Clinton's "East Room mea culpa" may have been "a gripping moment, but it turned out to be just one scene in a kaleidoscopic day of astonishing moments."⁷⁸ The next such moment came a few hours later. At 2:45 p.m., CNN became the first news organization to post the full text of the modestly named "Referral to the United States House of Representatives Pursuant to Title 28, United States Code, Section 595c"—otherwise known as the Starr Report.

The media overwhelmingly cast the Prayer Breakfast speech in the context of the Starr Report, which dominated the news on September 12. Although the picture on the front page of the *New York Times* was from the Prayer Breakfast, the lead columns—left, center, and right—were each dedicated to the report. On the lower right side of the paper, below the fold, squeezed between three articles on the Starr Report, was a lonely account of the Prayer Breakfast speech. But even there, the first sentence placed the speech in the context of the report. The first thing columnist James Bennet told his readers was that Clinton admitted he had sinned "just hours before the world was presented a painstaking account by prosecutors of when, where and how."⁷⁹

This relative disregard for the Prayer Breakfast speech should not suggest a paucity of references to the genre of confession. Indeed, the papers of September 12 and the following weeks were saturated with confessional references, but as was the case on August 17, the bulk of these were in response to the witch-hunt politics of the Starr investigation. The standard comparisons to Miller, Hawthorne, and Kafka were rolled out once more. Thus, just as the grand jury testimony of August 17 was constituted as a coerced confession, so also was the Starr Report. Indeed, if the media accounts can be trusted, the Starr Report was *the* primary confessional event of September 11, 1988. To be sure, the Prayer Breakfast speech received its fair share of coverage, and as I noted above, journalists and academics turned August 17–September 11 comparisons into a minor critical industry. But given the contours of the media coverage, a Prayer Breakfast speech–Starr Report comparison is far easier to justify. For as Bennet noted, the Starr Report read as the perfect complement to Clinton's Prayer Breakfast confession: the latter asking forgiveness for the actions described in the former. In this section, I return the Prayer Breakfast speech to its original context, a context dominated by the public release of the Starr Report. So contextualized, a rather different lesson emerges. Far from the opposite of his August 17 confession and a lesson on the importance of contrition, the speech appears strikingly similar to the August 17 Map Room speech. Like that speech, this one was crafted in response to the excesses of the Starr examination: it was designed as a model for a public, democratic confession, one that holds in equipoise two styles widely considered to be mutually exclusive: humble contrition and legal argument.

The Starr Report as a Coerced Confession

The Starr Report attacked Clinton's August 17 grand jury testimony on two primary grounds. First, Clinton inappropriately engaged in legal arguments, and second, he did not provide sufficient details. Taken together, these points constitute the OIC's primary complaint against what they understood as Clinton's "limited confession." In this sense, the Starr Report, whatever else it was, was also a partisan style guide for public confession. Although it does not announce itself as such, and although the entire document makes no reference to confession as a rhetorical practice, the public reception of the document leaves no doubt that its prescriptions of detailed disclosure without mitigating legal arguments was, for a wide swath of the American population, a recipe for confession.

The Starr Report condemned nothing with more energy than Clinton's infamous penchant for legalisms. The report consistently decried Clinton's "semantic defense" and his "detailed parsing of ... words."[80] From the perspective of the Starr Report and, no doubt, the country at large, the example par excellence of such semantic parsing was Clinton's grand jury claim that the truthfulness of his lawyer's statement—"there is no sex of any kind" with Ms. Lewinsky—"depends on what the meaning of the word 'is' is." If the word "is" restricts the scope of his lawyer's claim to the present tense, Clinton reasoned, then it was a true statement, for at the time the claim was made there was in fact no sex of any kind. From the perspective of the OIC, however, "the President's linguistic parsing is unreasonable."[81]

Clinton's legal parsing earned him the censure of, among others, Maureen Dowd—no friend of Starr or his report. In her *New York Times* column, she memorably attacked Clinton as the "wizard of is." She saw in his legal hairsplitting nothing but narcissism: "He tries to make words subjective, insisting they mean only what he wants them to. Just as he made the Democratic Party about himself, and the Democratic Conventions about himself, and the Presidency about himself, he tries to make the language about himself." This linguistic narcissism, Dowd concluded, perverts our language and corrupts our thought. Like the OIC, Dowd could see no place for recourse to finely parsed legal definitions. This momentary allegiance of Maureen Dowd and the OIC is illustrative of just how widespread was the opposition to Clinton's legalisms. From here, however, Dowd and the OIC parted ways. Dowd simply demanded that Clinton "find a way to reconnect words and meaning."[82] The Starr Report, however, treated Clinton's semantic parsings and legalisms as justification for the inclusion of an overwhelming amount of salacious detail.

The Starr Report's level of explicit detail has been widely noted. *U.S. News and World Report* called the level of detail "breathtaking";[83] the *New York Times* noted that "there is no end" to the facts accumulated in Starr's report;[84] and even the *Wall Street Journal*, which, along with *Newsweek*, represented Starr's journalistic home turf, suggested that Starr deserved a "penalty flag" for "piling it on." "Nearly all," the *Journal*'s editorial continued, "accuse Mr. Starr of stepping over the line by including details in his report that seem gratuitous and embarrassing to the president."[85] As David Kendall and his colleagues put it in the White House's Initial Response, the report is "so loaded with irrelevant and unnecessary graphic and salacious allegations that only one conclusion is possible: its principal purpose is to damage the President."[86] Indeed, from Kendall's perspective, the salacious details were so overwhelming that the report was literally reducible to them: "The OIC report is left with nothing but the details of a private sexual relationship, told in graphic details with the intent to embarrass."[87]

While the fact of the details is well-known, Starr's rationale for providing excessive details is less so. The report claims in multiple places that it was not the sexually explicit nature of the case that required the sexually explicit details.[88] Rather, the details were a response to Clinton's legalisms. Consider the report's defense of its own "Narrative":

> The Narrative is lengthy and detailed. It is the view of this Office that the details are crucial to an informed evaluation of the testimony, the credibility of witnesses, and the reliability of other evidence. Many of the details reveal highly personal information; many are sexually explicit. This is unfortunate, but it is essential. The President's defense to many of the allegations is based on a close parsing of the definitions that were used to describe his conduct. We have, after careful review, identified no manner of providing the information that reveals the falsity of the President's statements other than to describe his conduct with precision.[89]

The essential but unfortunate detail is here cast as a response to the president's rhetorical choices. Clinton sought recourse in the "close parsing of definitions," so the report responded with recourse to precise description. Among other things, we have here a contest over rhetorical style: the style of the report justified by the style of Clinton's "limited confession": "In his grand jury testimony, the President relied heavily on a particular interpretation of 'sexual relations' as defined in the Jones deposition. Beyond insisting that this conduct did not fall within the Jones definition, he refused to answer questions about the nature of his physical contact with Ms. Lewinsky. . . . This strategy . . . mandates that this Referral set forth evidence of an explicit nature that otherwise would be omitted."[90] For these reasons, the Starr Report was filled with stories of blow jobs, phone sex, Oval Office masturbation, and, famously, cigars. Nor did it simply report these activities; it was careful to report the exact minute and location of each, the levels of undress, the placement of hands relative to clothes, and the measures taken to muffle the inevitable sounds. Thus was Clinton's legal parsing met by Starr's sexual accountancy.

The Starr Report explicitly stated that if Clinton had simply confessed these misdeeds, they would not need to be rehearsed in such detail. Instead of admitting them, however, Clinton sought recourse to arcane legalisms. Thus the Starr Report cast itself as a sort of confessional corrective: providing the details that Clinton omitted, and omitting the legalisms he clung to: "Unfortunately, the nature of the President's denials requires that the contrary evidence be set forth in detail. If the President, in his grand jury appearance, had admitted the sexual activity recounted by Ms. Lewinsky and conceded that he lied under oath in his civil deposition, these particular descriptions would be superfluous."[91] That is to say, if Clinton had just confessed according to the OIC's definition of confession, the OIC would not now have to provide the substance of that confession. But given Clinton's "continued contention that his civil deposition testimony was legally accurate" and his "refusal to answer related questions," the "detail is critical."[92] The Starr Report, in other words, casts itself as providing the confession that Clinton refused to give.[93]

Perhaps the most compelling evidence that the Starr Report's twin demands of full disclosure without legal argument constituted a demand for an invasive, overreaching confession is its reception in the news media. In the weeks that followed the publication of the Starr Report, the news media struggled to define the nature of the document. It was evident immediately that the report was not simply a legal document, and thus the categories of law were insufficient to describe its rhetorical force. Rather than law or legal precedent, journalists explained the report with recourse to literature. As the literary critic James Wood noted, the report is "not a neutral legal account, but a literary confection."[94] Accordingly, news reports once again bristled with references to Nathaniel Hawthorne's *Scarlet Letter*, Arthur Miller's *Crucible*, Dostoevsky's Grand Inquisitor, and Koestler's *Darkness at Noon*. When the journalists didn't turn to these literary examples, they turned directly to the historical episodes that inspired them—the Salem witch trials of Hawthorne's *Scarlet Letter* and the McCarthyism that motivated Miller's *Crucible*. Tellingly, confession plays a significant role in each of these historical and literary referents—but it is confession in the witch-hunt mode.

The struggle to define the Starr Report was nowhere more conspicuous than in an op-ed piece for the *New York Times* by the well-known literary critic Stephen Greenblatt. Greenblatt described the Report as a "peculiar literary production" with a "nonfiction novel" "inserted at the core" of its legal argument. This nonfiction novel has "many elements of comedy" as well as "many pornographic elements." But Greenblatt insisted that the report was neither comedy nor pornography; the text was not really all that funny and its sex rarely suggested ecstatic pleasure. The only genre into which the Starr Report fits comfortably, Greenblatt contended, is the "documents of the witchcraft trials." In these trials, Greenblatt explained, "the accused were publicly stripped and shaved and searched with minute attention until the witch's mark' was discovered, and, under enough pressure, the confessions tumbled out." The Starr Report, Greenblatt concluded, "is our version of the documents that proudly published these confessions." For Greenblatt, the report is a record of Clinton's confessions, not because it records a mea culpa or expresses contrition, but because within its pages it tells the story of the "minute attention" focused on a publicly stripped and shaven president. Greenblatt concluded that the report "is not finally about sex or even about perjury. It is about the power of narrative to expose everything, about the ripping away of dignity and respect, about what unleashed and merciless state authorities can do to a person, even to the President himself."[95] It is thus about the power of confession: that narrative form which, when stripped of legal argument as it is in the Starr Report and placed in a witch-hunt tradition, is unmatched in its powers of exposure. The form of confession pursued in the Starr Report is indeed merciless: shorn of any rhetorical style that might contain its jurisdiction, it constitutes a game of "gotcha" that strips those whom it exposes and robs them of "dignity and respect."

The wider media possessed neither Greenblatt's eloquence nor his literary expertise. They did, however, share his fundamental thesis. They, too, read the Starr Report as the record of an excessive confession. As they confirmed Greenblatt's reading, they also provided his reading with a force he could have never alone produced: the force of public opinion. From across the political spectrum, the media repeated different versions Greenblatt's claims ad nauseam. This suggests that his office in Harvard's English Department did not overly determine his reading of the report. On the contrary, journalists who had doubtless never heard of Greenblatt or New Historicism interpreted the Starr Report in the same manner: not as a legal document but as a confessional narrative in the tradition of Hawthorne and Miller.

The *New York Times* even called on Arthur Miller himself to pen an op-ed on the Clinton "extravaganza." Apparently only one so well versed in both literature and the excesses of confession could interpret rightly Kenneth Starr and his tactics. While Miller noted both similarities and differences between the abuses of Salem's forced confessions and Starr's crusade, he ended on a hopeful note. Perhaps the excesses of Salem, he mused, provided inspiration for the Fifth Amendment—constitutional protection against forced confessions. Miller's hope was that the excesses of the Starr investigation might function similarly: they might inspire a revulsion against the form of confession provided by the Starr Report.[96] If the sentiments consistently expressed in the news media can be trusted, Miller's hope was fully realized in 1998.

Time magazine put it this way: "Whatever else the Clinton–Lewinsky scandal may ultimately be viewed as—grounds for impeachment, epic tabloid sideshow or the latest outbreak of puritan hysteria in the culture that gave us *The Scarlet Letter*—it already provides a cautionary tale about the dangers of instant intimacy."[97] Writing in the *New Statesman*, Michael Bywater argued that Starr has the "smirk of the inquisitor": "A plague on both their houses, but a bigger plague—a slow, deliquescing plague, with sores and exudates—upon Starr for being a Puritan and a hypocrite."[98] Andrew Sullivan accused Starr of confusing conservatism and puritanism.[99] The influential Dallas clergyman T. D. Jakes was even more explicit, arguing on network television that the investigation embodied "the spirit of the lynch man" that once "led to the burning of witches in Salem, the lynching of black people."[100] *Newsweek* referred to the Starr-led attack on Clinton as "sexual McCarthyism" and Starr himself as a "dour-faced Puritan."[101]

Mari Blecher suggested in *USA Today* that the Clinton sex scandal could help high school English teachers teach Hawthorne's *Scarlet Letter*, Miller's *Crucible*, and Shakespeare's *Othello*. The modern news media stands in for the scaffolding erected at the center of Hawthorne's New England village, enabling private sins to be publicly displayed. Similarly, "students might also compare Ken Starr to the husband character, Roger Chillingworth, who, in his obsessive pursuit of Dimmesdale, ultimately destroys himself." And just like Miller's John Proctor, whose refusal to confess to charges of adultery occasioned the Salem witch trials, Clinton's legal evasions have ignited a twentieth-century version of the witch hunt.[102] Blecher's connection of the scaffolding and television was not lost on the *New York Times'* Anthony Lewis, who opined, "Today, when you turn on the Sunday television 'news' programs, you might be watching Mr. Starr's prosecutors rehearsing. They sound like a crowd at an *auto-da-fé*, a burning at the stake in the Inquisition."[103]

The *New York Times* columnist Frank Rich agreed. Grouping Starr with the likes of Pat Robertson and Dr. James Dobson, Rich argued that the *Starr Report* was threatening not so much for over-the-top salacious detail, but for the "vision of what America might be like if the Starrs, Robertsons and Dobsons were in power." What is this vision of America, proper to Starr but "chilling" to Rich and the "rest of us"? It is an America modeled on Miller's *Crucible*: "The two-thirds of the people in this land who reject such invasive politics, many of them far more honorable than Bill Clinton, would rather have a piggish President they don't admire, and perhaps actively deplore, in the White House than lend any vindication to the crusade of a zealous prig out of *The Crucible*."[104] Walter Shapiro aptly summarized the reception of the Starr Report: "The world's news media drew historical analogies to the scandal, almost always in defense of Clinton, often mentioning the Salem witch trials and the McCarthyism of the 1950s, but also reading back to the Spanish inquisition."[105]

Formally speaking, of course, there was nothing about the Starr Report that suggested it was a confession. It was, after all, a "narrative" written in the third person. Yet, as its public reception demonstrates, these formal characteristics hardly kept it from being read in confessional terms. The message was overwhelming: from the *New York Times* to *USA Today*, the Starr Report was placed in a witch-hunt tradition of public confession. So placed, Kenneth Starr was the guilty party and Bill Clinton the victim of his unqualified power. As the French daily *Le Monde* put it, Starr was a monster "worthy of the reports of the Inquisition."[106] The German *Berliner Zeitung* was even harsher, claiming that "Starr [was] more successful than Stalin."[107]

This is the context into which Clinton delivered his Prayer Breakfast speech. And the first words of that speech suggested Clinton was well aware of this context. Although the public release of the Starr Report was still five hours away, he began his speech at 9:40 a.m. by insisting that although the Prayer Breakfast is always an "important day," this particular Prayer Breakfast fell on an "unusual and, I think, unusually important day."[108] Given that the only "unusual" event recorded on that day was the public release of the Starr Report, and given the fact that it had already been rumored for two days that Newt Gingrich was going to release it into the public domain, and finally, given the fact that Clinton's lawyers had already begun drafting their Preliminary Response to the Starr Report, it is a fair assumption that Clinton's September 11 confession was, for him as for the media, contextualized by the OIC's impending release.[109]

The Prayer Breakfast Speech

However much Clinton's Prayer Breakfast speech may have emphasized religious contrition, it was not, as the *New York Times* claimed, an "unmitigated confession."[110] In fact, Clinton was quite clear; he may have a "broken spirit," but he would also instruct his lawyers to "mount a vigorous defense" and use "all available appropriate arguments." This is precisely a *mitigated* confession, one qualified by legal argument. In this sense, there is little difference from Clinton's texts of August 17—on both occasions, Clinton wed confession and legal argument for the purposes of public discourse. The only difference between the speeches of August 17 and September 11 was one of emphasis. On the evening of August 17, the emphasis was on legal argument. To be sure, that speech contained enough confessional language that it registered as an attempted confession for nearly all who heard it, but the emphasis was clearly on Starr's infringement of Clinton's right to privacy.

On September 11, the distribution of emphasis was reversed: while Clinton explicitly retained his right to legal argument, the emphasis was solidly on contrition.

Critics have interpreted this shift in emphasis as evidence that Clinton learned from his mistakes and gradually got better at giving confessions. The *Los Angeles Times* conclusion that, over time, Clinton's confessions gradually approximated the religious ideal was mirrored by scores of academic critics—Bauer, as well as Koesten and Rowland, to name only the best—who argued that Clinton's confessional skills improved over time.[111] There are two issues with this interpretation. First, it takes a partisan definition of confession and posits it as the standard by which all confessions are to be measured. It was, recall, Starr and the OIC who argued that confession must be characterized in the first instance by contrition. Second, it minimizes, if not ignores, a foundational principle of textual analysis: texts are responsive to audiences. When this principle is recalled, the shift in emphasis between Clinton's speeches of August 17 and September 11 is rendered commonplace—even uninteresting. Whatever differences might exist between the two speeches can be largely attributed to the different audiences Clinton was addressing. Clinton spent the entire afternoon of August 17 facing a grand jury; thus it is hardly surprising that his testimony and his address to the nation that evening featured legal arguments. Indeed, the White House's formal name for the speech is "Remarks to the Nation on Testimony Before the Independent Counsel's Grand Jury."[112] In a text so named, how could the emphasis be on anything but legal arguments? On September 11, by contrast, Clinton's audience was filled with clergy. Accordingly, his religious language, his consistent recourse to the Bible, and his reliance on Jewish liturgy reflect less a shift in Clinton's vision of confession than they do a change in the composition of his audience. The tendency of elite journalists like John Harris and rhetorical critics like Benoit and Blaney, Bauer, and Lee and Barton to interpret the Prayer Breakfast speech as the pinnacle of Clinton's confessional tour is simply trivial. Such a conclusion minimizes the elementary fact that the Prayer Breakfast speech was given at a prayer breakfast.

Not only was it given at prayer breakfast, it was given by a president renowned for playing to the crowd. If we take Howard Kurtz's analysis in *Spin Cycle* seriously, in which he argues that the Clinton administration was to an unprecedented degree playing always and only "to the cameras"; or if we believe the Parry-Gileses' argument that Clinton's disclosures were "carefully crafted, highly scripted exercises" in hyperreality; or if we credit Hogan's description of Clinton as the quintessential "poll-driven, focus-group-tested, made-for-television president," then we have little ground for reading the contrition of the Prayer Breakfast speech as evidence that Clinton had finally realized that contrition was the best mode of confession.[113] Indeed, as Gormley makes clear, sometimes Clinton confessed simply because a confession was politically expedient. Of September 1998, Gormley writes, "The Clinton White House recognized that it was now 'fighting for survival.' Clinton's handlers made accommodations whenever possible to those whose support he relied upon to survive. If the president needed to suffer through extra rubber-chicken dinners to help allies in Congress, he did it. If he needed to eat crow along with the meal, so that voters could hear repentance in his voice, Bill Clinton served it up."[114] On this account, a confession was in the same category as "rubber-chicken dinners"—both were last-ditch political maneuvers designed to save the presidency. In short, the Prayer Breakfast speech was given by a president with a storied capacity for spin who found himself in a situation that required all his resources. All this suggests that the differences between the two confessions can be attributed to basic demographics.

Once we take into account Clinton's varied audiences and discount the differences between speeches accordingly, the confessions of August 17 and September 11 look remarkably similar: both are composed of two basic styles, religious contrition and legal argument. The accomplishment of both is the intertwining of these styles in a relation of mutual dependence. And the result, in both cases, is a distinctively public—even democratic—vision of confession.

While scholars and pundits have noted the coexistence of confession and legal argument in Clinton's September 11 address, this coexistence is most often mentioned as an imperfection, evidence that Clinton can progress still further in pursuit of a religious confession. As Michiko Kakutani put it in the *New York Times*, Clinton's confession was a "contemporary blend of legalistic defensiveness and self-abnegating moralism. . . . Some form of mea culpa perhaps but not exactly words that conjure up the elevated world of classical tragedy: Job on the ash-heap, Lear on the heath, Ahab on the quarterdeck."[115] Or as the pundits at the *National Journal* put it, Clinton's Prayer Breakfast confession exemplified his "latest two-track strategy of repenting his sins while resorting to preposterous semantic games." In the opinion of the *National Journal*, this recourse to legal argument is the "most disingenuous" moment of the entire speech; they, like Starr, would have preferred an unmitigated confession.[116] As Blaney and Benoit put it, Clinton's "persistence" in resorting to legal argument threatened to "reduce the effectiveness of his professed contrition."[117] Lee and Barton argue that Clinton's comment that he will instruct his lawyers to mount a vigorous defense "disrupts the tone of the confession" and "undermines" Clinton's claims to mend his ways.[118]

In pursuing this argument, each of these critics is forced to read Clinton's invocations of legal argument as exceptional, or out of keeping with an otherwise confessional text. But the very form of Clinton's Prayer Breakfast speech suggests that confession and legal argument are not disconsonant. Indeed, the text suggests, sometimes explicitly, that the two discursive forms work in tandem: "Legal language must not obscure the fact that I have done wrong." Three paragraphs later Clinton returned to the symbiosis of these rhetorical styles: "I am grateful for those who have stood by me and who say that in this case and many others, the bounds of privacy have been excessively and unwisely invaded. That may be. Nevertheless, in this case, it may be a blessing, because I still sinned."[119] In this quotation, confession and legal argument spring from the same source: the excesses of the Starr investigation. While Clinton is grateful for those who have responded to Starr with legal arguments, he is quick to insist that the same excesses that require legal argument also require a confession. Far from being disconsonant, the two styles grow organically, as it were, from the same source.

In sum, there are no grounds for reading the September 11 speech as an authentic moment of religious contrition, proof that Clinton learned from his early confessional failures, or as a vast departure from the strategy of August 17. On the union of legal argument and public confession, Clinton was, from January 26, 1992, forward, remarkably consistent. Nor are there grounds for reading Clinton's recourse to legal argument as a flaw in an otherwise contrite document. Indeed, Clinton suggests legal argument is a required corrective for public confession; it prevents the confession from becoming criminally invasive. On this matter, I stand with A. M. Rosenthal: Clinton has given us a gift, teaching us democracy's requirements of public confession.

Conclusion: Clinton and a Democratic Confession

Looking back on the scandal years later, Clinton remembered 1998 in remarkably positive terms. In an interview with Ken Gormley, Clinton reflected, "You know, my family stayed together and Hillary stayed with me and my daughter got through this, it was all pretty wonderful in a certain way. I mean, the overall thing was terrible, [but] the American people got [it]."[120]

One wonders what, precisely, the American people "got." It is difficult to know for sure, but the language is eerily similar to Clintons' 1992 response to the Gennifer Flowers scandal. In that *60 Minutes* interview, Clinton defended his democratically attuned theory of confession as follows: "You know, I have acknowledged wrongdoing, I have acknowledge[d] causing pain in my marriage. I have said things to you tonight and to the American people from the beginning that no American politician ever has. I think most Americans who are watching this tonight, they'll know what we're saying, they'll get it, and they'll feel that we have been more than candid. And I think what the press has to decide is: Are we going to engage in a game of gotcha?" When Clinton claimed that the "American people got [it]," perhaps he was referring to his view of confession. They "got" that confession, if it is to be democratically serviceable, must know its limits. It must be "candid" and "acknowledge wrongdoing," but it need not elaborate. They "got" that Starr's unchecked pursuit of the president—and his demand that no detail go unconfessed—constituted a dangerous game of "gotcha" and violated an important zone of privacy. They understood that, in a democratic polity, contrition and legal argument are not "rhetorically disconsonant." Rather, the two are rhetorically symbiotic: they feed off each other and stand as mutual correctives for the excesses of the other. When Clinton said the American people "got [it]," it was almost as if he was saying that they got the fact that democracy required a new form of confession, one tempered by its classical antithesis, legal argument.

If this indeed was what the American people took away from the Lewinsky scandal, it would not be by accident. The symbiosis of legalisms and contrition is a central argument of the last document the White House released prior to Clinton's impeachment trial. Discussing the "Trial Memorandum of William Jefferson Clinton" is the perfect way to conclude this chapter. In addition to the legal arguments carefully compiled, and in addition to the step-by-step refutations of the Starr Report, the memorandum insisted on the fundamental compatibility of confession and legal argument.

Perhaps the most distinctive thing about the memorandum is the sheer number of references to Clinton's various confessions. "Nothing in this Trial Memorandum," the document began, should obscure the fact of Clinton's confessions. By his "own admission," it continued, he "is guilty of personal failings. As he has publicly stated, 'I don't think there is a fancy way to say that I have sinned.' He has misled his family, his friends, his staff, and the Nation about the nature of his relationship with Ms. Lewinsky. He hoped to avoid exposure of personal wrongdoing so as to protect his family and himself and to avoid public embarrassment. He has acknowledged that his actions were wrong." Following this reference to the Prayer Breakfast confession, the memorandum reminded its readership that Clinton also confessed to the grand jury: "No one who watched the videotape of this grand jury testimony had any doubt that the President was admitting to an improper physical relationship with Ms. Lewinsky." Twenty-six pages later, the claim was even stronger: "No one who heard the President's August 17 speech or watched the President's videotaped grand jury testimony had any doubt that he had admitted to an ongoing physical relationship with Ms. Lewinsky." Two pages after that, the memorandum reprinted the entirety of Clinton's grand jury testimony. All told, the memorandum explicitly recalled Clinton's various confessions eleven times. More important, it treated the various public confessions—the grand jury testimony, the August 17 Map Room speech, and the Prayer Breakfast speech—as interchangeable. The grand jury testimony was just as much a confession as the Map Room speech, and the Map Room speech was just as much a confession as the September 11 Prayer Breakfast speech. Unlike the criticisms of so many journalists and academic critics, Clinton's memorandum refused to hierarchize the various attempts at confession or to judge them by an external, Starr-provided standard. From the perspective of Clinton's legal team, his gradual approximation of the religious confession was simply irrelevant. Despite the much-rehearsed variance between the speeches of August 17 and September 11, all of Clinton's confessions were united in the memorandum by one decisive fact: each of them combined legal argument with public confession.

On this score, it is important to note that if the memorandum highlighted the fact of Clinton's confessions, it expended equal energy reclaiming a positively valenced understanding of legal argument: "In rebutting the allegations contained in the articles of impeachment, this brief refers to the facts as well as to laws, legal principles, court decisions, procedural safeguards, and the Constitution itself.... These principles are not 'legalisms' but rather the very essence of the 'rule of law' that distinguishes our Nation from others." In the opinion of the administration, "legalisms" were central to the democratic project. They constitute the "rule of law" that protects individuals from the dangers of arbitrary power.

One particular way legalisms protect democracy, the memorandum suggested, is by tempering the danger of public confession. While the constant references to witch hunts suggested that Kenneth Starr was guilty of overstepping the line that protected the sanctity of the private sphere, the memorandum argued that Clinton's recourse to legal arguments "protects against partisan overreaching." So defined, legal argument does not stand in opposition to confession, but rather acts as a safeguard internal to it. Consider the careful intertwining of legal argument and confession in the following quotation: "[Clinton] declined to describe, because of personal privacy and institutional dignity considerations, certain specifics about his conduct with Ms. Lewinsky, but he indicated his willingness to answer, and he did answer, the other questions put to him about his relationship with her. No one who watched the videotape of this grand jury testimony had any doubt that the President was admitting to an improper physical relationship with Ms. Lewinsky."[121] In sum, legal arguments are not "meaningless legal jargon." They have real-world applications, the most important of which is as a safeguard against the "extraordinary overreaching" of which the Starr Report was so dramatically guilty.

This is Clinton's underappreciated contribution to the history of confession. When the OIC demanded his confession, he consented. Indeed, he not only provided numerous public confessions, but, as the memorandum illustrates, his administration constantly reminded the public of these confessions. And yet the substance of these confessions was not what the OIC had in mind. As Wisenberg made plain on August 17, and as the Starr Report made plain on September 11, the OIC wanted an unqualified admission of fault and an unchecked relinquishing of legal rights. On this count, Clinton would not budge. He recognized clearly that, under such a definition of confession, he could not possibly retain the presidency. So he responded to the OIC's demands with his own understanding of confession. According to this understanding, which he had deployed with success following the Gennifer Flowers accusations, a truly public confession holds in equipoise the competing demands of legal protections and religious contrition. Indeed, every confessional statement Clinton made—the grand jury testimony, the August 17 speech, and the Prayer Breakfast speech—were each characterized by precisely this balance. And if we can trust the memorandum, everything beyond this fundamental equipoise—such as his references to Scripture and his humility (or his lack thereof)—were inessential fluff, rubber-chicken dinners added for the audience of the moment. But this balance, this union of legal argument and humble contrition, was Clinton's original and important contribution to the history of confession. If I sing of it rather too loudly, it is because twelve years of scholarship have drowned this lesson in platitudes about humility, repentance, and Clinton's gradual approximation of the religious confession.

CONCLUSION:
JAMES FREY AND TWENTY-FIRST-CENTURY CONFESSIONAL CULTURE

On January 8, 2006, the investigative website the *Smoking Gun* incited a media firestorm by reporting that James Frey's memoir *A Million Little Pieces* was filled with "fabrications, falsehoods, and other fakery." Four months earlier, Oprah Winfrey had given Frey undreamt-of fame by selecting his first-person story of recovery from drug addiction for the October 2005 installment of Oprah's Book Club. Then, after fifteen Oprah-inspired weeks atop the *New York Times* Best Seller list, the *Smoking Gun* revealed that Frey was not the malevolent thug that he made himself out to be: he spent a few hours in a local police station rather than three months in a cell block reserved for "violent and felonious offenders," there was never a fight with the cops, never an attempt to incite a riot, never a 0.29 blood alcohol test, and he was never booked on charges of "Felony Mayhem."[1]

Three days later, Frey appeared on CNN's *Larry King Live* to defend *A Million Little Pieces*. Rather than contest the charges of fabrication, Frey sought recourse in the genre of his book: "I wrote a memoir." According to Frey, "A memoir is a subjective retelling of events," one that emphasizes an "essential truth" rather than factual fidelity. In this case, Frey explained, *A Million Little Pieces* told the "essential truth" of addiction and recovery, a truth that historical inaccuracies could never compromise. Every time King questioned Frey's facts, Frey returned to the capacious and protective fold of memoir: "You know, it's a memoir, it's a selective recollection of my life."[2]

Oprah Winfrey fought back. "A memoir means it's the truth of your life," she argued on her January 26 show—a show dedicated to Frey and his newly exposed *Million Little Pieces*. In response to Winfrey's definition of memoir, Frey's Doubleday editor Nan A. Talese countered that memoir's only requirement was that it "strike" the reader as "authentic" and "valid"—a test, she claimed, that Frey passed with flying colors. For the duration of the hour, Frey, Talese, Winfrey, and her high-profile guests functioned as literary critics, debating the boundaries of the memoir and the obligations of memoirists and their publishers.[3] Thus were the pages and programs of the U.S. mainstream media momentarily preoccupied with what, under other circumstances, would have seemed a pedantic, ivory-tower topic: genre theory. Yet in the weeks that followed the expose, the sheer success of *A Million Little Pieces*, Frey's insistence that it was a memoir, speculation that it might be better labeled a confession, and the deep anger of Oprah Winfrey transformed journalists, celebrities, writers, and ordinary citizens into ad hoc literary critics.

For three reasons, the story of the James Frey controversy makes a perfect conclusion to *Confessional Crises and Cultural Politics in Twentieth-Century America*. First, like the six twentieth-century stories I have told thus far, the Frey controversy is about a moment in which confessional hermeneutics— the act of determining precisely which texts count as confessions—became a politically loaded activity. Second, in the Frey controversy we can see the continued relevance of the four arguments I've pursued throughout *Confessional Crises and Cultural Politics in Twentieth-Century America*: that confessional hermeneutics are a powerful form of intervention into cultural politics, that the genre of confession has been formed and reformed by the diverse political commitments of those who have deployed it, that virtually any text can become a confession, and that the power of confession lies in its vexed relationship to authenticity. The fact that Frey brought each of these issues to the fore in 2006 is a powerful reminder that confessional crises are not a historical curiosity, relegated to the past. They are, rather, a pressing feature of twenty-first-century cultural politics, and all indications suggest that they will grow only more pressing in the coming years. Third, the crisis Frey incited was not simply over the classification of *A Million Little Pieces*; it was also a crisis over the place of confession in public life. By looking at the brouhaha sparked by Frey's decision to reclassify his novel, we may see with particular clarity some of the vexing issues haunting our twenty-first-century confessional culture.

A Million Little Pieces as a Confession

When decisions over whether particular texts count as confessions are extracted from the academy and pursued by actors seeking partisan gains, the criteria by which such decisions are made bear little resemblance to the criteria used to make similar decisions within the academy. The debate over the proper categorization of *A Million Little Pieces* is instructive. It was driven not by considerations of recurrent formal characteristics, semantic similarities, typologies of the audience, descriptions of recurrent "rhetorical situations," styles of prosody, or the "social action" of the text.[4] Rather, old-fashioned politicking drove the generic descriptions of *A Million Little Pieces*.

Vanity Fair reports that Frey initially spun the book as a novel to spare his family any "undue embarrassment." After eighteen rejections, however, Frey changed his tune. The publishing market at the time was particularly rough on novelists but particularly kind to memoirists.[5] The recent successes of Frank McCourt's *Angela's Ashes* and Augusten Burroughs's *Running with Scissors* had turned memoirs into "cash cows for the publishing houses."[6] Thus, without changing a single word, Frey and his agent reclassified *A Million Little Pieces*. It was now a memoir.[7] The results were immediate: Nan A. Talese/Doubleday offered Frey $50,000 for the manuscript. Although he told his publisher, "I think of this book more a work of art or literature than I do a work of memoir or autobiography," in April 2003 it was nonetheless released as a memoir.[8] Thus, from its very inception, *A Million Little Pieces* was a memoir only because, politically speaking, it needed to be one. Despite the fact that Frey wrote it as a novel, and despite the further fact that he registered his misgivings regarding Doubleday's *Million Little Pieces*-as-memoir marketing scheme, the politics of publishing trumped the designs of the author. When, two and a half years later, Oprah Winfrey could barely contain her excitement, the reluctant memoirist James Frey became the best-selling American author of 2005.[9]

Frey's reluctance was short-lived. In the firestorm of 2006, the vaguely defined contours of memoir were his only shelter. Although the "memoir defense" was not foolproof—many critics reacted with Winfrey, claiming that the distinguishing characteristic of a memoir was its truthfulness[10]—Frey and his publisher held relentlessly to the line that "memoir cannot be held to the same standard as history or biography."[11] As a means of contesting this claim, and applying the norms of truthfulness that apply in "history or biography" to the genre of memoir, Frey's critics emphasized the kinship of memoir and confession.[12] While memoir is a notoriously murky genre—admitting of both Winfrey's and Talese's definitions—confession's religious history can, when needed, provide it with an aura of truthfulness.[13] As the distinguished critic Daniel Mendelsohn noted, "The need for certain kinds of memoirs to be true goes back to Augustine's 'Confessions.'"[14]

Thus labeling *A Million Little Pieces* a confession, as Brian Williams did on *NBC Nightly News*, served to highlight the moral unacceptability of Frey's fabrications: his "searing piece of self-confession is actually, in large part, a work of fiction."[15] Here the disjunction between "confession" and "fiction" emphasized the nobility of Frey's purported genre and the inadequacy of his execution. Similarly, the *Philadelphia Inquirer*'s Karen Heller defined memoir as a "literary confession" and shortly thereafter accused Frey of being a "sham opportunist, mining sales out of pretense."[16] Although Frey himself suggested on numerous occasions that *A Million Little Pieces* should be understood in the tradition of Henry Miller, Jack Kerouac, and Charles Bukowski—"icons of male debauchery"—his critics just as insistently located it in the tradition of Augustine's *Confessions*—an icon of truthfulness.[17] Unsurprisingly, after the *Smoking Gun* expose, neither Frey nor any of his supporters ever once called *A Million Little Pieces* a confession, for so labeling the text was just as politically motivated as labeling it a memoir: to call it a confession was to emphasize the extent to which it violated norms of truthfulness. Thus, by the spring of 2006 *A Million Little Pieces* was a (successful) memoir to Frey and his devotees and a (failed) confession to his critics. The line separating the memoir from the confession now served double duty, separating as well Frey's friends from his foes.

By 2008, however, things were looking up for James Frey. HarperCollins bought his (well-labeled) novel *Bright Shiny Morning* for an estimated $1.5 million, and the "high-decibel debates about the murky rules of memoir" were a thing of the past.[18] So, too, it seems, was Frey's need for memoir: "I don't *care*, if somebody calls [*A Million Little Pieces*] a memoir, or a novel, or a fictionalized memoir, or what. I could care less what they call it. The thing on the side of the book means nothing. Who knows what it is. It's just a *book*. It's just a *story*. It's just a book that was written with the intention to break a lot of rules in writing. I've broken a lot of rules in a lot of ways. So be it."[19] While it might be true that Frey no longer cared how his book was labeled, it was certainly not true that "the thing on the side of the book means nothing." His initial misgivings about turning his novel into a memoir and, even more, the "high-decibel debates" over his doing so indicate that "the thing on the side of book" mattered a great deal to a great number of people.

For better or worse, *A Million Little Pieces* was never "just a story": depending on whom you asked, it was a novel-turned-memoir-turned-confession-turned-"just a book." The repeated transformations in the symbolic career of *A Million Little Pieces* illustrate what we might call *genre politics*: in 2003 James Frey was a reluctant memoirist because he needed to publish his book, in 2006 he was an insistent memoirist because he needed to shield himself from those who indicted his text as a failed confession, and in 2008 he was "just" a rule-breaking story writer because his need for memoir abated as quickly as did the media scrutiny. In every instance, Frey's reclassifications of the book cannot be separated from the shifting political economy that made such reclassifications possible. If *A Million Little Pieces* counted as a confession for some of Frey's critics, this categorization cannot be separated from their censure of his text.

Confessional Crises and Cultural Politics in Twentieth-Century America has argued that this point is generalizable if not universal. That is, it has argued that debates over the classification of a text are not reducible to determining the proper shelf on which a text should be displayed in Barnes & Noble. Rather, *Confessional Crises and Cultural Politics in Twentieth-Century America* assumes that debates over the proper classification of a text are political debates of the first order. As such, they constitute an important, if often overlooked, form of cultural intervention.

Moreover, the willingness of Frey's critics to call *A Million Little Pieces* a confession is important. It is a powerful reminder that when it comes to confession, political needs trump textual characteristics. No substantive definition of confession—especially an Augustinian one—could possibly encompass Frey's text. As I suggested above, *A Million Little Pieces* became a confession simply because, from the perspective of Frey's critics, it needed to be one. Yet the sheer fact that, of all books, *A Million Little Pieces* could become an Augustinian confession marks a strong challenge to the conventional wisdom. It complicates the nearly universal assumption that every study of confession must begin by offering a substantive definition of what counts as a confession. From the perspective of these prescriptions, *A Million Little Pieces* would never count—its substantive content as well as its formal construction assures this. The critic would thus be reduced to either ignoring the numerous and accomplished people who called it a confession or, more likely, suggesting that these people were wrong to do so. In either case, the critic would be blind to the political power the text wielded simply because it was labeled a confession by partisan advocates.

Frey, Confession, and the Politics of Authenticity

A Million Little Pieces was not James Frey's only confession. Eighteen days after the *Smoking Gun* exposed his fraudulent claims, Frey "confess[ed] his sins on Oprah's daytime talk show."[20] All are agreed on this count. The *New York Times* described the show as an hour-long "mea culpa" in which Frey "grovel[ed] for forgiveness" and "admitted to extensive fabrications."[21] In his Oprah "confessional," Andrew Potter wrote, "Frey conceded that pretty much everything in The Smoking Gun report was accurate and that, consequently, pretty much everything in his book was a pack of lies."[22] Yet, unlike the case regarding *A Million Little Pieces*, it seems that no one expected *this* confession to be authentic. Potter, for example, described it as a "calculated and profoundly cynical" confession. The sheer fact that a category exists for a calculated and cynical confession is evidence that there is not a straightforward relationship between confession and authenticity.[23]

Confessional Crises and Cultural Politics in Twentieth-Century America has argued for a complex, historically nuanced understanding of the relationship between authenticity and confession. On the one hand, as Peter Brooks has put it, Western society has made "confessional speech a prime mark of authenticity."[24] On the other hand, to the extent that a confession is extracted by force, its purchase on authenticity is compromised. Frey's January 26 confession belongs to this latter tradition. The *New York Times* media critic Virginia Heffernan described it as follows: The "book's phony 'hitting bottom' was nothing compared to the chastening—the emasculation, really—that [Frey] received yesterday on 'The Oprah Winfrey Show.'" Oprah came out, "whip in hand," and "savag[ed] Mr. Frey, hammering him with questions and heaving deep sighs of fury until he stammered with cartoonish diffidence: 'I—I—I—.'"[25] The language of torture—emasculation, whip, savaged, stammering—is significant. Foucault notes, "Since the Middle Ages, torture has accompanied [confession] like a shadow, and supported it when it could go no further."[26] As a January 27 *New York Times* editorial makes plain, Frey's on-air confessional was provided for in just this fashion: "Oprah did her best to force him . . . to admit the extent of his deception." Similarly, the *Washington Post*'s Howard Kurtz wrote that Oprah "lectured the sheepish-looking author and his publisher in an emotional hour of televised penance." And finally, the *New York Daily News* aptly noted that a "furious Oprah Winfrey ripped literary liar James Frey into 'A Million Little Pieces' on her show."[27] Given Winfrey's "fury" and her "savagery," is there any surprise that Frey's confession was "stammered with cartoonish indifference"? And can there be any surprise that those who called *A Million Little Pieces* a confession and demanded its authenticity made no similar demands of Frey's January 26 confession? The distance between Brian Williams and Virginia Heffernan neatly captures the vexed relationship between confession and authenticity. Both commentators deployed the genre of confession. Williams called *A Million Little Pieces* a confession and demanded that it be authentic; Heffernan called Frey's January 26 performance a confession and thereby called into question its authenticity. This tension is at the heart of our confessional culture.

As Peter Brooks has demonstrated, the U.S. legal system has long recognized that confessions produced by force are not authentic and cannot be trusted. Indeed, the 1966 Supreme Court case *Miranda v. Arizona*, the origin of the now-storied "Miranda rights," was motivated by the need to distinguish which types of confession could be trusted and which could not. Writing for the Court, Chief Justice Earl Warren argued that, for a confession to be valid, the defendant must be able "to tell his story without fear."[28] The very presence of compulsion—"of whatever nature or however infused"—compromises the truth value of the confession.[29] Indeed, the presence of compulsion shifts the meaning of confession, turning it from a discourse of authenticity to one that reflects nothing more than the power relation that produced it.

Indeed, well beyond the American legal system there is wide consensus that a coerced confession cannot be trusted. Writing in the *New Republic*, and using the example of the Inquisition to condemn American waterboarding, the historian Anthony Grafton argued, "The conclusion—drawn by the vast majority of modern scholars who have studied this material—is that torture could compel ordinary Jews, law-abiding craftsmen, and housewives and teenagers, to confess fantastic crimes. Torn from their normal lives, imprisoned, subjected to terrifying, intense pain, most of them would, quite simply, say anything. Only the bravest held up for long—and, with just a few exceptions, even they eventually broke as well."[30] And as Elaine Scarry eloquently reminds us, "saying anything" is the functional equivalent of saying nothing all. She argues that the confession, when extracted by force, is simply another way of saying, "Yes, all is almost gone now, there is almost nothing left now, even this voice, the sounds that I am making, no longer form my words, but the words of another." And, of course, a confession that is composed of another's words is no confession at all: "The prisoner has almost no voice—his confession is a halfway point in the disintegration of language, an audible objectification of the proximity of silence—the torturer and the regime have doubled their voice since the prisoner is now speaking their words."[31]

There are, of course, substantial differences between the Inquisition, waterboarding, and Winfrey's extraction of James Frey's January 26 confession. But the ubiquitous language of torture deployed to explain Frey's confession suggests that, material differences notwithstanding, the tortured prisoner became a heuristic through which Frey's confession was better understood. Indeed—and this is my larger point—*Confessional Crises and Cultural Politics in Twentieth-Century America* has argued that, historically speaking, the tortured prisoner has provided an important template for understanding the political work of confession. It was this heuristic, after all, that allowed the Black Power advocate John Oliver Killens to delegitimize Styron's novel: "We know what confessions of black men are worth in these times in the dear old southland. We know how these confessions are brought about and with what methods of persuasion." In other words, because it might well have been extracted by force and on threat of pain, "we would not rely too heavily on Nat's so-called confession."[32] The same heuristic was on display in the fall of 1998. When President Clinton confessed numerous times to an inappropriate relationship with Monica Lewinsky, he was compared to none other than Hawthorne's Hester Prynne, and the *New York Times* called on *The Crucible* playwright Arthur Miller to pen an editorial. Like Killens, Clinton was cashing in on what Supreme Court Justice Byron White called "a deep-seated distrust of all confessions."[33]

Confessional Crises and Cultural Politics in Twentieth-Century America has argued that, taken together, the competing notions of authenticity and coercion have provided the confession its political potency. On the one hand, confession can be the discourse of authenticity par excellence. On the other hand, it can be an inauthentic discourse that signals the abuse of power. The fact that both traditions of confession fit comfortably within the confines of the American confessional imagination turns the genre of confession into a powerful but volatile political resource.

Confessional Hermeneutics as Cultural Politics

On the January 26 episode of the *Oprah Winfrey Show*, the Poynter Institute's Roy Clark responded to the James Frey controversy by suggesting that publishers be required to "label what's going on in the book": "I think that there should be a statement of method in the beginning of every memoir that describes the degree of accuracy." Clark's idea was well received, as it reflected a widely shared anxiety that books be well labeled; Winfrey talked about publisher's obligation to "categorize" a book correctly, and the *Washington Post*'s Richard Cohen asked Frey if he would be willing to "move [his book] to the fiction shelf."[34] One might wonder why so many people cared so much about the proper categorization of a text. *Confessional Crises and Cultural Politics in Twentieth-Century America* suggests the following: Clark, Winfrey, and Cohen pursued questions of categorization because, historically speaking, such questions are never innocent. Such questions—ostensibly categorical—are often politically loaded. In every episode examined here, the crises were driven by the fact that questions of categorization were heuristics for larger cultural debates. *Confessional Crises and Cultural Politics in Twentieth-Century America* has charted how contests over the definition of confession have intersected with questions of sexuality, class, race, violence, religion, and democracy.

The case of James Frey is no different. In the spring of 2006, the controversy over the categorization of *A Million Little Pieces* was a heuristic for a larger controversy over twenty-first-century confessional culture. The Frey controversy was thus a confessional crisis in two senses of the word. First, as with every other crisis examined here, the crisis was incited by a text that, depending on one's politics, may or may not have been a confession. Second, unlike the other crises examined here, in which such debates were calibrated to external political issues (sexuality, race, etc.), the debate over *A Million Little Pieces* was part of a larger debate about the place of confession itself in twenty-first-century America. Nearly every critic who commented on the case of James Frey commented also on what the case taught us about our twenty-first-century confessional culture.

Among Frey's most hostile critics was the influential *New York Times* writer Michiko Kakutani. Like many others, Kakutani argued that *A Million Little Pieces* was a product of America's confessional culture; in her view, Frey "rode the crest" of "our obsession with navel gazing," reality television, the blogosphere, and the sheer ubiquity of "television-talk-show confessions." Accordingly, Kakutani used her review call into question not simply Frey's text, but also the larger confessional culture that made it possible. The Frey scandal "is not," she wrote, "just a case about truth-in-labeling or the misrepresentations of one author." To the contrary, "it is a case about how much value contemporary culture places on the very idea of truth." To her mind, the verdict is an unhappy one. Frey's text, she claimed, represents "the logical if absurd culmination of several trends that have been percolating away for years."

Kakutani argued that *A Million Little Pieces* demonstrated the "willful self-absorption and shameless self-promotion embraced by the 'Me Generation' and its culture of narcissism." Further, it was a product of "deconstructionists" and their "fashionably nihilistic view of the world." Neither historians, nor "postmodernists," nor "radical feminists," nor "multiculturalists" escaped her rage. All of these, she argued, were collusive partners in the confessional culture that made *A Million Little Pieces* possible. If Frey's text was a "petty," ultimately trivial manifestation of these forces, the danger lurking in Frey's text was quite real. Kakutani argued that "the dangers of such relativistic theories are profound." They create an environment "in which the testimony of a witness to the Holocaust . . . can actually be questioned." In sum, Kakutani argued that Frey's text was fiction, and the failure to so label it was indicative of a culture in which relativism compounds cynicism and displaces the "old idea" of objective truth.[35]

Kakutani's review was admittedly one of the most extreme. Yet her basic impulse of reading *A Million Little Pieces* as a heuristic for confessional culture was widely repeated. For the *Washington Post*'s Jonathon Yardley, Frey was the most "notorious" contributor to the endless catalog of "confessions" that is the "Age of Memoir." Like Kakutani, his verdict is pessimistic: "What the memoir boom has in fact given us is too many dull or forgettable memoirs, precious few of which have enriched our literature, but most of which have simply encouraged the narcissism of their authors."[36] Or consider the accomplished writer Richard Siklos: "A disturbing question lurks behind the literary scandal that won't die: Does authenticity still matter?" His answer, too, is negative: "Ours is a culture that loosened its grip on reality quite a while ago."[37] Consider finally the response of the American essayist Mary Karr. Like the above critics, she, too, faulted Frey for the "label slapped on the jacket of the book." Such labels matter a great deal, she argued, and Frey's failure to get the label right signals large-scale cultural decay. She laments the fact that objective truth has lost so much ground in recent decades that "memoirists have begun to employ novelistic devices to improve the genre's literary prospects."[38]

Kakutani, Yardley, Siklos, Karr—four accomplished writers, four identical verdicts. In each case, the debate over the proper categorization of *A Million Little Pieces* was a heuristic, providing an opportunity to critique twenty-first-century confessional culture. Without endorsing their critique of our confessional culture, I stress that their shared impulse to turn *A Million Little Pieces* into such a heuristic underscores a fundamental argument of *Confessional Crises and Cultural Politics in Twentieth-Century America*: debates over the classification of texts are also interventions into cultural politics. In the case at hand, those who questioned the confessional status of *A Million Little Pieces* did so in order to question the status of the wider confessional culture. With apologies to Richard Siklos, who argued that the Frey story "had legs mostly because of Oprah Winfrey," *Confessional Crises and Cultural Politics in Twentieth-Century America* suggests that, in addition to Winfrey's influence, the Frey story "had legs" because it made available a powerful form of cultural intervention. Cultural critics of all stripes latched on to the controversy and used it as a mechanism by which to criticize American culture writ large. In this, they were simply appropriating what was, by 2006, at least a century-old rhetorical technique. It is almost as if the James Frey pundits had surveyed twentieth-century American history, identified confessional hermeneutics as a powerful form of intervening into matters of sexuality, class, race, violence, religion, and democracy, and turned the same venerable weapon on confessional culture itself.

Conclusion: Confessional Anxiety and Confessional Crises

The entries of Kakutani, Yardley, Siklos, and Karr into the Frey debate are indicative of a widespread confessional anxiety. Each of these writers suggests that as the once-distinct line between fact and fiction blurs, so, too, does the public's capacity to demarcate precisely which texts count as confessions. According to Yardley, the market is so saturated with "confessions" that "it is just about impossible to separate what little wheat there may be from the vast ocean of chaff."[39] It is precisely this inability to make generic distinctions that produced the nervousness, confusion, uncertainty, irritation, unreliability, ambivalence, and anxiety I documented in the introduction. This anxiety may well be the reason the Frey controversy burned so brightly. When Frey relabeled his book, he touched on a well-prepared cultural nerve.

Confessional Crises and Cultural Politics in Twentieth-Century America bears witness to just how well prepared that nerve was. Confessional anxiety—by virtually every account the predominant feature of our confessional age—is the result of a long history of confessional crises. Since Macfadden deployed confessions to fight Comstock, politically minded authors have been doing exactly what Macfadden (and Frey) did: reclassifying texts to cash in on the promise of political gain. There is no question it has been an effective strategy; *Confessional Crises and Cultural Politics in Twentieth-Century America* has recorded how the strategy found purchase in some of America's most intractable cultural issues. That the act of relabeling a text a confession has influenced debates over sexuality, class, race, violence, religion, and democracy should not suggest that these issues share some structural alliance with the genre of confession or that they are somehow uniquely liable to this sort of intervention. Quite the contrary, the strategy's influence in these arenas should simply suggest that confessional hermeneutics is an incredibly powerful form of rhetorical argument. We might look to any major issue of twentieth-century America—urbanism, industrialism, or foreign policy, just to name a few—and expect to find therein the influence of confessional hermeneutics.

Beyond matters of effectiveness, however, there is no question that the twentieth-century habit of reclassifying texts as confessions has produced the twenty-first century's confessional anxiety. It is certainly true, as Kakutani and her colleagues have made abundantly clear, that the arbitrary reclassification of texts has blurred the line between fact and fiction. Indeed, in each of the confessional crises examined here, the truth or falsity of the texts in question was figured always and only with recourse to political needs. *Look*'s account of the Till murder, Styron's novel, Swaggart's sermon, and Starr's report: all these were labeled confessions simply because such a classification was required by pressing political issues.

Frey's critics are wrong, however, on the solution to this anxiety. Working on the assumption that confessional anxiety is a novel phenomenon, a product of postmodernity, they call for a return to a time when everyone knew just what a confession was. Mary Karr, for example, called would-be memoirists to cling ("like a marsupial") to the "outdated" notion of "objective truth." While she recognized that perfect objectivity was impossible, she nonetheless heralded truth as the ultimate antidote to confessional anxiety.[40] *Confessional Crises and Cultural Politics in Twentieth-Century America*, however, suggests that the blurred line between fact and fiction is not a French import. Long before the advent of postmodernity, the line was blurred by politically motivated actors who recognized the personal gain to be had by reclassifying texts. Given this, if there is a balm to our confessional anxiety, it may well lie in a new understanding of what precisely the confession has become. To the extent we recognize that confession has become a mode of ideological intervention, we will recognize also the powerful incentives driving activists to play fast and loose with the boundaries of the genre, and we will cease to be surprised when the line between fact and fiction disappears altogether. From the perspective of *Confessional Crises and Cultural Politics in Twentieth-Century America*, in other words, James Frey was in the cards from the get-go. Of course he reclassified his book; given the long history of political gains to be had by doing so, who among us wouldn't?

NOTES

Introduction

1. Mendelsohn, "But Enough About Me."
2. It is now commonplace to claim that we live in a "confessional culture." Two of the better descriptions of this culture belong to Peter Brooks and Ben Yagoda. See Brooks, *Troubling Confessions*, 140; and Yagoda, *Memoir*, 28–29. However, confessional culture's classic description—part of which is quoted in virtually every analysis of confession except this one—belongs to Michel Foucault. See *History of Sexuality*, 59.
3. Confessional crises are thus analogous to what Edward Schiappa has called "definitional ruptures." Such "ruptures," he argues, are moments in time in which particular circumstances require a people to "address the issue of how words are defined." Correspondingly, I am interrogating six moments in which the word "confession" lost it self-evident character and no longer seemed a ubiquitous, normal part of American life. Rather, in each crisis, confession itself became a widely contested practice and the subject of national debate. Schiappa, *Defining Reality*, 9.
4. Mailloux, *Reception Histories*, 54, 55.
5. McChesney, *Political Economy of Media*.
6. Brooks, *Troubling Confessions*, 11.
7. Ibid., 3.
8. Ibid., 3, 81, 87, 64. See also: "There is something inherently unstable and unreliable about the speech-act of confession, about its meaning and motives" (23).
9. Yardley, "Shelve Them Under Navel-Gazing."
10. Shields, *Reality Hunger*, 35.
11. Mendelsohn, "But Enough About Me."
12. Mailloux, *Reception Histories*, 55–56. Mailloux's work on reception history has gained wide acceptance and been used to rethink the place of cultural studies within the humanities writ large. See Cain, *Reconceptualizing American Literary/Cultural Studies*. More recently, see Goldstein and Machor, *New Directions in American Reception Study*. These demonstrate the prestigious, interdisciplinary acceptance of the critical practice to which Mailloux gave early voice and which informs my work.
13. Lazare, *On Apology*, 26, 25, 24.
14. Williams, *Culture and Society*, xix (emphasis mine).
15. Mailloux, *Reception Histories*, 77.
16. Working in an explicitly pragmatist tradition (like Mailloux), Schiappa argues, "Definitions always serve interests and advance values, and they always require the exercise of power." Schiappa, *Defining Reality*, 177. Building on Schiappa's work, Zarefsky argues, "Questions of the form, 'What is X?' are not susceptible to answer because they are overly abstracted from the world of experience in which people's own values and commitments determine what X means. The 'real nature' of X, in other words, is a matter of how X is used in communication." Zarefsky, "Definitions," 4.
17. Bauer, *Art of the Public Grovel*, 4, 89, 76, 143–45, 150.

18. Foucault, *Abnormal*, 70, 82, 84, 85, 171; and *History of Sexuality*, 63–68.

19. It is difficult to overstate the importance of this distinction in Foucault's account of confession. As he put it in a 1980 lecture at Dartmouth, the modern confession "is much more concerned with thoughts than with actions. . . . So much so that the primary material for scrutiny and for the examination of the self is an area anterior to actions." Foucault, "About the Beginning of the Hermeneutics of the Self," 216–17. See also Foucault, "Writing the Self," 235; Foucault and Sennett, "Sexuality and Solitude," 6; and Foucault, *Technologies of the Self*, 30, 45.

20. For a detailed explanation of this shift in Foucault's theory of confession, see Tell, "Rhetoric and Power."

21. Mailloux, "Rhetorical Hermeneutics in Theory," 5–6. See also Mailloux, *Reception Histories*, 55–56.

22. I use the term "political economy" advisedly. In 2004 Robert McChesney wrote that political economy "addresses the nature of the relationship between media of communication systems on the one hand and the broader social structure of society on the other." Substituting "the genre of confession" for "media of communication systems," this is precisely my own methodology. McChesney, "Making a Molehill out of a Mountain," 43.

23. Brooks, *Troubling Confessions*, 9.

24. Qtd. in French, *Rebellious Slave*, 259.

25. Hicks, "Writer Challenges Brownell to Act in Till Kidnap–Murder Case."

26. Schultze, *Televangelism and American Culture*, 58.

27. Anon., "Heckler Calls Swaggart a Hypocrite."

28. No one has better championed (or documented) the capacity of ordinary citizens to engage in sophisticated literary argument than Rosa A. Eberly has. In the aptly titled *Citizen Critics*, Eberly uses the term "citizen critic" to describe "a person who produces discourses of common concern from an ethos of citizen first and foremost—not as an expert or spokesperson for a workplace or as member of a club or organization." Eberly, *Citizen Critics*, 1.

29. Rich, "Truthiness 101."

Chapter 1

1. Johnston, "Great Macfadden," June 21, 1941, 9.
2. Gerbner, "Social Role of the Confession Magazine," 29.
3. Johnston, "Great Macfadden," June 21, 1941, 9.
4. Manchester, "True Stories," 27; MacMullen, "Pulps and Confessions," 99; and Fabian, "Making a Commodity of Truth," 52, 51.
5. Hatton, "True Stories," 60.
6. Bowen, "Macfadden, the Bare Torso King, and His Shoddy Sex Magazines," 3.
7. Garrett, "Another True Story," 9–11.
8. Villard, "Sex, Art, Truth, and Magazines," 389. There were some exceptions: In 1924 the American Medical Association explained *True Story* as a "so-called confession type," and the historian Frederick Lewis Allen recognized it as a confession magazine as early as 1931. However, even if *True Story* was occasionally classified as a "confession magazine" in the 1920s, such labels never bore much explanatory weight. Both the American Medical Association and Frederick Lewis Allen, for example, classify *True Story* as a confession magazine only in passing, and quickly move to more pressing characteristics. To call *True Story* a confession in the 1920s was never sufficient; some started there, but none ended there. See Anon., "Exploiting the Health Interest II," 744; and Allen, *Only Yesterday*, 87.

9. Anon., "False Hypocrites," 32; Anon., "Tin from Sin," 80; Taylor, "Physical Culture, III," 42.
10. Peterson, *Magazines in the Twentieth Century*, 258.
11. Taft, "Bernarr Macfadden," 630.
12. Mandziuk, "Confessional Discourse and Modern Desires," 175.
13. As *Scribner's* would later note, *True Story*'s early evasion of the word "confession" is particularly conspicuous when *True Story* is compared with its primary 1920s competitor, W. H. Fawcett's *True Confessions*—which, as its title suggests, differed from *True Story* because it did not "shy away from the word 'confession.'" Manchester, "True Stories," 29.
14. Heyn, *Book of True Stories*, v, vii.
15. Waugh, "Bernarr Macfadden," 85.
16. Although this story is much repeated, the best rendition belongs to Robert Ernst. See *Weakness Is a Crime*, 41–44.
17. Oursler, *True Story of Bernarr Macfadden*, 179.
18. Thus William R. Hunt: Comstock's "antics in [the] days before the event accomplished far more than Macfadden's advertisements in creating the sensation that brought the crowd out." Hunt, *Body Love*, 2. For Comstock's official title, see Waugh, "Bernarr Macfadden," 89. The phrase "vile handbills" is from Broun and Leach, *Anthony Comstock*, 237.
19. Hunt, *Body Love*, 1.
20. Waugh, "Bernarr Macfadden," 78–79.
21. Ernst, *Weakness Is a Crime*, 44; and Waugh, "Bernarr Macfadden," 91.
22. Macfadden, "Comstock, King of the Prudes," December 1905, 561–63. Also: "His distorted mind sees nothing in all the beautiful works of art, in all the superior specimens of human perfection, but the reflection of the vileness which his mentality has created" (561).
23. Foucault, *History of Sexuality*, 15–50.
24. Macfadden, "Comstock, King of the Prudes," 1906, 162.
25. Ibid., 163. The theory of Comstockery holds that it is the "hiding of all knowledge which shall enable youth to avoid evil." Macfadden, "Comstock, King of the Prudes," December 1905, 561–63.
26. Macfadden, "Comstock, King of Prudes," 1906, 163.
27. Foucault, *Discipline and Punish*, 27.
28. Waugh, "Bernarr Macfadden," 83, 81.
29. Macfadden quoted in ibid., 95.
30. Ernst, *Weakness Is a Crime*, 42.
31. Waugh, "Bernarr Macfadden," 99.
32. Welford, "Growing to Manhood in Civilized (?) Society." Because the first page of each installment identifies Welford as editor, it is cited as such. However, historians agree that John R. Coryell wrote it at the urging of Macfadden. See Ernst, *Weakness Is a Crime*, 47; Waugh, "Bernarr Macfadden," 97; and Oursler, *True Story of Bernarr Macfadden*, 190.
33. Ernst, *Weakness Is a Crime*, 47.
34. Welford, "Growing to Manhood in Civilized (?) Society," October 1906, 343.
35. Ibid., December 1906, 501, 502.
36. Ibid., March 1907, 218.
37. Ibid., December 1906, 502, 497.
38. Ibid., February 1907, 129.
39. Earle, "Brief on Behalf of Plaintiff-in-Error," 5; Ernst, *Weakness Is a Crime*, 47; Macfadden, "Is the Editor Guilty?" 363.
40. Macfadden, "Is the Editor Guilty?" 363.
41. Ibid., 364.
42. Macfadden, *Macfadden Prosecution*, 1.

43. Earle, "Brief on Behalf of Plaintiff-in-Error," 16; *Macfadden v. United States.*
44. Earle, "Brief on Behalf of Plaintiff-in-Error," 13.
45. Macfadden, "Is the Editor Guilty?" 365.
46. Ernst, *Weakness Is a Crime*, 47–48.
47. Oursler, *True Story of Bernarr Macfadden*, 213–14.
48. Anon., "Telling the Whole Truth," 66.
49. Oursler, *True Story of Bernarr Macfadden*, 214.
50. Anon., "Telling the Whole Truth," 66 (emphasis mine).
51. Oursler, *True Story of Bernarr Macfadden*, 214.
52. Ibid., 188–89.
53. Ibid., 214.
54. Anon., "Reality and Truth," 2.
55. Oursler, *True Story of Bernarr Macfadden*, 234 (emphasis mine).
56. Ibid., 233.
57. Ernst, *Weakness Is a Crime*, 49.
58. Macfadden, "Comstock, King of the Prudes," December 1905, 563.
59. Oursler, *True Story of Bernarr Macfadden*, 214.
60. Ibid., 235.
61. Garrett, "Another True Story," 10.
62. Anon., "Experience," 2.
63. Ernst, *Weakness Is a Crime*, 80.
64. See, for example, Macfadden, "Experience," 13; Macfadden, "Reared Amidst Falsehoods," 17; Macfadden, "Fortune in Prizes for *True Story*," 17.
65. Ernst, *Weakness Is a Crime*, 82.
66. Anon., "Telling the Whole Truth," 65. See also Macfadden, "Imitations of *True Story*," 25; and Macfadden, "*True Story* Imitators," 17.
67. Variations on this triple formulation are commonplace. See, for example, Anon., "Why's for the Wise," 2; "Brevity and Levity," 2; and "Have *You* Attained Success—or Missed It," 48.
68. Fabian, "Making a Commodity of Truth," 52.
69. Anon., "Don't Miss This," 2.
70. Anon., "What *Is* the *True Story* Idea?" 2.
71. Anon., "More About the *True Story* Idea," 2.
72. Anon., "Telling the Whole Truth," 158.
73. Anon., "Readers and Writers," 2.
74. Anon., "Open to Everybody," 2.
75. Mencken, "American Idealist," 125.
76. Oursler, *True Story of Bernarr Macfadden*, 219–21 (emphasis mine).
77. Gerbner, "Social Role of the Confession Magazine," 34.
78. Ibid., 33.
79. Anon., "Experience," 2.
80. Oursler, *True Story of Bernarr Macfadden*, 217.
81. Johnston, "Great Macfadden," June 28, 1941, 20.
82. Ibid.; and Oursler, *True Story of Bernarr Macfadden*, 217.
83. Macfadden and Gauvreau, *Dumbbells and Carrot Strips*, 223–24.
84. Johnston, "Great Macfadden," June 28, 1941, 91.
85. Anon., "True Stories—or Fictions," 2.
86. Kemble, *Behind the Girl on the Magazine Cover*, 19.
87. Adams, *Mr. America*, 107.
88. See, for example, Bowen, "Macfadden, the Bare Torso King, and His Shoddy Sex Magazines."
89. Macfadden, "Comstock, King of the Prudes," 1906, 163.

90. Macfadden, "Reared Amidst Falsehoods," 17.
91. Macfadden, "Ideals That Scorch the Soul," 13.
92. Macfadden, "Experience," 13.
93. Anon., "Telling the Whole Truth," 65. See also James, "Book and Life Experience," 7; Anon., "Face the Naked Truth," 13; Macfadden, "Reared Amidst Falsehoods," 17.
94. Macfadden, *True Story Magazine*," 18.
95. Ibid.
96. Oursler, *True Story of Bernarr Macfadden*, 230.
97. See, for example, Anon., "*True Story Magazine*: A Great Moral Force: A Minister Commends *True Story* and Other Readers Tell the Part It Plays in Their Lives," 66; "*True Story Magazine*: A Great Moral Force," October 1923, 64; "*True Story Magazine*: A Great Moral Force," February 1924, 12; "*True Story Magazine* a Great Moral Force"; "Making of a Million," 39; and "Page of Letters," 67.
98. "*True Story Magazine*: A Great Moral Force," October 1923, 66.
99. Macfadden, "Imitations of *True Story*," 25.
100. "Although heretofore we have never mentioned Comstock in the pages of this magazine, yet we have nevertheless fought his principles with the utmost intensity almost from the first issue of this publication." Macfadden, "Comstock, King of the Prudes," December 1905, 563.
101. On this reaction, see Ernst, *Weakness Is a Crime*, 77.
102. See Tell, "Jimmy Swaggart's Secular Confession"; and chapter 5, below.
103. Mullins, "Nudes, Prudes, and Pigmies," 28.
104. Hart, "Contemporary Scholarship in Public Address," 292.

Chapter 2

1. Stuart, "Bernarr Macfadden," 8.
2. Ernst, *Weakness Is a Crime*, 81.
3. Hunt, *Body Love*, 89, 85.
4. Marchand, *Advertising the American Dream*, 56.
5. Ibid., 54.
6. Qtd. in ibid., 71.
7. See published lists of advertisers: Anon., "Congratulations, *Good Housekeeping*!" 3; and "Luxuries of the Rich Within Their Reach," 62.
8. Anon., "No Limit to Their Wants," 55.
9. Anon., "Congratulations, *Good Housekeeping*!" 40; and "Hail Columbia," 37.
10. Anon., "Hail Columbia," 37.
11. Anon., "Luxuries of the Rich Within Their Reach," 63.
12. Anon., "No Limit to Their Wants," 54.
13. Anon., "Hail Columbia," 37.
14. Anon., *86% of America*, v.
15. Anon., *American Economic Evolution*, 16.
16. Ibid., 32–33.
17. Anon., *86% of America*, v.
18. Anon., *American Economic Evolution*, 33, 38.
19. Anon., "No Limit to Their Wants," 55.
20. Qtd. in Cohen, *Making a New Deal*, 100.
21. Qtd. in Cohen, *Consumer's Republic*, 20.
22. Ibid., 18.
23. Pells, *Radical Visions and American Dreams*, 11–12.

24. Cohen, *Making a New Deal*, 99–158; and Kim, "Confession, Control, and Consumption," 11–19.
25. Pells, *Radical Visions and American Dreams*, 21.
26. Cohen, *Making a New Deal*, 102.
27. Pells, *Radical Visions and American Dreams*, 12.
28. Anon., *American Economic Evolution*, 52.
29. Anon., "Do You Know How to Read Your Newspaper?" 40.
30. Anon., "Congratulations, *Good Housekeeping!*" 39.
31. Anon., "No Limit to Their Wants," 55.
32. Anon., "Great Experiment," 13.
33. Anon., "Congratulations, *Good Housekeeping!*" 39.
34. Anon., *American Economic Evolution*, 77.
35. Anonymous, "No Limit to Their Wants," 55.
36. Anon., *American Economic Evolution*, 36, 37.
37. Ibid., 12, 14, 8.
38. Anon., *History and Magazines*, n.p.
39. Ibid.
40. Anon., "Great Experiment," 13.
41. Anon., *American Economic Evolution*, 42–43.
42. Anon., "Turning Point," 2.
43. Anon., "Two Million," 2.
44. Anon., *History and Magazines*, n.p. See also Anon., "Do You Know How to Read Your Newspaper?" 40.
45. Anon., "Do You Know How to Read Your Newspaper?" 37.
46. Anon., *American Economic Evolution*, 51, 12, 47, 34, 78, 9, 82–83.
47. Anon., *History and Magazines*, n.p.
48. Anon., *American Economic Evolution*, 9.
49. Hatton, "True Stories," 167; and Oursler, *True Story of Bernarr Macfadden*, 213.
50. Freud, *Standard Edition*, 2:210–11.
51. Freud, *Interpretation of Dreams*, 81.
52. Anon., *American Economic Evolution*, 12.
53. Freud, *Interpretation of Dreams*, 136.
54. Allen, *Only Yesterday*, 85–87.
55. Loughery, *Other Side of Silence*, 115, 113.
56. Fishbein, *Fads and Quackery in Healing*, 350.
57. Ibid., 351.
58. Gay, *Freud Reader*, 678.
59. Freud, *Standard Edition*, 20:189.
60. Foucault, *History of Sexuality*, 59.
61. Gerbner, "Social Role of the Confession Magazine," 32, 40.
62. Mandziuk, "Confessional Discourse and Modern Desires," 181.
63. Honey, "Confession Formula and Fantasies of Empowerment," 305.
64. Macfadden, "Riches of Life," 31; "Revenge Isn't Sweet," 17; "Love of Life," 17; and "Heart That Thrills," 17.

Chapter 3

1. William Bradford Huie to Dan Mich, October 23, 1955, William Charvat Collection of American Fiction, Box 39, Folder 353c.
2. William Bradford Huie to Basil Walters, October 18, 1955, William Charvat Collection of American Fiction, Box 39, Folder 353c.

3. William Bradford Huie to Dan Mich, October 25, 1955, William Charvat Collection of American Fiction, Box 39, Folder 353c.
4. Raines, *My Soul Is Rested*, 388–89.
5. William Bradford Huie to Dan Mich, October 17, 1955, William Charvat Collection of American Fiction, Box 39, Folder 353c.
6. Huie to Mich, October 23, 1955.
7. Raines, *My Soul Is Rested*, 388.
8. Huie, interviewed by *Eyes on the Prize*.
9. Consent and Release, October 28, 1955, William Charvat Collection of American Fiction, Box 39, Folder 353.
10. William Bradford Huie to Roy Wilkins, October 12, 1955, William Charvat Collection of American Fiction, Box 39, Folder 353c.
11. Huie to Walters, October 18, 1955.
12. Huie to Mich, October 17, 1955.
13. Huie to Mich, October 25, 1955.
14. David Terry argues, "We tend to associate confession with feelings of guilt or shame." "Once Blind, Now Seeing," 213. See also Sharon Downey: in confession "one sought forgiveness for past transgressions and appealed for divine intervention in the future." "Evolution of the Rhetorical Genre of Apologia," 49.
15. Huie, *Wolf Whistle, and Other Stories*, 37, 38.
16. John L. Whitten to William Bradford Huie, November 23, 1956, William Charvat Collection of American Fiction, Box 39, Folder 353b.
17. Baldwin, *Blues for Mister Charlie*, xiv.
18. Hicks, "Writer Challenges Brownell to Act in Till Kidnap–Murder Case."
19. FBI, "Prosecutive Report of Investigation," 7, 89.
20. Ibid., 86.
21. Huie, *Wolf Whistle, and Other Stories*, 20.
22. At the time of the Till trial, Adams was the editor of the Global News Network, an agency serving the black press. Her column "Straight Ahead" appeared in more than fifty African American newspapers. See Metress, *Lynching of Emmett Till*, 214.
23. Halttunen, *Murder Most Foul*, 1–2.
24. Hicks, "Hicks Lays Careful Plans for Rapid Travel in Mississippi," 2.
25. Hicks, "Sheriff Kept Key Witness Hid in Jail During Trial."
26. Anon., "Dr. Howard to Tell of Mississippi Story."
27. Adams, *Time Bomb*, 9, 17.
28. Payne, "Mamie Bradley's Untold Story."
29. Anon., "Dr. Howard to Tell of Mississippi Story."
30. On the Baltimore speech, see Howard, "Terror Reigns in Mississippi." For a review of the lecture circuit nationwide, and for numbers on the speeches in Detroit and Chicago (and a different New York meeting), see Anon., "Lynch Case Verdict Stirs the Whole Nation." For the New York speech referred to above, see Anon., "Mass Meet." For the Cleveland speech, see Richardson, "Clevelanders Rally Behind Mother of Lynching Victim."
31. Huie, *Wolf Whistle, and Other Stories*, 32.
32. Huie to Walters, October 18, 1955.
33. Huie to Wilkins, October 12, 1955.
34. Huie to Walters, October 18, 1955.
35. Anon., "Approved Killing in Mississippi," *Chicago Defender*; and "Approved Killing in Mississippi," *Daily Corinthian*, 8.
36. Anon., "Editor's Note," *Look*, 46.
37. Hicks, "Sheriff Kept Key Witness Hid in Jail During Trial."

38. Anon., "You Are There," 1.
39. Hicks, "Sheriff Kept Key Witness Hid in Jail During Trial," 1; and "Hicks Lays Careful Plans for Rapid Travel in Mississippi," 2.
40. Adams, *Time Bomb*, 10, 6.
41. Qtd. in Anon., "Dixie Lynch Lie Is So Old It Stinks," 2.
42. Anon., "Bryant and Milam Deny Look Story," 1. See also Anon., "Milam Denies Look Article Quotes; May Sue Magazine," 1.
43. Anon., "Ask New Till Probe," *Philadelphia Afro-American*, 2.
44. Anon., "Pair Denies Till Article in Magazine," 1.
45. William Bradford Huie to James E. Mills, January 21, 1956, William Charvat Collection of American Fiction, Box 39, Folder 353d.
46. Anon., "Till Expose by Writer Shakes Dixie," 1.
47. William Bradford Huie to Jean Franklin, February 1, 1956, William Charvat Collection of American Fiction, Box 39, Folder 353d.
48. Huie to Walters, October 18, 1955.
49. Anon., "Dr. Howard to Tell of Mississippi Story," 1.
50. Anon., "'Look' Story Causes Furor," 1A.
51. Anon., "Wm. Bradford Huie Charges Milam, Bryant Killed Till," 1.
52. Anon., "Ask New Till Probe," *Philadelphia Afro-American*, 2.
53. Anon., "Suspects in Till Murder Case Will Be Retried," 4.
54. Anon., "You Are There," 1; and Roberts and Klibanoff, *Race Beat*, 93.
55. Hicks, "Writer Challenges Brownell to Act in Kidnap–Murder Case," 2.
56. Anon., "Ask New Till Probe," *Philadelphia Afro-American*, 2.
57. Anon., "NAACP Asks Mississippi to Reopen Till Murder," D1.
58. Qtd. in Anon., "Admit They're Slayers of Emmett Till," 12.
59. Anon., "'I Told the Truth,' Huie Tells Courier," 3; and "Judge Jordan Says Can Still Indict Pair on Kidnapping," 1.
60. Anon., "Suspects in Till Murder Case Will Be Retried," 4.
61. Anon., "Ask New Till Probe," *Baltimore Afro-American*, 1. This is a different version of the article than that appearing in the *Philadelphia Afro-American*. See notes 41, 50, and 56.
62. Roberts and Klibanoff, *Race Beat*, 98.
63. "Huie to Walters, October 18, 1955."
64. Consent and Release, October 28, 1955.
65. Houck and Grindy, *Emmett Till and the Mississippi Press*, 150.
66. Huie to Wilkins, October 12, 1955.
67. Huie to Mich, October 17, 1955.
68. Huie to Walters, October 18, 1955.
69. Huie to Mich, October 23, 1955.
70. Huie to Mich, October 17, 1955.
71. William Bradford Huie to Dan Mich, October 21, 1955, William Charvat Collection of American Fiction, Box 39, Folder 353c.
72. Anon., "Investigation Proceeds of Slaying of Boy in Mississippi," 1.
73. Houck and Grindy, *Emmett Till and the Mississippi Press*, 22, 35.
74. Ibid., 92.
75. Howard, "Terror Reigns in Mississippi."
76. Hicks, "Sheriff Kept Key Witness Hid in Jail During Trial," 1.
77. Adams, *Time Bomb*, 17, 19.
78. FBI, "Prosecutive Report of Investigation," 110.
79. Ibid., 90.
80. Ibid., 92–95.

81. Houck and Grindy, *Emmett Till and the Mississippi Press*, 151.
82. Monteith, "Murder of Emmett Till in the Melodramatic Imagination," 39.
83. Qtd. in FBI, "Prosecutive Report of Investigation," 16.
84. Howard, "Terror Reigns in Mississippi."
85. Qtd. in FBI, "Prosecutive Report of Investigation," 18. For the "archsegregationist" label, see Houck and Grindy, *Emmett Till and the Mississippi Press*, 126.
86. Whitaker, "Case Study in Southern Justice," 16.
87. McMillen, *Citizens' Council*, 19.
88. Ibid., vii.
89. Ibid., 11.
90. Whitaker, "Case Study in Southern Justice," 22.
91. Whitfield, *Death in the Delta*, 29.
92. FBI, "Prosecutive Report of Investigation," 18.
93. McMillen, *Citizens' Council*, 26.
94. Qtd. in Whitfield, *Death in the Delta*, 26, 27.
95. Houck and Grindy, *Emmett Till and the Mississippi Press*, 7.
96. Qtd. in ibid., 23.
97. Qtd. in Whitfield, *Death in the Delta*, 28.
98. Houck and Grindy, *Emmett Till and the Mississippi Press*, 23–30.
99. Anon., "Recent Attacks on Mississippi," 1.
100. Whitfield, *Death in the Delta*, 30.
101. FBI, "Prosecutive Report of Investigation," 17.
102. Whitfield, *Death in the Delta*, 27.
103. Houck and Grindy, *Emmett Till and the Mississippi Press*, 6.
104. Anon., "Review of 1955 in Mississippi," 1.
105. Coleman: "I assume that the NAACP wanted an acquittal for propaganda purposes, and unfortunately the jury, being stirred up as they were, proceeded to give them that propaganda." Anon., "Say Coleman Cites NAACP, Diggs for Till Case Outcome," 2.
106. Houck and Grindy, *Emmett Till and the Mississippi Press*, 60.
107. J. J. Breland to W. W. Malone, September 26, 1955, William Charvat Collection of American Fiction, Box 39, Folder 353a. See also J. J. Breland to B. B. Allen, September 26, 1955, William Charvat Collection of American Fiction, Box 39, Folder 353a.
108. J. J. Breland to Frederick Sullins [sic], October 18, 1955, William Charvat Collection of American Fiction, Box 39, Folder 346.
109. Whitfield, *Death in the Delta*, 27, 30.
110. Huie to Walters, October 18, 1955.
111. Ibid.
112. William Bradford Huie to John L. Whitten, October 30, 1956, William Charvat Collection of American Fiction, Box 39, Folder 353b.
113. Huie, "Shocking Story of Approved Murder in Mississippi," 49.
114. Houck and Grindy, *Emmett Till and the Mississippi Press*, 150.
115. Consent and Release, October 28, 1955.
116. Ethridge, "Mississippi Notebook," 2.
117. Tell, "'Shocking Story' of Emmett Till and the Politics of Public Confession."
118. Anon., "Ask New Till Probe," *Baltimore Afro-American*, 2; and Adams, *Time Bomb*, 17.
119. 1961, 1972, 1976, 1978, 1980, 1981, 1984, and 2001.
120. The list could go on. Kareem Abdul-Jabbar, Myrlie Evers, Langston Hughes, and Eldridge Cleaver are among the scores of Americans who worked to ensure the circulation of Till's story. For an almost-complete listing of the ways the story of Emmett Till has been taken up and circulated, see Metress, *Lynching of Emmett Till*.

121. Houck and Grindy, *Emmett Till and the Mississippi Press*, 5. Although the FBI announced in March 2006 that there would be no new federal charges levied, the reinvestigation has not been without consequence: in September 2005 the Senate passed the "Till Bill," creating a federal unit dedicated to the reexamination of civil rights trials. See Houck and Grindy, *Emmett Till and the Mississippi Press*, 157.
122. Qtd. in Houck and Grindy, *Emmett Till and the Mississippi Press*, 150.
123. Beito and Beito, "Why It's Unlikely the Emmett Till Murder Mystery Will Ever Be Solved."
124. Monteith, "Murder of Emmett Till in the Melodramatic Imagination," 40.
125. FBI, "Prosecutive Report of Investigation," 50, 88.
126. Houck and Grindy, *Emmett Till and the Mississippi Press*, 151.

Chapter 4

1. Although we cannot know precisely how much money Gray made from "The Confessions of Nat Turner," we do know that a Richmond publisher reprinted a second edition less than a year after the original was published in Baltimore. We know, too, that Gray sold approximately forty thousand copies of the pamphlet. It is for these reasons that Henry Tragle refers to Gray as "a man with an eye for a good thing." Tragle, *Southampton Slave Revolt of 1831*, 402–4.
2. Sokolov, "Into the Mind of Nat Turner," 3, 67.
3. Barzelay and Sussman, "William Styron on *the Confessions of Nat Turner*," 31.
4. These figures are quoted in Sokolov, "Into the Mind of Nat Turner," 65.
5. Qtd. in Tragle, *Southampton Slave Revolt of 1831*, 51.
6. French, *Rebellious Slave*, 6.
7. Joseph, *Black Power Movement*, xi.
8. Rudwick and Meier, "Black Violence in the Twentieth Century," 226.
9. Aptheker, *Nat Turner's Slave Rebellion*, iv.
10. "Editor's Note," *Negro Digest*, 30.
11. Sartre, "Wretched of the Earth," 80; and Bhabha, "Preface," xxxv.
12. Thus Harold Cruse wrote of Turner's rebellion in 1967, "These historical episodes of force and violence in Negro history have become hallowed as prototypical examples of the revolutionary potential in the Negro presence in America." Cruse, *Crisis of the Negro Intellectual*, 350. Fanon himself recognized the importance of such a strategy: "In order to retain their stamina and their revolutionary capabilities, the people also resort to retelling certain episodes in the life of the community." Fanon, *Wretched of the Earth*, 30. On the "urgent" need for an "anti-racist historiography," see Aptheker, "An Address," 105.
13. Killens, "Meaning and Measure of Black Power," 33.
14. Hamilton, "Our Nat Turner and William Styron's Creation," 74.
15. Davis, "Nat Turner," 231.
16. Clarke, "Introduction," vii.
17. West, *Letters to My Father*, 132.
18. William Styron to Philip Roth, August 19, 1964, Library of Congress Manuscript Division, Box 33, Folder 5; and Anon., *William Styron: A Portrait*. On several occasions, Styron did acknowledge that Turner was a trendy topic, but he denied being motivated by such local concerns. For example: "And the theme of a slave revolt certainly does, I think, on the surface smack of grabbing a bandwagon and climbing on, but this book has been a long time germinating and was on my mind far in advance of what we call the present Negro civil rights movement." Canzoneri and Stegner, "Interview with William Styron," 37. On other occasions, however, he seemed completely unaware of Turner's timeliness.

In a 1967 interview for *Yale Alumni Magazine*, for example, Styron opined that Turner's rebellion was forgotten "about a year" after it happened. Lewis and Woodward, "Slavery in the First Person," 34.

19. Strine, "Confessions of Nat Turner," 265. Addison Gayle, Jr., argued that Styron's Turner "reassur[ed] white Americans who had begun to believe that Malcolm X, Stokely Carmichael, and H. Rap Brown posed a threat to the maintenance of the great society." Gayle, *Black Situation*, 183.

20. "In Styron's version, Nat is portrayed as sick, ineffective, almost losing control of the insurrection as it takes place and regaining it only with the intervention of Nelson, one of his assistants." Delany, "A Psychologist Looks at *The Confessions of Nat Turner*," 12.

21. Canzoneri and Stegner, "Interview with William Styron," 39.

22. Bennett, "Nat's Last White Man," 5.

23. Qtd. in French, *Rebellious Slave*, 256.

24. Hairston, "William Styron's Nat Turner," 70.

25. Hamilton, "Our Nat Turner and William Styron's Creation," 73–74.

26. Stone, *Return of Nat Turner*, 147–48.

27. Rudwick and Meier, "Black Violence in the Twentieth Century," 225.

28. The line dividing Styron's supporters from his critics was largely racial. Although there were exceptions (James Baldwin and John Hope Franklin supported the novel, Wilfred Sheed and Herbert Aptheker did not), the racial division was so consistent that the participants in the debate self-identified as either "white critics" or "black critics."

29. Robinson, *Black Movements in America*, 36–38; and Hahn, *Nation Under Our Feet*, 55–56.

30. Fanon: "Challenging the colonial world is not a rational confrontation of viewpoints. It is not a discourse on the universal, but the impassioned claim by the colonized that their world is fundamentally different." Because "Western values"—even the value of reasonableness—are complicit with the violence of colonialism, Fanon is explicit that "dialogue" and "discussion" are out of the question as a strategy of social justice. He argues that such a strategy is characteristic of the colonized intellectual, who has "invested his aggression in his barely veiled wish to be assimilated to the colonizer's world." Moreover, it is for this reason Fanon argues that social justice requires eradicating the "superstructure" of the colonists. Fanon, *Wretched of the Earth*, 6, 22, 11.

31. Taylor, "Contentions of William Styron," 11.

32. Aptheker, "Note on History," 376.

33. Aptheker, "Truth and Nat Turner," 544.

34. West, *Letters to My Father*, 132.

35. For background on the Aptheker–Styron debate, see Shapiro, "Impact of the Aptheker Thesis."

36. Elkins, *Slavery*, 2–23.

37. Styron, "Overcome," 18.

38. Phillips, *American Negro Slavery*, 321, 328, 342, 514, 329.

39. Elkins, *Slavery*, 11.

40. Styron, "Overcome," 18.

41. Bracey, "Foreword," 3.

42. Aptheker, *American Negro Slave Revolts*, 374.

43. Styron, "Overcome," 19.

44. This is Elkins's characterization of Phillips. See Elkins, *Slavery*, 10.

45. Styron, "Overcome," 19.

46. Taylor, "Contentions of William Styron," 9, 11.

47. Genovese, "Rebelliousness and Docility in the Negro Slave," 43.

48. Elkins, *Slavery*, 17, 1.

49. Ibid., 22.

50. Ibid., 81, 82, 62. Elkins makes his point powerfully: the slave "could look to none but his master, the one man to whom the system has committed his entire being: the man upon whose will depended his food, his shelter, his sexual connections, whatever moral instruction he might be offered, whatever 'success' was possible within the system, his very security—in short, everything" (102).
51. Ibid., 82.
52. Ibid., 89, 84, 85.
53. Styron, "Overcome," 19.
54. Aptheker, "Note on History," 376.
55. Duberman, "Confessions of Nat Turner," 9.
56. Bennett, "Nat's Last White Man," 7.
57. In *The Sound and the Fury*, Faulkner writes first person sections for Benjy, Quentin, and Jason. Yet none of these is a black figure. Significantly, Dilsey's section is the only one *not* narrated in the first person. For more on the Styron–Faulkner connection, see Canzoneri and Stegner, "Interview with William Styron," 40.
58. Styron, "This Quiet Dust," 126, 137, 138.
59. Styron's critics, black and white alike, noted the Victorian prose of his Nat Turner. See Rahv, "Through the Midst of Jerusalem," 8; Sokolov, "Into the Mind of Nat Turner," 66; Thelwell, "Back with the Wind," 81; and Hairston, "William Styron's Nat Turner," 67.
60. Canzoneri and Stegner, "Interview with William Styron," 39–40.
61. Plimpton, "William Styron," BR2.
62. Lewis and Woodward, "Slavery in the First Person," 35.
63. Barzelay and Sussman, "William Styron on *The Confessions of Nat Turner*," 32, 31, 33.
64. Canzoneri and Stegner, "Interview with William Styron," 40.
65. Fanon's *Wretched of the Earth*, which according to Bhabha was spreading across American college campuses like "wildfire," devotes many pages to the fundamentally Manichaean organization of society: an oppressed "species" and an oppressor "species" that share absolutely nothing in common. See Bhabha, "Preface," xxi; and Fanon, *Wretched of the Earth*, 5, 6, 14, 43, 50.
66. Gilman, "White Standards and Negro Writing," 25.
67. William Styron to Philip Roth, January 29, 1973, Library of Congress Manuscript Division, Box 33, Folder 5.
68. Gilman, "White Standards and Negro Writing," 25, 30, 29.
69. Ibid., 30.
70. Gilman, "More on Negro Writing," 25.
71. Gilman, "Nat Turner Revisited," 23, 24.
72. Gilman, "More on Negro Writing," 37.
73. Gilman, "Nat Turner Revisited," 23.
74. Stone, *Return of Nat Turner*, 3.
75. Canzoneri and Stegner, "Interview with William Styron," 38.
76. Styron, "This Quiet Dust," 139; Taylor, "Contentions of William Styron," 13; and Lewis and Woodward, "Slavery in the First Person," 33–34.
77. Tragle, *Southampton Slave Revolt*, 401–2.
78. Styron, "This Quiet Dust," 139.
79. Lewis and Woodward, "Slavery in the First Person," 33.
80. Woodward, "Confessions of a Rebel," 25.
81. Ibid.
82. O'Connell, "Styron's Nat Turner," 373.
83. Sokolov, "Into the Mind of Nat Turner," 65, 66.
84. Hostile and racially inflected reviews appeared in black newspapers such as the *New York Amsterdam News*; alternative publications like the *Village Voice*, the *New Leader*, and *The Worker*; black journals like *Negro Digest*, *The Crisis*, and *Freedomways*; popular

magazines like *Psychology Today*, *Esquire*, and *Ebony*; and, eventually, elite publications such as the *New York Review of Books* and *The Nation*.

85. Styron, "Nat Turner Revisited."
86. French, *Rebellious Slave*, 262. The most powerful critique of *William Styron's Nat Turner* belonged to Genovese. See his "Nat Turner Case."
87. On these points, see Sussman, "Case Against William Styron's Nat Turner," 20–23; Durden, "William Styron and His Black Critics," 181–87; and Muse, "Failure of a Mission," 102–3.
88. Killens, "Confessions of Willie Styron," 36.
89. Aptheker, "Note on History," 375–76.
90. Clarke, "Introduction," ix.
91. Killens, "Confessions of Willie Styron," 42.
92. Clarke, "Introduction," ix, viii.
93. Sussman, "Case Against William Styron's Nat Turner," 22.
94. Killens, "Confessions of Willie Styron," 37.
95. Delany, "Psychologist Looks at *The Confessions of Nat Turner*," 13.
96. Harding, "Exchange on 'Nat Turner,'" 32.
97. Delany, "Psychologist Looks at *The Confessions of Nat Turner*," 11.
98. Killens, "Confessions of Willie Styron," 36, 43.
99. Clarke, "Introduction," viii.
100. Williams, "Manipulation of History and of Fact," 45, 47, 45.
101. Bennett, "Nat's Last White Man," 8, 11, 13, 15, 11, 5, 16, 12, 11, 7.
102. Ibid., 5.
103. Hairston, "William Styron's Nat Turner," 71, 67, 70, 72.
104. Ibid., 70; Hairston, "William Styron's Dilemma," 10.
105. Hairston, "William Styron's Nat Turner," 72.
106. Hairston, "William Styron's Dilemma," 8.
107. Ibid., 11, 8; Hairston, "William Styron's Nat Turner," 72.
108. Hairston, "William Styron's Dilemma," 9, 11.
109. Thelwell, "Back with the Wind," 80.
110. "The other and perhaps the most crucial question raised by these essayists [the ten black writers] is whether a white, particularly a Southern-born one, may hope to speak for a black, especially a famous militant one." Durden, "William Styron and His Black Critics," 186.
111. Killens, "Confessions of Willie Styron," 37.
112. Killens, "Confessions of Willie Styron," 36.
113. Thelwell, "Back with the Wind," 80, 81.
114. Killens, "Confessions of Willie Styron," 44.
115. Gayle, *Black Situation*, 183–84.
116. Harding, "You've Taken My Nat and Gone," 32.
117. Halttunen, *Murder Most Foul*, 1–2.
118. Foucault, *Discipline and Punish*, 92; Browne, "This Unparalleled and Inhuman Massacre," 310.
119. Hairston, "William Styron's Dilemma," 9.

Chapter 5

1. Duin, "Swaggart Admits Sin, Begs Forgiveness as He Leaves Pulpit."
2. Harris, "Swaggart Steps Down for 'Sin.'"
3. Anon., "Plea for Mercy."

4. Seaman, *Swaggart*, 341.
5. Ostling, "Now It's Jimmy's Turn," 46.
6. Schultze, *Televangelism and American Culture*, 104.
7. Giuliano, *Thrice-Born*, 107.
8. Swaggart, "Apology Sermon," 120.
9. Muro, "Jimmy Swaggart Faithful Forgive."
10. Wright, *Saints and Sinners*, 50.
11. Fontaine and Fontaine, *Jimmy Swaggart*, 66.
12. Swaggart, "Apology Sermon," 119.
13. The leak came from "Assemblies of God Officials." See Anon., "After 3 Months, Swaggart Rises Again."
14. Qtd. in Duin, "Swaggart Plays Penitence to Hilt."
15. Qtd. in Harris, "Swaggart Steps Down for 'Sin.'"
16. Some three weeks after the confession, Swaggart promised that he would "someday" provide the details of his sin. To my knowledge, this day has yet to arrive. See Anon., "Swaggart Promises His Followers That Someday He'll Specify Sin."
17. Miller, "Sinning Clerics," 7.
18. Schultze, *Televangelism and American Culture*, 85.
19. Bauer, *Art of the Public Grovel*, 144–45, 150.
20. Brooks, *Troubling Confessions*, 2, 73.
21. Thus Susan Wise Bauer, who understands the modern public confession exclusively in Christian terms, defines confession thus: "A confession is an admission of fault: I am sorry because I did wrong. I sinned." *Art of the Public Grovel*, 2.
22. Fliegelman, *Declaring Independence*, 49.
23. Darsey, *Prophetic Tradition and Radical Rhetoric in America*, 6. I intentionally borrow Darsey's language to capture the relationship between Swaggart's confession and the eighteenth-century tradition of confession. Darsey argues that radical rhetoric in America has its "primitive source" in the prophetic tradition of the Old Testament. His argument is not, of course, that American radicals were consciously thinking of the Old Testament as they composed their arguments. Darsey's argument, rather, is that even without conscious emulation, the Old Testament tradition provides the clearest theoretical resources with which these latter-day radicals may be understood. In the same way, I argue that Rousseau provides the clearest theoretical explanation for Swaggart's rhetorical choices, without claiming that Swaggart was even aware of Rousseau.
24. Anne Hartman is correct that Foucault has "dominated critical conversation so thoroughly that it is difficult to conceptualize confession in other terms." "Confession as a Cultural Form," 537.
25. Foucault, *History of Sexuality*, 21, 61. Foucault's line-going-straight theory in this regard has rightly been criticized by some of his best readers. See Macey, *Lives of Michel Foucault*, 257; and Foucault, *Power/Knowledge*, 199.
26. Hart, "Contemporary Scholarship in Public Address," 292.
27. Giuliano, *Thrice-Born*, 53–54, 56, 64.
28. Medhurst, "Filled with the Spirit," 565.
29. Harding, *Book of Jerry Falwell*, x–xi.
30. Ostling, "TV's Unholy Row," 60.
31. Ibid., 60–64.
32. Ostling, "Now It's Jimmy's Turn," 47.
33. Qtd. in Harris, "Swaggart Steps Down for 'Sin.'"
34. Harris, "Swaggart Steps Down for 'Sin.'"
35. Qtd. in Duin, "Swaggart Admits Sin, Begs Forgiveness as He Leaves Pulpit."
36. Qtd. in Anon., "Plea for Mercy."

37. Qtd. in Buursma, "Swaggart Confesses, Leaves Pulpit."
38. King, "Church Orders 2-Year Rehabilitation for Swaggart."
39. Stepp, "Church Disciplines Swaggart."
40. Qtd. in Harris, "Swaggart Steps Down for 'Sin.'"
41. Kaufmann, "Fall of Jimmy Swaggart," 35.
42. Muro, "Jimmy Swaggart Faithful Forgive."
43. Marcus, "Foe Who Also Lost Church Urges Prayers for Swaggart."
44. Swaggart, "Apology Sermon," 122–23.
45. "'What is iniquity?' . . . It is a perversity of the will, twisted away from the supreme substance, yourself, O God, and towards lower things." Augustine, *Confessions*, 7.16.22. Or as R. A. Markus puts it, "Perverse self-love, rooted in pride, is the basic disorder in the human self and the basic force disruptive in society." Markus, *Saeculum*, xviii.
46. Augustine, *Literal Meaning of Genesis*, 11.15.19.
47. Mathewes, *Theology of Public Life*, 31–32.
48. Markus, *Saeculum*, xviii.
49. On Augustine, confession, and rhetoric more generally, see Tell, "Augustine and the 'Chair of Lies'"; and Tell, "Augustinian Political Theory and Religious Discourse in Public Life."
50. Swaggart, "Apology Sermon," 119.
51. Rousseau, *Social Contract and Discourse on the Origin of Inequality*, 7.
52. Deneen, *Democratic Faith*, 2.
53. Starobinski, *Jean-Jacques Rousseau*, 18.
54. Taylor, *Sources of the Self*, 368–92.
55. Rousseau, *Confessions*, 270.
56. Starobinski, "Eloquence and Liberty," 205.
57. Rousseau, *Confessions*, 647.
58. Peters, *Speaking into the Air*, 65; and Taylor, *Secular Age*, 19.
59. Rousseau, "Essay on the Origin of Languages," 295, 306, 318.
60. Ibid., 296.
61. Ibid., 295.
62. Scott, "Rousseau and the Melodious Language of Freedom," 815.
63. Rousseau, "Essay on the Origin of Languages," 295.
64. Derrida, *Of Grammatology*, 226.
65. Rousseau, "Essay on the Origin of Languages," 297, 300, 296.
66. Ibid., 296.
67. Derrida, *Of Grammatology*, 315.
68. Rousseau, "Essay on the Origin of Languages," 300.
69. Derrida, *Of Grammatology*, 315.
70. Rousseau, "Essay on the Origin of Languages," 315.
71. Rousseau, *Emile*, 214, 345, 43.
72. Rousseau, *Confessions*, 507–8 (emphasis mine). Rousseau also praises unreflectivity in the *Second Discourse*: "I almost dare to affirm that the state of reflection is a state contrary to nature and that the man who meditates is a depraved animal." Rousseau, *First and Second Discourses*, 110.
73. Rousseau, *Confessions*, 187, 50, 201.
74. Ibid., 462 (emphasis mine).
75. Starobinski, *Jean-Jacques Rousseau*, 137.
76. Garver, "Derrida on Rousseau on Writing," 663.
77. Derrida, *Of Grammatology*, 97, 161.
78. Giuliano, *Thrice-Born*, 3.
79. Swaggart, "Apology Sermon," 119.
80. Fliegelman, *Declaring Independence*, 26–27.

81. Swaggart, "Comeback Sermon," 124 (emphasis mine).
82. Ibid., 124.
83. For example: "And to be frank and plain and honest with you I would not blame you, I do not blame you, for not sending us one dime or dollar. And I want that to sink in because I mean it from my heart." Swaggart, "Comeback Sermon," 128.
84. Ibid., 132.
85. Derrida, *Of Grammatology*, 275.
86. Rousseau, "Essay on the Origin of Languages," 300.
87. Fliegelman, *Declaring Independence*, 28.
88. Rousseau, *Confessions*, 608. See also: "It is impossible for me to introduce any order into the events of my narrative" (586). And this: "The further I advance into my narrative, the less order and sequence I am able to introduce into it" (608). Likewise Rousseau asserts that his panegyric that prefigures the *Second Discourse* must be excused from societal conventions: "If I were unfortunate enough to be guilty of some indiscreet excess in this lively effusion of my heart, I beg you to pardon it as the tender affection of a true patriot." Rousseau, *First and Second Discourses*, 90.
89. Swaggart, "Comeback Sermon," 131.
90. Medhurst, "Filled with the Spirit," 556, 566.
91. Giuliano, *Thrice-Born*, 66.
92. Ibid., 68–69.
93. KCPQ-TV, Channel 13, Tacoma, Washington, "The Jimmy Swaggart Telecast," May 24, 1987, qtd. in Peck, *Gods of Televangelism*, 1.
94. Schudson, "Why Conversation Is Not the Soul of Democracy," 298, 307.
95. Bell, *Cultural Contradictions of Capitalism*, 132, 22–34, xv.
96. Habermas, "Modernity Versus Postmodernity," 6.
97. Augustine: "I must now carry my thoughts back to the abominable things I did in those days, the sins of the flesh which defiled my soul. I do this, my God, not because I love those sins, but so that I may love you. For love of your love I shall retrace my wicked ways." *Confessions*, 2.1.1.
98. Swaggart, "Apology Sermon," 119.
99. Giuliano, *Thrice-Born*, 61.
100. Ibid., 61–62.
101. Ibid., 61.
102. Swaggart, "Apology Sermon," 122.
103. Qtd. in Wuthnow, "Religion and Television," 211.
104. Swaggart, "Apology Sermon," 123.
105. For this formulation I am indebted to both Stephen H. Browne and Ralph Ellison. Browne writes of Crispus Attucks, "The more American he becomes, seemingly, the less African American he remains." "Remembering Crispus Attucks," 121. In *Invisible Man*, Ellison's narrator wonders what it means to become "more human": "Did [it] mean that I had become less of what I was, less a Negro?" *Invisible Man*, 354.
106. Daley, "So What's a Little Forgiveness Cost?"
107. Farrell, *Norms of Rhetorical Culture*, 10–12.
108. Garsten, *Saving Persuasion*, 12. I take Garsten's term to be synonymous with Jay Fliegelman's "nonrhetorical rhetoric." See Fliegelman, *Declaring Independence*, 49.
109. Garsten, *Saving Persuasion*, 12.

Chapter 6

1. Kurtz, *Spin Cycle*, 301.
2. Shapiro, "Simply Enough for Survival."

3. Gormley, *Death of American Virtue*, 413–18.
4. Clinton, "Remarks at the White House Correspondents' Association Dinner," 713.
5. Grossman, "Sex Scandal's Other Lure."
6. Qtd. in Gormley, *Death of American Virtue*, 513.
7. Gorman, "President Regrets"; Anon., "Excerpts from Apologies by Clinton"; Anon., "Always Having to Say You're Sorry"; and "Who's Sorry Now?" Moreover, the *New York Times*' list was published prior to the well-known Prayer Breakfast confession of September 11, and each of these lists, with the exception of that from *People Weekly*, was published before Clinton's apology to the grand jury was made public on September 21.
8. A fair number of scholars also attended to the August 28 Massachusetts confession, but this text was consistently dismissed as a "run-up" to the September 11 speech. See, for example, Bauer, *Art of the Public Grovel*, 158; Koesten and Rowland, "Rhetoric of Atonement"; and Lee and Barton, "Clinton's Rhetoric of Contrition."
9. Lee and Barton, "Clinton's Rhetoric of Contrition," 233.
10. Qtd. in Gormley, *Death of American Virtue*, 672.
11. On the existence and contours of such a tradition, see Morone, *Hellfire Nation*.
12. Foucault, *History of Sexuality*, 59.
13. Clinton, "Address to the Nation on Testimony Before the Independent Counsel's Grand Jury," 1638.
14. McGrory, "Enough of Starr's Smut"; and Hogan, "Public Opinion and Journalistic Voyeurism."
15. Toobin, *Vast Conspiracy*, 320.
16. Clinton, "Remarks at a Breakfast with Religious Leaders," 1763.
17. Anon., "Shame at the White House."
18. Qtd. in Rogers and Cummings, "Top Democrats in Congress Want Clinton to Stop Legalisms and Just 'Talk Straight.'"
19. Glaberson, "Legal Gamesmanship May Take Toll."
20. Purdum, "Starr's Report Paints a Many-Sided Portrait."
21. Brodie, "Too Little, Too Late, Say Media"; and Toobin, *Vast Conspiracy*, 320.
22. Qtd. in Lee and Barton, "Clinton's Rhetoric of Contrition," 226.
23. Simons, "Dilemma-Centered Analysis of Clinton's August 17th Apologia," 445.
24. Blaney and Benoit, *Clinton Scandals and the Politics of Image Restoration*, 102.
25. As Lee and Barton explained, "Phrasing that puts the speaker in the best light . . . [is] hostile to the purposes of the sacrament." "Clinton's Rhetoric of Contrition," 225.
26. Watanabe, "Religions Reflect Different Points on Moral Compass," A16.
27. Lee and Barton, "Clinton's Rhetoric of Contrition," 219.
28. Clinton, "Address to the Nation on Testimony Before the Independent Counsel's Grand Jury," 1638.
29. Toobin, *Vast Conspiracy*, 320.
30. Ibid.
31. Clinton and Clinton, "Governor and Mrs. Bill Clinton Discuss Adultery."
32. Didion, "Clinton Agonistes," 16–23.
33. Office of the Independent Counsel, "Referral to the United States House of Representatives," 3:460.
34. Ibid., 3:460–61.
35. Kendall et al., "Preliminary Memorandum," § III.
36. Kendall et al., "Submission by Counsel for President Clinton to the Committee on the Judiciary of the United States House of Representatives," § II.C. Thus Todd S. Purdum in the *New York Times*: "Yet nowhere in the 4 hours and 3 minutes of his ordeal in the Map Room on the afternoon of Aug. 17 did Mr. Clinton display any emotion rawer than the anger he unleashed in his televised speech to the nation that night. Instead, in

muted and mournful tones in supposedly secret testimony that he made clear he knew would become public, Mr. Clinton actually said, 'I'm sorry,' for misleading his senior aides about his relationship with Monica S. Lewinsky—two words that it took him 18 more days to utter in public." See "Staring Straight Into Camera, President Reveals Many Sides."

37. Toobin, *Vast Conspiracy*, 312.
38. Office of the Independent Counsel, "Referral to the United States House of Representatives," 3:461.
39. Qtd. in Drinkard, "From Talk Shows to Polls."
40. Office of the Independent Counsel, "Referral to the United States House of Representatives," 3:461.
41. Ibid., 3:561.
42. Kendall et al., "Initial Response to Referral of Office of Independent Counsel," § Allegation #1.
43. Kendall et al., "Submission by Counsel for President Clinton to the Committee on the Judiciary of the United States House of Representatives," § Introduction.
44. Edwards and Totenberg, "Reaction to Video Tape."
45. The formal construction of the statement bears witness to the allegiance of confession and legal argument. Sentence 1 acknowledges wrongdoing; sentence 2 makes a legal argument based on the stipulated definition of "sexual relations"; sentence 3 argues that the inappropriate encounters ended at Clinton's own insistence; sentence 4 acknowledges inappropriate "sexual banter"; and sentences 5 and 6 express regret and accept responsibility. The sentences flow seamlessly into one another without conjunctions, explanations, or elaborations; this paratactical arrangement suggests the perfect complementarity of confession and legal argument. See Office of the Independent Counsel, "Referral to the United States House of Representatives," 3:460–61.
46. Office of the Independent Counsel, "Referral to the United States House of Representatives," 3:551.
47. United States House of Representatives, "Trial Memorandum of the United States House of Representatives," § Article I: False and Misleading Statements, Reason for the Falsity.
48. Ibid., § Introduction.
49. Office of the Independent Counsel, "Referral to the United States House of Representatives," 3:555.
50. Wisenberg even paternalistically reminded Clinton of what it meant that he took an oath! Office of the Independent Counsel, "Referral to the United States House of Representatives" 3:522. As Gormley makes clear, Wisenberg was the leading hawk in the OIC and, to a far greater extent than Starr, the prosecutor whose resolve did the most to turn the investigation into an inquisition. Gormley, *Death of American Virtue*, 456, 549.
51. Office of the Independent Counsel, "Referral to the United States House of Representatives," 3:528.
52. Gormley, *Death of American Virtue*, 539–40.
53. Harris, "Playing Many Roles, Assuredly."
54. Shales, "Only Show in Town."
55. Pressley, "'Crucible' Is Full of Heat, Suspense."
56. O'Brien, "How Cruel."
57. Nelson, "Not Very Grand Inquisitor," 10.
58. Caryn, "Clinton's Role of a Lifetime Breaks Cinema's Rules."
59. Fineman, "Enough Already."
60. Anon., "Starr Findings."
61. Shapiro, "It's Time to Say That Enough Is Enough."

62. Qtd. in Didion, "Clinton Agonistes," 16.
63. Bennett, *Death of Outrage*, 42.
64. For the complete text of the Shrum draft, see Toobin, *Vast Conspiracy*, 311.
65. Gormley, *Death of American Virtue*, 557.
66. Toobin, *Vast Conspiracy*, 311, 318.
67. Gormley, *Death of American Virtue*, 553.
68. Qtd. in Toobin, *Vast Conspiracy*, 317.
69. Clinton, "Address to the Nation on Testimony Before the Independent Counsel's Grand Jury," 1638.
70. Gormley, *Death of American Virtue*, 553.
71. Clinton, "Address to the Nation on Testimony Before the Independent Counsel's Grand Jury," 1638.
72. Ibid.
73. Ibid., 1638–39.
74. Clinton, "Remarks at a Breakfast with Religious Leaders," 1762–63.
75. Harris, "For Clinton, a Day to Atone but Not Retreat."
76. Coles, "Nation Face-to-Face with 'Yuck Factor.'"
77. Blaney and Benoit, *Clinton Scandals and the Politics of Image Restoration*, 104.
78. Harris, "For Clinton, a Day to Atone but Not Retreat."
79. Bennet, "Tearful Clinton Tells Group of Clerics, 'I Have Sinned.'"
80. Office of the Independent Counsel, "Referral to the United States House of Representatives," vol. 1, § Grounds, VI.B, Summary of the President's Grand Jury Testimony.
81. Ibid., vol. 1, § Grounds, I.A.6.
82. Dowd, "Wizard of Is."
83. Duffy, "Clinton's Days of Shame."
84. Winerip, "Starr Report Recalls Outlook of a Preacher in Rural Texas."
85. Anon., "Test of Faith."
86. Kendall et al., "Initial Response to Referral of Office of Independent Counsel," § Introduction.
87. Kendall et al., "Preliminary Memorandum of the President of the United States Concerning Referral of the Office of the Independent Counsel," § Executive Summary.
88. Office of the Independent Counsel, "Referral to the United States House of Representatives," vol. 1, § Introduction, Significance of the Evidence of Wrongdoing.
89. Ibid., vol. 1, § Introduction, The Contents of the Referral.
90. Ibid., vol. 1, § Narrative, I.C.2.
91. Ibid., vol. 1, § Grounds I.A.2, Monica Lewinsky's Testimony.
92. Ibid.
93. Thus this account in *Time*: "As numbing and repetitive as any porn, the narrative is clinical and sad, a recitation of furtive gropings and panicky zipping-ups between two profoundly needy people, one of whom happened to be the leader of the free world. While Clinton's lawyers thunder that the endless tawdry details serve no purpose but to 'humiliate the President and force him from office,' Starr argues that Clinton himself made them necessary. Starr's office had originally planned to confine the seamier material to a secret sex appendix, a Starr ally told TIME. But because the President lied so long and hard, the report maintains, Starr had no choice but to include the particulars that proved that, despite Clinton's parsing of the term and even by the tortuous definition used in the Paula Jones deposition, Clinton and Lewinsky had sex, and Clinton lied to cover it up." Pooley et al., "High Crimes?" 42.
94. Wood, "Madame Lewinsky," 16.
95. Greenblatt, "Story Told with Evil Intent," A31.

96. Miller, "Salem Revisited," A31.
97. Kirn, "Papa Bill, Mama Linda, Baby Monica," 26.
98. Bywater, "Come on Down, Mr. Starr," 46–47.
99. Sullivan, "Going Down Screaming," 48.
100. Qtd. in Rabinowitz, "Taste—de gustibus."
101. Alter, "Shaming the Shameless," 47; and Klaidman and Thomas, "Falling Starr," 35.
102. Blecher, "Shakespeare, Hawthorne, Miller, Sex-Scandal Pundits All."
103. Lewis, "To the Stake."
104. Rich, "Pig vs. Prig."
105. Shapiro, "It's Time to Say That Enough Is Enough."
106. Qtd. in Whitney, "Stupefaction in France, but Calls for Resignation in Britain."
107. Qtd. in Shapiro, "It's Time to Say That Enough Is Enough."
108. Clinton, "Remarks at a Breakfast with Religious Leaders," 1762.
109. Gormley, *Death of American Virtue*, 571–72.
110. Anon., "Shame at the White House."
111. Watanabe, "Starr Report."
112. Clinton, "Address to the Nation on Testimony Before the Independent Counsel's Grand Jury," 1638.
113. Kurtz, *Spin Cycle*, xx; Parry-Giles and Parry-Giles, *Constructing Clinton*, 2; Hogan, "Public Opinion and Journalistic Voyeurism."
114. Gormley, *Death of American Virtue*, 585.
115. Kakutani, "American Drama Replete with Ironies."
116. Germond and Witcover, "Bobbing, Weaving, and Ludicrous Semantics," 2192.
117. Blaney and Benoit, *Clinton Scandals and the Politics of Image Restoration*, 102.
118. Lee and Barton, "Clinton's Rhetoric of Contrition," 233.
119. Clinton, "Remarks at a Breakfast with Religious Leaders," 1763.
120. Qtd. in Gormley, *Death of American Virtue*, 679.
121. Kendall et al., "Trial Memorandum of President William Jefferson Clinton."

Conclusion

1. Anon., "Million Little Lies."
2. Frey, "Interview with James Frey."
3. Frey, "James Frey and the *Million Little Pieces* Controversy."
4. This is a partial list of the parsing mechanisms used by professional critics. In 1980 Walter Fisher addressed himself to the question of how academics demarcated genres. After a two-page catalog of different parsing techniques, he could conclude only that genres are demarcated "variously." See Fisher, "Genre," 295. The mechanisms have only multiplied in the intervening thirty years. For two good (and recent) summaries, see Devitt, *Writing Genres*; and Benoit, "Beyond Genre Theory."
5. Yagoda, *Memoir*, 231, 239.
6. Peretz, "James Frey's Morning After."
7. Wyatt, "Best-Selling Memoir Draws Scrutiny"; and Wyatt, "Live on 'Oprah,' a Memoirist Is Kicked out of the Book Club."
8. Qtd. in Peretz, "James Frey's Morning After."
9. On Oprah's excitement, see Frey, "The Man Who Kept Oprah Awake at Night."
10. See, in particular, Kakutani, "Bending the Truth a Million Little Ways."
11. Wyatt, "Writer Says He Made up Some Details." For Talese's public comments, see Oates, "Writing Non-fiction" (her comments follow Oates's presentation).
12. On the kinship of memoir and confession, see Shields, *Reality Hunger*, 102.

13. On the "murkiness" of memoir, see Yagoda, *Memoir*, 2.
14. Mendelsohn, "But Enough About Me."
15. Williams, "Book 'A Million Little Pieces' May Not Be a Work of Fact."
16. Heller, "Intuition."
17. The quotation is taken from Peretz, "James Frey's Morning After."
18. Keller, "Look Beyond the Fact That It's Not All Truth."
19. Peretz, "James Frey's Morning After."
20. Robertson, "False Memoir Syndrome."
21. Carr, "Oprahness Trumps Truthiness"; Dargis, "Harrowing Tales of the Deceitfulness of Hearts from a Highly Deceitful Author"; and Wyatt, "Frey Says Falsehoods Improved His Tale."
22. Potter, *Authenticity Hoax*, 139, 137.
23. Ibid., 139.
24. Brooks, *Troubling Confessions*, 4.
25. Heffernan, "Ms. Winfrey Takes a Guest to the Televised Woodshed."
26. Foucault, *History of Sexuality*, 59.
27. Anon., "On Oprah's Couch"; Kurtz, "Oprah Throws Book at Herself"; and Hutchinson, "Soap Oprah!"
28. Qtd. in Brooks, *Troubling Confessions*, 11.
29. Ibid., 69. Brooks is quoting Justice Felix Frankfurter in *Culombe v. Connecticut*.
30. Grafton, "Say Anything," 24.
31. Scarry, *Body in Pain*, 35, 36.
32. Killens, "Confessions of Willie Styron," 39–40.
33. Qtd. in Brooks, *Troubling Confessions*, 11.
34. Frey, "James Frey and the *Million Little Pieces* Controversy."
35. Kakutani, "Bending the Truth in a Million Little Ways."
36. Yardley, "Shelve Them Under Navel-Gazing."
37. Siklos, "I Cannot Tell a Lie (from an Amplification)."
38. Karr, "His So-Called Life."
39. Yardley, "Shelve Them Under Navel-Gazing."
40. Karr, "His So-Called Life."

BIBLIOGRAPHY

Adams, Mark. *Mr. America: How Muscular Bernarr Macfadden Transformed the Nation Through Sex, Salad, and the Ultimate Starvation Diet.* New York: Harper, 2009.
Adams, Olive Arnold. *Time Bomb: Mississippi Exposed and the Full Story of Emmett Till.* New York: Mississippi Regional Council of Negro Leadership, 1956.
Allen, Frederick Lewis. *Only Yesterday: An Informal History of the 1920s.* New York: HarperCollins, 2000.
Alter, Jonathan. "Shaming the Shameless." *Newsweek*, September 28, 1998.
Anonymous. "Admit They're Slayers of Emmett Till." *New York Amsterdam News*, January 14, 1956.
———. "After 3 Months, Swaggart Rises Again." *Houston Chronicle*, May 22, 1988.
———. "Always Having to Say You're Sorry." *Newsweek*, September 21, 1998.
———. *American Economic Evolution.* New York: Macfadden Publications, 1930.
———. "Approved Killing in Mississippi." *Chicago Defender*, January 14, 1956.
———. "Approved Killing in Mississippi." *Daily Corinthian*, January 11, 1956.
———. "Ask New Till Probe." *Baltimore Afro-American*, January 21, 1956.
———. "Ask New Till Probe." *Philadelphia Afro-American*, January 21, 1956.
———. "Brevity and Levity." *True Story*, August 1923.
———. "Bryant and Milam Deny Look Story." *Greenwood Commonwealth*, January 13, 1956.
———. "Congratulations, *Good Housekeeping*! But Why the Detour?" *Printer's Ink*, June 14, 1928.
———. "Dixie Lynch Lie Is So Old It Stinks." *Baltimore Afro-American*, October 1, 1955.
———. "Don't Miss This." *True Story*, May 1920.
———. "Do You Know How to Read Your Newspaper?" *Printer's Ink*, January 14, 1926.
———. "Dr. Howard to Tell of Mississippi Story." *Atlanta Daily World*, January 22, 1956.
———. "Editor's Note." *Look*, January 24, 1956.
———. "Editor's Note." *Negro Digest* 14, no. 9 (1965): 29–30.
———. *86% of America.* New York: Macfadden Publications, 1927.
———. "Excerpts from Apologies by Clinton." *New York Times*, September 11, 1998.
———. "Experience." *True Story*, June 1925.
———. "Exploiting the Health Interest II: Type of Literature on Which 'Physical Culturists' and Macfaddists Thrive." *Hygeia* 2, no. 11 (1924): 744–48.
———. "Face the Naked Truth." *True Story*, April 1922.
———. "False Hypocrites." *Time*, February 14, 1927.
———. "The Great Experiment." *Chicago Tribune*, June 11, 1929.
———. "Hail Columbia." *Printer's Ink*, December 2, 1926.
———. "Have *You* Attained Success—or Missed It?" *True Story*, September 1920.
———. "Heckler Calls Swaggart a Hypocrite." *Houston Chronicle*, April 4, 1988.
———. *History and Magazines.* New York: True Story Magazine, 1941.
———. "Investigation Proceeds of Slaying of Boy in Mississippi." *Atlanta Daily World*, September 1, 1955.

———. "'I Told the Truth,' Huie Tells Courier." *Pittsburgh Courier*, January 21, 1956.
———. "Judge Jordan Says Can Still Indict Pair on Kidnapping." *Delta Democrat-Times*, January 13, 1956.
———. "'Look' Story Causes Furor: NAACP Demands Till Case Be Reopened." *Cleveland Call and Post*, January 21, 1956.
———. "Luxuries of the Rich Within Their Reach." *Printer's Ink*, July 7, 1927.
———. "Lynch Case Verdict Stirs the Whole Nation." *Baltimore Afro-American*, October 8, 1955.
———. "The Making of a Million." *True Story*, November 1923.
———. "Mass Meet: Crowd Bitter, Sad, Sullen." *New York Amsterdam News*, October 1, 1955.
———. "Milam Denies Look Article Quotes; May Sue Magazine." *Delta Democrat-Times*, January 10, 1956.
———. "A Million Little Lies: Exposing James Frey's Fiction Addiction: The Man Who Conned Oprah." *Smoking Gun*, January 8, 2006. http://www.thesmokinggun.com/archive/0104061jamesfrey1.html.
———. "More About the *True Story* Idea." *True Story*, November 1923.
———. "NAACP Asks Mississippi to Reopen Till Murder." *Cleveland Call and Post*, January 21, 1956.
———. "No Limit to Their Wants." *Printer's Ink*, June 23, 1927.
———. "On Oprah's Couch." *New York Times*, January 27, 2006.
———. "Open to Everybody." *True Story*, January 1926.
———. "Page of Letters." *True Story*, September 1924.
———. "Pair Denies Till Article in Magazine." *Atlanta Daily World*, January 13, 1956.
———. "A Plea for Mercy: Swaggart Says He Sinned, Will Stop Preaching." *San Francisco Chronicle*, February 22, 1988.
———. "Readers and Writers." *True Story*, February 1922.
———. "Reality and Truth." *True Story*, April 1925.
———. "Recent Attacks on Mississippi." *Greenwood Commonwealth*, January 24, 1956.
———. "Review of 1955 in Mississippi." *Jackson Clarion-Ledger*, January 1, 1956.
———. "Say Coleman Cites NAACP, Diggs for Till Case Outcome." *Delta Democrat-Times*, January 12, 1956.
———. "Shame at the White House." *New York Times*, September 12, 1998.
———. "Starr Findings." *Newsweek*, October 19, 1998.
———. "Suspects in Till Murder Case Will Be Retried." *New York Amsterdam News*, January 21, 1956.
———. "Swaggart Promises His Followers That Someday He'll Specify Sin." *Houston Chronicle*, March 7, 1988.
———. "Telling the Whole Truth: In Which We Reveal the Mechanical Operation of the Great *True Story* Reading Department." *True Story*, April 1924.
———. "Test of Faith: Clinton Loyalists Are Distraught, Disgusted, and Sadly Supportive—Their Allegiance to the Man, Not the Cause Is Frayed; President's Polls Stay up—Penalize Starr for 'Piling On.'" *Wall Street Journal*, September 14, 1998.
———. "Till Expose by Writer Shakes Dixie." *Chicago Defender*, January 21, 1956.
———. "Tin from Sin." *Time*, March 25, 1957.
———. "True Stories—or Fictions." *True Story*, December 1923.
———. "*True Story Magazine*: A Great Moral Force: A Minister Commends *True Story* and Other Readers Tell the Part It Plays in Their Lives." *True Story*, September 1923.
———. "*True Story Magazine*: A Great Moral Force." *True Story*, October 1923.
———. "*True Story Magazine*: A Great Moral Force." *True Story*, February 1924.

———. "*True Story Magazine*: A Great Moral Force." *True Story*, April 1924.
———. "The Turning Point." *True Story*, December 1924.
———. "Two Million." *True Story*, May 1924.
———. "What *Is* the *True Story* Idea?" *True Story*, September 1922.
———. "Who's Sorry Now?" *People Weekly*, September 28, 1998.
———. "Why's for the Wise." *True Story*, October 1920.
———. *William Styron: A Portrait*. Films for the Humanities. 1982.
———. "Wm. Bradford Huie Charges Milam, Bryant Killed Till: No Others Implicated, He Says in Magazine Expose." *Chicago Defender*, January 14, 1956.
———. "You Are There." *Baltimore Afro-American*, September 24, 1955.
Aptheker, Herbert. "An Address." *Journal of Negro History* 57, no. 1 (1972): 99–105.
———. *American Negro Slave Revolts: On Nat Turner, Denmark Vessey, Gabriel, and Others*. New York: Columbia University Press, 1993.
———. *Nat Turner's Slave Rebellion: Together with the Full Text of the So-Called "Confessions" of Nat Turner Made in Prison in 1831*. New York: Humanities Press, 1966.
———. "A Note on History." *The Nation*, October 16, 1967.
———. "Truth and Nat Turner: An Exchange." *The Nation*, April 22, 1968.
Augustine. *Confessions*. Translated by R. S. Pine-Coffin. New York: Penguin Classics, 1961.
———. *The Literal Meaning of Genesis*. Translated by John Hammond Taylor. New York: Newman Press, 1982.
Baldwin, James. *Blues for Mister Charlie*. New York: Vintage International, 1995.
Barzelay, Douglas, and Robert Sussman. "William Styron on *The Confessions of Nat Turner*: A Yale Lit Interview." *Yale Literary Magazine* 137 (Fall 1968): 24–35.
Bauer, Susan Wise. *The Art of the Public Grovel: Sexual Sin and Public Confession in America*. Princeton: Princeton University Press, 2008.
Beito, David T., and Linda Royster Beito. "Why It's Unlikely the Emmett Till Murder Mystery Will Ever Be Solved." *History News Network: Because the Past Is the Present, and the Future Too*, April 26, 2004. http://hnn.us/articles/4853.html.
Bell, Daniel. *The Cultural Contradictions of Capitalism*. New York: Basic Books, 1996.
Bennet, James. "Tearful Clinton Tells Group of Clerics, 'I Have Sinned.'" *New York Times*, September 12, 1998.
Bennett, Lerone, Jr. "Nat's Last White Man." In *William Styron's Nat Turner: Ten Black Writers Respond*, edited by John Henrik Clarke, 3–16. Boston: Beacon Press, 1968.
Bennett, William J. *The Death of Outrage: Bill Clinton and the Assault on American Ideals*. New York: Free Press, 1998.
Benoit, William L. "Beyond Genre Theory: The Genesis of Rhetorical Action." *Communication Monographs* 67, no. 2 (2000): 178–92.
Bhabha, Homi K. "Preface." In *The Wretched of the Earth*, by Frantz Fanon. New York: Grove Press, 2004.
Blaney, Joseph R., and William L. Benoit. *The Clinton Scandals and the Politics of Image Restoration*. Westport, Conn.: Praeger, 2001.
Blecher, Mari. "Shakespeare, Hawthorne, Miller, Sex-Scandal Pundits All." *USA Today*, September 22, 1998.
Bowen, N. H. "Macfadden, the Bare Torso King, and His Shoddy Sex Magazines." *Detroit Saturday Night*, May 3, 1924.
Boyle, David. *Authenticity: Brands, Fakes, Spin, and the Lust for Real Life*. New York: HarperCollins, 2004.
Bracey, John H. "Foreword: 40th Anniversary Edition." In *American Negro Slave Revolts: On Nat Turner, Denmark Vessey, Gabriel, and Others*, by Herbert Aptheker. New York: Columbia University Press, 1993.

Brodie, Ian. "Too Little, Too Late, Say Media." *The Times*, August 19, 1998.
Brooks, Peter. *Troubling Confessions: Speaking Guilt in Law and Literature*. Chicago: University of Chicago Press, 2000.
Broun, Heywood, and Margaret Leach. *Anthony Comstock: Roundsman of the Lord*. New York: Albert and Charles Boni, 1927.
Browne, Stephen H. "Remembering Crispus Attucks: Race, Rhetoric, and the Politics of Commemoration." *Quarterly Journal of Speech* 85, no. 2 (1999): 169–87.
———. "'This Unparalleled and Inhuman Massacre': The Gothic, the Sacred, and the Meaning of Nat Turner." *Rhetoric and Public Affairs* 3, no. 3 (2000): 309–32.
Bruce, Steve. *Pray TV: Televangelism in America*. New York: Routledge, 1990.
Buursma, Bruce. "Swaggart Confesses, Leaves Pulpit—for Now." *Chicago Tribune*, February 22, 1988.
Bywater, Michael. "Come on Down, Mr. Starr." *New Statesman*, October 2, 1998.
Cain, William, ed. *Reconceptualizing American Literary/Cultural Studies: Rhetoric, History, and Politics in the Humanities*. New York: Garland Publishing, 1996.
Canzoneri, Robert, and Page Stegner. "An Interview with William Styron." *Per/Se* 1 (Summer 1966): 37–44.
Carr, David. "Oprahness Trumps Truthiness." *New York Times*, January 30, 2006.
Caryn, James. "Clinton's Role of a Lifetime Breaks Cinema's Rules." *New York Times*, September 22, 1998.
Clarke, John Henrik. "Introduction." In *William Styron's Nat Turner: Ten Black Writers Respond*, edited by John Henrik Clarke, vii–x. Boston: Beacon Press, 1968.
Clinton, William J. "Address to the Nation on Testimony Before the Independent Counsel's Grand Jury." *Weekly Compilation of Presidential Documents* 34, no. 34 (1998): 1638–39.
———. "Remarks at a Breakfast with Religious Leaders." *Weekly Compilation of Presidential Documents* 34, no. 37 (1998): 1762–63.
———. "Remarks at the White House Correspondents' Association Dinner." *Weekly Compilation of Presidential Documents* 34, no. 18 (1998): 713–15.
Clinton, William J., and Hillary Clinton. "Governor and Mrs. Bill Clinton Discuss Adultery." *60 Minutes*, NBC, January 26, 1992. http://lexisnexis.com/.
Cohen, Lizabeth. *A Consumer's Republic: The Politics of Mass Consumption in Postwar America*. New York: Knopf, 2003.
———. *Making a New Deal: Industrial Workers in Chicago, 1919–1939*. Cambridge: Cambridge University Press, 1990.
Coles, Joanna. "Nation Face-to-Face with 'Yuck Factor.'" *The Times*, September 12, 1998.
Cruse, Harold. *The Crisis of the Negro Intellectual*. New York: William Morrow, 1967.
Daley, Steve. "So What's a Little Forgiveness Cost?" *Chicago Tribune*, February 25, 1988.
Dargis, Manohla. "Harrowing Tales of the Deceitfulness of Hearts from a Highly Deceitful Author." *New York Times*, March 10, 2006.
Darsey, James. *The Prophetic Tradition and Radical Rhetoric in America*. New York: New York University Press, 1997.
Davis, Ossie. "Nat Turner: Hero Reclaimed." *Freedomways* 8, no. 3 (1968): 230–32.
Delany, Lloyd Tom. "A Psychologist Looks at *The Confessions of Nat Turner*." *Psychology Today*, January 1968.
Deneen, Patrick J. *Democratic Faith*. Princeton: Princeton University Press, 2005.
Derrida, Jacques. *Of Grammatology*. Translated by Gayatri Chakravorty Spivak. Baltimore: Johns Hopkins University Press, 1976.
Devitt, Amy. *Writing Genres*. Carbondale: Southern Illinois University Press, 2004.
Diamond, Suzanne. *Compelling Confessions: The Politics of Personal Disclosure*. Madison: Fairleigh Dickinson University Press, 2010.

Didion, Joan. "Clinton Agonistes." *New York Review of Books*, October 22, 1998.
Dowd, Maureen. "The Wizard of Is." *New York Times*, September 16, 1998.
Downey, Sharon. "The Evolution of the Rhetorical Genre of Apologia." *Western Journal of Communication* 57 (Winter 1993): 42–64.
Drinkard, Jim. "From Talk Shows to Polls: Calls for Compromise Starr's Allegations Not Seen as Knockout Punch to Presidency." *USA Today*, September 14, 1998.
Duberman, Martin. "The Confessions of Nat Turner: A Novel by William Styron." *Village Voice*, December 14, 1967.
Duffy, Brian. "Clinton's Days of Shame: Crisis in the White House." *U.S. News and World Report*, September 21, 1998.
Duin, Julia. "Swaggart Admits Sin, Begs Forgiveness as He Leaves Pulpit." *Houston Chronicle*, February 22, 1988.
———. "Swaggart Plays Penitence to Hilt." *Houston Chronicle*, February 27, 1988.
Durden, Robert F. "William Styron and His Black Critics." *South Atlantic Quarterly* 68 (1969): 181–87.
Earle, Henry M. "Brief on Behalf of Plaintiff-in-Error, Bernarr Macfadden." In *The Macfadden Prosecution: A Curious Story of Wrong and Oppression Under the Postal Laws*. New York: Macfadden Publications, 1908.
Eberly, Rosa A. *Citizen Critics: Literary Public Spheres*. Urbana: University of Illinois Press, 2000.
Edwards, Bob, and Nina Totenberg. "Reaction to Video Tape." *Morning Edition*, NPR, September 22, 1998. http://lexisnexis.com/.
Elkins, Stanley M. *Slavery: A Problem in American Institutional and Intellectual Life*. Chicago: the University of Chicago Press, 1967.
Ellison, Ralph. *Invisible Man*. New York: Vintage International, 1980.
Ernst, Robert. *Weakness Is a Crime: The Life of Bernarr Macfadden*. Syracuse: Syracuse University Press, 1991.
Ethridge, Tom. "Mississippi Notebook." *Jackson Clarion-Ledger*, January 19, 1956.
Fabian, Ann. "Making a Commodity of Truth: Speculations on the Career of Bernarr Macfadden." *American Literary History* 5, no. 1 (1993): 51–76.
Fanon, Frantz. *The Wretched of the Earth*. Translated by Richard Philcox. New York: Grove Press, 2004.
Farrell, Thomas B. *Norms of Rhetorical Culture*. New Haven: Yale University Press, 1993.
FBI. "Prosecutive Report of Investigation Concerning [the Murder of Emmett Till]." 2006. http://vault.fbi.gov/Emmett%20Till%20/.
Fineman, Howard. "Enough Already." *Newsweek*, October 5, 1998.
Fishbein, Morris. *Fads and Quackery in Healing: An Analysis of the Foibles of the Healing Cults, with Essays on Various Other Peculiar Notions in the Health Field*. New York: Blue Ribbon Books, 1932.
Fisher, Walter R. "Genre: Concepts and Applications in Rhetorical Criticism." *Western Journal of Speech Communication* 44 (Fall 1980): 288–99.
Fliegelman, Jay. *Declaring Independence: Jefferson, Natural Language, and the Culture of Performance*. Stanford: Stanford University Press, 1993.
Fontaine, Charles R., and Lynda K. Fontaine. *Jimmy Swaggart: To Obey God Rather Than Men*. Crockett, Tex.: Kerusso Company, 1989.
Foucault, Michel. *Abnormal: Lectures at the Collège de France, 1974–1975*. Edited by Arnold I. Davidson. Translated by Graham Burchell. New York: Picador Press, 2003.
———. "About the Beginning of the Hermeneutics of the Self: Two Lectures at Dartmouth." *Political Theory* 21, no. 2 (1993): 198–227.
———. *Discipline and Punish: The Birth of the Prison*. Translated by Alan Sheridan. New York: Vintage Books, 1995.

———. *An Introduction.* Vol. 1, *The History of Sexuality.* Translated by Robert Hurley. New York: Vintage Books, 1990.

———. *Power/Knowledge: Selected Interviews and Other Writings, 1972–1977.* Edited by Colin Gordon. New York: Pantheon Books, 1980.

———. *Technologies of the Self: A Seminar with Michel Foucault.* Edited by L. H. Martin, H. Gutman, and P. H. Hutton. Amherst: University of Massachusetts Press, 1988.

———. "Writing the Self." In *Foucault and His Interlocutor*, edited by A. I. Davidson, 234–48. Chicago: University of Chicago Press, 1997.

Foucault, Michel, and Richard Sennett. "Sexuality and Solitude." *London Review of Books*, May 21, 1981.

French, Scot. *The Rebellious Slave: Nat Turner in American Memory.* Boston: Houghton Mifflin, 2004.

Freud, Sigmund. *The Interpretation of Dreams.* Translated by Joyce Crick. Oxford: Oxford University Press, 2008.

———. *The Standard Edition of the Complete Psychological Works of Sigmund Freud.* 24 vols. Edited and translated by James Strachey, with Anna Freud. London: Hogarth Press and the Institute of Psychoanalysis, 1976.

Frey, James. "Interview with James Frey." *Larry King Live*, CNN, January 11, 2006. http://transcripts.cnn.com/TRANSCRIPTS/0601/11/lkl.01.html.

———. "James Frey and the *Million Little Pieces* Controversy." *Oprah Winfrey Show*, January 26, 2006. http://www.lexisnexis.com/.

———. "The Man Who Kept Oprah Awake at Night: *A Million Little Pieces*." *Oprah Winfrey Show*, October 26, 2005. http://www.lexisnexis.com/.

Garrett, Oliver H. P. "Another True Story." *New Yorker*, September 19, 1925.

Garsten, Bryan. *Saving Persuasion: A Defense of Rhetoric and Judgment.* Cambridge: Harvard University Press, 2006.

Garver, Newton. "Derrida on Rousseau on Writing." *Journal of Philosophy* 77, no. 11 (1977): 663–73.

Gay, Peter, ed. *The Freud Reader.* New York: Norton, 1995.

Gayle, Addison, Jr. *The Black Situation.* New York: Horizon Press, 1970.

Genovese, Eugene D. "The Nat Turner Case." *New York Review of Books*, September 12, 1968.

———. "Rebelliousness and Docility in the Negro Slave: A Critique of the Elkins Thesis." In *The Debate over Slavery: Stanley Elkins and His Critics*, edited by Ann J. Lane, 43–74. Urbana: University of Illinois Press, 1971.

Gerbner, George. "The Social Role of the Confession Magazine." *Social Problems* 6, no. 1 (1958): 29–40.

Germond, Jack W., and Jules Witcover. "Bobbing, Weaving, and Ludicrous Semantics." *National Journal*, September 19, 1998.

Gilman, Richard. "More on Negro Writing." *New Republic*, April 13, 1968.

———. "Nat Turner Revisited." *New Republic*, April 27, 1968.

———. "White Standards and Negro Writing." *New Republic*, March 9, 1968.

Giuliano, Michael James. *Thrice-Born: The Rhetorical Comeback of Jimmy Swaggart.* Macon: Mercer University Press, 1999.

Glaberson, William. "Legal Gamesmanship May Take Toll." *New York Times*, September 24, 1998.

Goldstein, Philip, and James L. Machor, eds. *New Directions in American Reception Study.* Oxford: Oxford University Press, 2008.

Gorman, Siobhan. "The President Regrets." *National Journal*, September 14, 1998.

Gormley, Ken. *The Death of American Virtue: Clinton vs. Starr.* New York: Crown, 2010.

Grafton, Anthony. "Say Anything." *New Republic*, November 5, 2007.

Greenblatt, Stephen. "A Story Told with Evil Intent." *New York Times*, September 22, 1998.
Grossman, Cathy Lynn. "Sex Scandal's Other Lure: Call to Repentance." *USA Today*, September 21, 1998.
Habermas, Jurgen. "Modernity Versus Postmodernity." *New German Critique* 22 (Winter 1981): 3–14.
Hahn, Steven. *A Nation Under Our Feet: Black Political Struggles in the Rural South from Slavery to the Great Migration.* Cambridge: Harvard University Press, 2003.
Hairston, Loyle. "William Styron's Dilemma: Nat Turner in the Rogue's Gallery." *Freedomways* 8, no. 1 (1968): 7–11.
———. "William Styron's Nat Turner: Rogue-Nigger." In *William Styron's Nat Turner: Ten Black Writers Respond*, edited by John Henrik Clarke, 66–72. Boston: Beacon Press, 1968.
Halttunen, Karen. *Murder Most Foul: The Killer and American Gothic Imagination.* Cambridge: Harvard University Press, 1998.
Hamilton, Charles V. "Our Nat Turner and William Styron's Creation." In *William Styron's Nat Turner: Ten Black Writers Respond*, edited by John Henrik Clarke, 73–78. Boston: Beacon Press, 1968.
Harding, Susan Friend. *The Book of Jerry Falwell: Fundamentalist Language and Politics.* Princeton: Princeton University Press, 2000.
Harding, Vincent. "An Exchange on 'Nat Turner.'" *New York Review of Books*, November 7, 1968.
———. "You've Taken My Nat and Gone." In *William Styron's Nat Turner: Ten Black Writers Respond*, edited by John Henrik Clarke, 23–33. Boston: Beacon Press, 1968.
Harris, Art. "Swaggart Steps Down for 'Sin'; Evangelist's Fall Is Latest Casualty in a Year of Scandal." *Washington Post*, February 22, 1988.
Harris, John F. "For Clinton, a Day to Atone but Not Retreat; at Prayer Breakfast, President Apologizes—and Pledges Legal Defense." *Washington Post*, September 12, 1998.
———. "Playing Many Roles, Assuredly." *Washington Post*, September 2, 1998.
Hart, Roderick P. "Contemporary Scholarship in Public Address: A Research Editorial." *Western Journal of Speech Communication* 50 (Summer 1986): 283–95.
Hartman, Anne. "Confession as a Cultural Form." *Victorian Studies* 4 (Summer 2005): 535–56.
Hatton, Jacqueline A. "True Stories: Working-Class Mythology, American Confessional Culture, and *True Story Magazine*." Ph.D. diss., Cornell University, 1997.
Heffernan, Virginia. "Ms. Winfrey Takes a Guest to the Televised Woodshed." *New York Times*, January 27, 2006.
Heller, Karen. "Intuition: Letting It All out, No Matter How Sorry." *Philadelphia Inquirer*, February 5, 2006.
———. "Look Beyond the Fact That It's Not All Truth." *The Record*, February 7, 2006.
Heyn, Ernest V., ed. *The Book of True Stories.* Garden City, N.Y.: Blue Ribbon Books, 1948.
Hicks, James L. "Hicks Lays Careful Plans for Rapid Travel in Mississippi." *Baltimore Afro-American*, September 24, 1955.
———. "Sheriff Kept Key Witness Hid in Jail During Trial." *Cleveland Call and Post*, October 8, 1955.
———. "Writer Challenges Brownell to Act in Till Kidnap–Murder Case." *The Afro-American*, January 21, 1956.
Hogan, J. Michael. "Public Opinion and Journalistic Voyeurism: The Lesson of the Clinton Apology." *Journal of American Communication* 2, no. 2 (1999). http://www.ac-journal.org/journal/vol2/Iss2/editorials/hogan/index.html.
Honey, Maureen. "The Confession Formula and Fantasies of Empowerment." *Women's Studies* 10, no. 3 (1984): 303–20.

Houck, Davis W., and Mathew A. Grindy. *Emmett Till and the Mississippi Press.* Jackson: University Press of Mississippi, 2008.

Howard, T. R. "Terror Reigns in Mississippi: The Address of Dr. T. R. Howard." *Baltimore Afro-American*, October 8, 1955.

Huie, William Bradford. Interviewed by *Eyes on the Prize: America's Civil Rights Years (1954–1965)*. Washington University Libraries, Film and Media Archive, Henry Hampton Collection, August 1979. http://digital.wustl.edu/e/eop/eopweb/hui0015.1034.050williambradfordhuie.html.

———. "The Shocking Story of Approved Murder in Mississippi." *Look*, January 1956.

———. *Wolf Whistle, and Other Stories*. New York: New American Library, 1959.

Hunt, William R. *Body Love: The Amazing Career of Bernarr Macfadden.* Bowling Green: Bowling Green State University Popular Press, 1989.

Hutchinson, Bill. "Soap Oprah! 'I Feel That You Betrayed Millions of Readers,' She Tells Author." *New York Daily News*, January 27, 2006.

James, George Wharton. "Book and Life Experience." *True Story*, January 1921.

Johnston, Alva. "The Great Macfadden." *Saturday Evening Post*, June 21, 1941.

———. "The Great Macfadden." *Saturday Evening Post*, June 28, 1941.

Joseph, Peniel E., ed. *The Black Power Movement: Rethinking the Civil Rights–Black Power Era.* New York: Routledge, 2006.

Kakutani, Michiko. "An American Drama Replete with Ironies." *New York Times*, September 12, 1998.

———. "Bending the Truth a Million Little Ways." *New York Times*, January 17, 2006.

Karr, Mary. "His So-Called Life." *New York Times*, January 15, 2006.

Kaufmann, Joanne. "The Fall of Jimmy Swaggart." *People Weekly*, March 7, 1988.

Keller, Julia. "Look Beyond the Fact That It's Not All Truth." *The Record*, February 7, 2006.

Kemble, Dorothy. *Behind the Girl on the Magazine Cover.* New York: Macfadden Publications.

Kendall, David E., Nicole K. Seligman, Emmet T. Flood, Max Stier, Glen Donath, Alicia L. Marti, Charles F. C. Ruff, Cheryl Mills, and Lanny A. Breurer. "Initial Response to Referral of Office of Independent Counsel." September 12, 1998. http://clinton4.nara.gov/textonly/WH/New/html/clinton9-12.html.

———. "Preliminary Memorandum of the President of the United States Concerning Referral of Office of the Independent Counsel." September 11, 1998. http://www.gpo.gov/fdsys/pkg/CDOC-105hdoc317/pdf/CDOC-105hdoc317.pdf.

———. "Submission by Counsel for President Clinton to the Committee on the Judiciary of the United States House of Representatives." December 8, 1998. http://clinton4.nara.gov/WH/New/html/scpc.html.

———. "Trial Memorandum of President William Jefferson Clinton: In re Impeachment of William Jefferson Clinton President of the United States." January 13, 1999. http://www.law.umkc.edu/faculty/projects/ftrials/clinton/clintonbrief.html.

Killens, John Oliver. "The Confessions of Willie Styron." In *William Styron's Nat Turner: Ten Black Writers Respond*, edited by John Henrik Clarke, 34–44. Boston: Beacon Press, 1968.

———. "The Meaning and Measure of Black Power." *Negro Digest* 16, no. 1 (1966): 31–37.

Kim, Eung-Sook. "Confession, Control, and Consumption: The Working-Class Market World of *True Story Magazine*." Ph.D. diss., University of Iowa, 1992.

King, Wayne. "Church Orders 2-Year Rehabilitation for Swaggart; Nature of Incident Unclear." *New York Times*, February 23, 1988.

Kirn, Walter. "Papa Bill, Mama Linda, Baby Monica." *Time*, October 5, 1998.

Klaidman, Daniel, and Evan Thomas. "A Falling Starr." *Newsweek*, October 5, 1998.

Koesten, Joy, and Robert C. Rowland. "The Rhetoric of Atonement." *Communication Studies* 55 (Spring 2004): 68–87.
Kurtz, Howard. "Oprah Throws Book at Herself; Talk-Show Host Apologizes for Defending Falsified Tale, Then Grills 'Pieces' Author." *Washington Post*, January 27, 2006.
———. *Spin Cycle: How the White House and the Media Manipulate the News*. New York: Simon and Schuster, 1998.
Lazare, Aaron. *On Apology*. Oxford: Oxford University Press, 2003.
Lee, Ronald, and Matthew H. Barton. "Clinton's Rhetoric of Contrition." In *Images, Scandal, and Communication Strategies of the Clinton Presidency*, edited by Robert E. Denton and Rachel L. Holloway, 219–46. Westport, Conn.: Praeger, 2003.
Lewis, Anthony. "To the Stake." *New York Times*, September 22, 1998.
Lewis, R. W. B., and C. Vann Woodward. "Slavery in the First Person." *Yale Alumni Magazine*, November 1967.
Library of Congress Manuscript Division. Phillip Roth Papers. Washington, D.C.
Loughery, John. *The Other Side of Silence: Men's Lives and Gay Identities: A Twentieth-Century History*. New York: Henry Holt, 1999.
Macey, David. *The Lives of Michel Foucault: A Biography*. New York: Vintage Books, 1995.
Macfadden, Bernarr. "Comstock, King of the Prudes." *Physical Culture*, December 1905.
———. "Comstock, King of the Prudes." *Physical Culture*, 1906.
———. "Experience: Greatest of Teachers." *True Story*, October 1923.
———. "A Fortune in Prizes for *True Story*." *True Story*, December 1925.
———. "The Heart That Thrills." *True Story*, May 1925.
———. "Ideals That Scorch the Soul." *True Story*, August 1922.
———. "Imitations of *True Story*." *True Story*, May 1924.
———. "Is the Editor Guilty?" *Physical Culture*, December 1907.
———. "The Love of Life." *True Story*, August 1925.
———. *The Macfadden Prosecution: A Curious Story of Wrong and Oppression Under the Postal Laws*. 1908.
———. "Reared Amidst Falsehoods." *True Story*, July 1925.
———. "Revenge Isn't Sweet." *True Story*, September 1925.
———. "The Riches of Life." *True Story*, March 1926.
———. "*True Story* Imitators." *True Story*, March 1925.
———. "*True Story Magazine*: A Great Moral Force." *True Story*, April 1924.
Macfadden, Mary, and Emile Gauvreau. *Dumbbells and Carrot Strips*. New York: Henry Holt, 1953.
Macfadden v. United States. No. 15 Circuit Court of Appeals, Third Circuit 165 F. 51, 1908.
MacMullen, Margaret. "Pulps and Confessions." *Harper's*, June 1937.
Mailloux, Steven. *Reception Histories: Rhetoric, Pragmatism, and American Cultural Politics*. Ithaca: Cornell University Press, 1998.
———. "Rhetorical Hermeneutics in Theory." In *Reconceptualizing American Literary/Cultural Studies: Rhetoric, History, and Politics in the Humanities*, edited by William E. Cain, 3–20. New York: Garland Publishing, 1996.
Manchester, Harland. "True Stories." *Scribner's*, August 1938.
Mandziuk, Roseann M. "Confessional Discourse and Modern Desires: Power and Please in *True Story Magazine*." *Critical Studies in Media Communication* 18, no. 2 (2001): 174–93.
Marchand, Roland. *Advertising the American Dream: Making Way for Modernity, 1920–1940*. Berkeley: University of California Press, 1985.
Marcus, Frances Frank. "Foe Who Also Lost Church Urges Prayers for Swaggart." *New York Times*, February 22, 1988.

Markus, R. A. *Saeculum: History and Society in the Theology of St. Augustine.* Cambridge: Cambridge University Press, 1970.
Mathewes, Charles. *A Theology of Public Life.* Cambridge: Cambridge University Press, 2007.
McChesney, Robert. "Making a Molehill out of a Mountain: The Sad State of Political Economy in U.S. Media Studies." In *Toward a Political Economy of Culture: Capitalism and Communication in the Twenty-First Century,* edited by Andrew Calabrese and Colin Sparks, 41–64. Lanham, Md.: Rowman and Littlefield, 2004.
———. *The Political Economy of Media: Enduring Issues, Emerging Dilemmas.* New York: Monthly Review Press, 2008.
McGrory, Mary. "Enough of Starr's Smut." *Washington Post,* September 24, 1998.
McMillen, Neil R. *The Citizens' Council: Organized Resistance to the Second Reconstruction, 1954–56.* Urbana: University of Illinois Press, 1971.
Medhurst, Martin J. "Filled with the Spirit: Rhetorical Invention and the Pentecostal Tradition." *Rhetoric and Public Affairs* 7, no. 4 (2004): 555–72.
Mencken, H. L. "An American Idealist." *American Mercury,* May 1930.
Mendelsohn, Daniel. "But Enough About Me: What Does the Popularity of Memoirs Tell Us About Ourselves?" *New Yorker,* January 25, 2010.
Metress, Christopher, ed. *The Lynching of Emmett Till: A Documentary Narrative.* Charlottesville: University of Virginia Press, 2002.
Miller, Arthur. "Salem Revisited." *New York Times,* October 15, 1998.
Miller, Donald E. "Sinning Clerics: The Double Indemnity of the Self-Exalted." *Los Angeles Times,* February 26, 1988.
Monteith, Sharon. "The Murder of Emmett Till in the Melodramatic Imagination: William Bradford Huie and Vin Packer in the 1950s." In *Emmett Till in Literary Memory and Imagination,* edited by Harriet Pollack and Christopher Metress, 31–52. Baton Rouge: Louisiana State University Press, 2008.
Morone, James A. *Hellfire Nation: The Politics of Sin in American History.* New Haven: Yale University Press, 2003.
Mullins, Greg. "Nudes, Prudes, and Pigmies: The Desirability of Disavowal in *Physical Culture.*" *Discourse* 15, no. 1 (1992): 27–49.
Muro, Mark. "Jimmy Swaggart Faithful Forgive; Will They Forget?" *Boston Globe,* February 26, 1988.
Muse, Edward B. "Failure of a Mission." *Crisis,* March 1968.
Nelson, Lars-Erik. "The Not Very Grand Inquisitor." *New York Review of Books,* November 5, 1998.
Oates, Joyce Carol. "Writing Non-fiction." C-SPAN Video Library, July 28, 2007. http://www.c-spanvideo.org/program/200282-1.
O'Brien, Geoffrey. "How Cruel: The Close Up." *New York Times,* September 22, 1989.
O'Connell, Shaun. "Styron's Nat Turner." *Nation,* October 16, 1967.
Office of the Independent Counsel, "Referral to the United States House of Representatives Pursuant to Title 28, United States Code, Section 595c." September 9, 1998. http://www.gpoaccess.gov/icreport/report/2toc.htm.
Ostling, Richard N. "Now It's Jimmy's Turn." *Time,* March 1988.
———. "TV's Unholy Row." *Time,* April 6, 1987.
Oursler, Fulton. *The True Story of Bernarr Macfadden.* New York: Lewis Copeland, 1929.
Parry-Giles, Shawn J., and Trevor Parry-Giles. *Constructing Clinton: Hyperreality and Presidential Image-Making in Postmodern Politics.* New York: Peter Lang, 2002.
Payne, Ethel. "Mamie Bradley's Untold Story: Installment VIII." *Chicago Defender,* June 8, 1956.
Peck, Janice. *The Gods of Televangelism.* Cresskill, N.J.: Hampton Press, 1993.

Pells, Richard H. *Radical Visions and American Dreams: Culture and Social Thought in the Depression Years*. New York: Harper and Row, 1973.
Peretz, Evgenia. "James Frey's Morning After." *Vanity Fair*, June 2008.
Peters, John Durham. *Speaking into the Air: A History of the Idea of Communication*. Chicago: University of Chicago Press, 1999.
Peterson, Theodore. *Magazines in the Twentieth Century*. Urbana: University of Illinois Press, 1964.
Phillips, Ulrich Bonnell. *American Negro Slavery: A Survey of the Supply, Employment, and Control of Negro Labor as Determined by the Plantation Regime*. Baton Rouge: Louisiana State University Press, 1966.
Plimpton, George. "William Styron: A Shared Ordeal." *New York Times*, October 8, 1967.
Pooley, Eric, J. F. O. McAllister, Jodie Morse, Elaine Shannon, and Michael Weisskopf. "High Crimes? Or Just a Sex Cover-Up?" *Time*, September 21, 1998.
Potter, Andrew. *The Authenticity Hoax: How We Get Lost Finding Ourselves*. New York: Harper, 2010.
Pressley, Nelson. "'Crucible' Is Full of Heat, Suspense." *Washington Times*, October 1, 1998.
Purdum, Todd S. "Staring Straight into Camera, President Reveals Many Sides." *New York Times*, September 22, 1998.
———. "Starr's Report Paints a Many-Sided Portrait." *New York Times*, September 14, 1988.
Rabinowitz, Dorothy. "Taste—de gustibus: Preachers, Pundits Now Tell Us How to Forgive." *Wall Street Journal*, September 18, 1998.
Radway, Janice. *Reading the Romance: Women, Patriarchy, and Popular Literature*. Chapel Hill: University of North Carolina Press, 1991.
Rahv, Philip. "Through the Midst of Jerusalem." *New York Review of Books*, November 23, 1967.
Raines, Howell. *My Soul Is Rested: Movement Days in the Deep South Remembered*. New York: Penguin, 1983.
Rich, Frank. "Pig vs. Prig." *New York Times*, September 23, 1998.
———. "Truthiness 101: From Frey to Alito." *New York Times*, January 22, 2006.
Richardson, Marty. "Clevelanders Rally Behind Mother of Lynching Victim." *Cleveland Call and Post*, September 24, 1955.
Roberts, Gene, and Hank Klibanoff. *The Race Beat: The Press, the Civil Rights Struggle, and the Awakening of a Nation*. New York: Knopf, 2006.
Robertson, Patricia. "False Memoir Syndrome." *Globe and Mail*, February 4, 2006.
Robinson, Cedric J. *Black Movements in America*. New York: Routledge, 1997.
Rogers, David, and Jeanne Cummings. "Top Democrats in Congress Want Clinton to Stop Legalisms and Just 'Talk Straight.'" *Wall Street Journal*, September 15, 1998.
Rousseau, Jean-Jacques. *Confessions*. Translated by Angela Scholar. New York: Oxford University Press, 1999.
———. *Emile: or, On Education*. Translated by Allan Bloom. New York: Basic Books, 1979.
———. "Essay on the Origin of Languages." In *Essay on the Origin of Languages, and Other Writings Related to Music*, vol. 7, *The Collected Writings of Rousseau*, edited and translated by John T. Scott, 289–332. Hanover: University Press of New England, 1998.
———. *The First and Second Discourses*. Edited and translated by Roger D. Masters and Judith R. Masters. New York: St. Martin's Press, 1964.
———. *The Social Contract and Discourse on the Origin of Inequality*. Translated by Lester G. Crocker. New York: Washington Square Press, 1967.
Rudwick, Elliott, and August Meier. "Black Violence in the Twentieth Century: A Study in Rhetoric and Retaliation." In *Along the Color Line: Explorations in the Black*

Experience, edited by August Meier and Elliott Rudwick, 224–37. Urbana: University of Illinois Press, 1976.
Sartre, Jean-Paul. "The Wretched of the Earth: Jean-Paul Sartre's Moving Preface to a Profoundly Significant Book." *Negro Digest*, 14, no. 9 (1965): 80–88.
Scarry, Elaine. *The Body in Pain: The Making and Unmaking of the World*. Oxford: Oxford University Press, 1985.
Schiappa, Edward. *Defining Reality: Definitions and the Politics of Meaning*. Carbondale: Southern Illinois University Press, 2003.
Schudson, Michael. "Why Conversation Is Not the Soul of Democracy." *Critical Studies in Media Communication* 14, no. 4 (1997): 297–309.
Schultze, Quentin J. *Televangelism and American Culture: The Business of Popular Religion*. Grand Rapids, Mich.: Baker Book House, 1991.
Scott, John T. "Rousseau and the Melodious Language of Freedom." *Journal of Politics* 59, no. 3 (1997): 803–29.
Seaman, Anne Rowe. *Swaggart: The Unauthorized Biography of an American Evangelist*. New York: Continuum, 1999.
Shales, Tom. "The Only Show in Town." *Washington Post*, September 22, 1998.
Shapiro, Herbert. "The Impact of the Aptheker Thesis: A Retrospective View of *American Slave Revolts*." *Science and Society* 48, no. 1 (1984): 52–73.
———. "It's Time to Say That Enough Is Enough." *USA Today*, September 18, 1998.
———. "Simply Enough for Survival." *USA Today*, January 28, 1998.
Shields, David. *Reality Hunger: A Manifesto*. New York: Knopf, 2010.
Siklos, Richard. "I Cannot Tell a Lie (from an Amplification)." *New York Times*, February 5, 2006.
Simons, Herbert W. "A Dilemma-Centered Analysis of Clinton's August 17th Apologia: Implications for Rhetorical Theory and Method." *Quarterly Journal of Speech* 86, no. 4 (2000): 438–53.
Sokolov, Raymond A. "Into the Mind of Nat Turner." *Newsweek*, October 16, 1967.
Starobinski, Jean. "Eloquence and Liberty." *Journal of the History of Ideas* 38, no. 2 (1977): 195–210.
———. *Jean-Jacques Rousseau: Transparency and Obstruction*. Translated by Arthur Goldhammer. Chicago: University of Chicago Press, 1988.
Stepp, Laura Sessions. "Church Disciplines Swaggart." *Washington Post*, February 23, 1988.
Stone, Albert E. *The Return of Nat Turner: History, Literature, and Cultural Politics in Sixties America*. Athens: University of Georgia Press, 1992.
Strine, Mary S. "The Confessions of Nat Turner: Styron's 'Meditation on History' as Rhetorical Act." *Quarterly Journal of Speech* 64, no. 3 (1978): 246–66.
Stuart, John. "Bernarr Macfadden: From Pornography to Politics." *New Masses*, May 19, 1936.
Styron, William. "Nat Turner Revisited." *American Heritage*, October 1992.
———. "Overcome." *New York Review of Books*, September 26, 1963.
———. "This Quiet Dust." *Harper's*, April 1965.
Sullivan, Andrew. "Going Down Screaming." *New York Times Magazine*, October 11, 1998.
Sussman, Robert. "The Case Against William Styron's Nat Turner." *Yale Literary Magazine*, Fall 1968.
Swaggart, Jimmy. "Apology Sermon." In *Thrice-Born: The Rhetorical Comeback of Jimmy Swaggart*, by Michael James Giuliano. Macon: Mercer University Press, 1999.
———. "Comeback Sermon." In *Thrice-Born: The Rhetorical Comeback of Jimmy Swaggart*, by Michael James Giuliano. Macon: Mercer University Press, 1999.
Taft, William H. "Bernarr Macfadden: One of a Kind." *Journalism Quarterly* 45 (Winter 1968): 627–33.

Taylor, Charles. *A Secular Age*. Cambridge: Cambridge University Press, 2007.
———. *Sources of the Self: The Making of the Modern Identity*. Cambridge: Harvard University Press, 1989.
Taylor, Robert. "The Contentions of William Styron: The Novelist Responds to Critics of *Nat Turner*." *Boston Sunday Globe Magazine*, April 20, 1969.
Taylor, Robert Lewis. "Physical Culture, III: Physician, Heal Thyself." *New Yorker*, October 28, 1950.
Tell, Dave. "Augustine and the 'Chair of Lies': Rhetoric in *The Confessions*." *Rhetorica* 28, no. 2 (2010): 384–407.
———. "Augustinian Political Theory and Religious Discourse in Public Life." *Journal of Communication and Religion* 30, no. 2 (2007): 213–35.
———. "Jimmy Swaggart's Secular Confession." *Rhetoric Society Quarterly* 39, no. 2 (2009): 124–46.
———. "Rhetoric and Power: An Inquiry into Foucault's Critique of Confession." *Philosophy and Rhetoric* 43, no. 2 (2010): 95–117.
———. "The 'Shocking Story' of Emmett Till and the Politics of Public Confession." *Quarterly Journal of Speech* 94, no. 2 (2008): 156–78.
Terry, David P. "Once Blind, Now Seeing: Problematics of Confessional Performance." *Text and Performance Quarterly* 26, no. 3 (2006): 209–28.
Thelwell, Mike. "Back with the Wind: Mr. Styron and the Reverend Turner." In *William Styron's Nat Turner: Ten Black Writers Respond*, edited by John Henrik Clarke, 79–92. Boston: Beacon Press, 1968.
Toobin, Jeffrey. *A Vast Conspiracy: The Real Story of the Sex Scandal That Nearly Brought Down a President*. New York: Random House, 1999.
Tragle, Henry Irving. *The Southampton Slave Revolt of 1831: A Compilation of Source Material*. Amherst: University of Massachusetts Press, 1971.
United States House of Representatives. "Trial Memorandum of the United States House of Representatives." 106th Cong., 1st sess., January 11, 1999. http://www.law.umkc.edu/faculty/projects/FTrials/clinton/senatebriefs.html.
Villard, Oswald Garrison. "Sex, Art, Truth, and Magazines." *Atlantic Monthly*, March 1926.
Watanabe, Teresa. "Religions Reflect Different Points on Moral Compass." *Los Angeles Times*, September 12, 1998.
———. "The Starr Report: Religions Reflect Different Points on Moral Compass." *Los Angeles Times*, September 12, 1998.
Waugh, Clifford Jerome. "Bernarr Macfadden: The Muscular Prophet." Ph.D. diss., State University of New York, 1979.
Welford, Robt. H., ed. "Growing to Manhood in Civilized (?) Society: The Personal Confessions of the Victim." *Physical Culture*, October 1906, 337–45; November 1906, 421–29; December 1906, 495–508; January 1907, 25–33; February 1907, 127–35; March 1907, 213–21.
West, James L., III, ed. *Letters to My Father: William Styron*. Baton Rouge: Louisiana State University Press, 2009.
Whitaker, Hugh Stephen. "A Case Study in Southern Justice: The Emmett Till Case." Master's thesis, Florida State University, 1963.
Whitfield, Stephen J. *A Death in the Delta: The Story of Emmett Till*. New York: Free Press, 1988.
Whitney, Craig R. "Stupefaction in France, but Calls for Resignation in Britain." *New York Times*, September 13, 1998.
William Charvat Collection of American Fiction. William Bradford Huie Papers. Ohio State University Libraries.

Williams, Brian. "Book 'A Million Little Pieces' May Not Be a Work of Fact." *NBC Nightly News*, NBC, January 10, 2006. http://www.lexisnexis.com/.
Williams, John A. "The Manipulation of History and of Fact: An Ex-Southerner's Apologist Tract for Slavery and the Life of Nat Turner; or, William Styron's Faked Confessions." In *William Styron's Nat Turner: Ten Black Writers Respond*, edited by John Henrik Clarke, 45–49. Boston: Beacon Press, 1968.
Williams, Raymond. *Culture and Society, 1780–1950*. New York: Columbia University Press, 1983.
Winerip, Michael. "Starr Report Recalls Outlook of a Preacher in Rural Texas." *New York Times*, September 13, 1998.
Withers, Ernest C. *Complete Photo Story of the Emmett Till Murder Case*. Memphis: Withers Photographers, 1955.
Wood, James. "Madame Lewinsky." *New Republic*, October 5, 1998.
Woodward, C. Vann. "Confessions of a Rebel: 1831." *New Republic*, October 7, 1967.
Wright, Lawrence. *Saints and Sinners: Walker Railey, Jimmy Swaggart, Madalyn Murray O'Hair, Anton LaVey, Will Campbell, Mathew Fox*. New York: Knopf, 1993.
Wuthnow, Robert. "Religion and Television: The Public and the Private." In *American Evangelicals and the Mass Media*, edited by Quentin J. Schultze, 199–214. Grand Rapids, Mich.: Academic Books, 1990.
Wyatt, Edward. "Best-Selling Memoir Draws Scrutiny." *New York Times*, January 10, 2006.
———. "Frey Says Falsehoods Improved His Tale." *New York Times*, February 2, 2006.
———. "Live on 'Oprah,' a Memoirist Is Kicked out of the Book Club." *New York Times*, January 27, 2006.
———. "Writer Says He Made up Some Details." *New York Times*, January 12, 2006.
Yagoda, Ben. *Memoir: A History*. New York: Riverhead, 2009.
Yardley, Jonathon. "Shelve Them Under Navel-Gazing." *Washington Post*, November 29, 2009.
Zarefsky, David. "Definitions." In *Argument in a Time of Change: Definitions, Frameworks, and Critiques*, edited by James F. Klumpp, 1–11. Annandale, Va.: National Communication Association, 1997.

INDEX

Adams, Mark, 37
Adams, Olive Arnold, 68–69, 71, 81, 88, 89
Allen, Frederick Lewis, 59, 193n. 8
The American Economic Evolution (Macfadden), 48–52, 53, 55
American Medical Association, 20, 193n. 8
anxiety. *See* confessional anxiety
Aptheker, Herbert, 92, 95–97, 98–99, 110, 111–12, 113, 115, 202n. 28
The Art of the Public Grovel (Bauer), 5, 7, 10–12
Assemblies of God
    coercion and, 120–22
    confessional crises and, 3
    confessional genre and, 120–22, 124, 127–28, 130, 136, 139, 140, 142
    confessional hermeneutics and, 3, 121–22, 124
    cultural politics and, 3, 120–22, 124, 139, 140, 142
    power and, 10–11, 126–27
Association of Citizens' Councils of Mississippi (ACCM), 16, 67, 77–79, 83–84, 86, 87
Augustine, Saint
    on confession, generally, 18, 22, 117, 129–31
    legal defense and, 152–53
    Million Little Pieces (Frey) and, 182, 183, 184
    Swaggart and, 122–23, 141
authenticity
    class and, 51–57
    Clinton and, 152, 158, 160, 187
    coercion and, 13–14, 185–87
    confessional anxiety and, 6, 105, 188–89, 191
    confessional crises and, 5, 13–14, 41–42, 93–94, 188–89, 191
    confessional genre and, 41–42, 43–44, 51–57, 70–72, 78–79, 88–90, 93–94, 100–105, 181, 184–87, 188–89, 191

confessional hermeneutics and, 13–14, 41–42, 78–79, 88–90, 93–94, 188–89
The Confessions of Nat Turner (Styron) and, 13, 93–94, 100–105, 187
cultural politics and, 38–42, 43–44, 51–57, 78–79, 88–90, 93–94, 100–105, 181, 184–87, 188–89, 191
emptiness of, 43–44, 55
Million Little Pieces (Frey) and, 180–81, 182–83, 184–87, 188–89
power and, 5, 13–14, 78–79, 88–90, 103–5, 181, 186, 187
race and, 78–79, 88–90, 93–94, 100–105
rhetorical style and, 35–37, 140
sexuality and, 38–42, 43–44, 54
"The Shocking Story" (Huie) and, 5, 69–72, 78–79, 88–90
Starr and, 14
Swaggart and, 140
True Story Magazine and, 34–42, 43–44, 51–57
violence and, 93–94
Authenticity (Boyle), 6
Authenticity Hoax (Potter), 5, 6
The Autobiography of Malcolm X, 103, 104

Bakker, Jim, 119, 122, 125–26
Bakker, Tammy Faye, 125
Baldwin, James, 66, 89, 105, 116, 202n. 28
Barton, Matthew H., 148, 152, 153, 166, 174, 175–76
Baton Rouge Family Worship Center, 17, 119
Bauer, Susan Wise
    on Clinton, 10, 166, 174
    on confession, generally, 5, 7, 10–12, 153, 205n. 21
    on Swaggart, 10–11, 122
Beauchamp, Keith A., 67, 89, 90
Begala, Paul, 163
Beito, David T., 66, 89

Beito, Linda Royster, 89
Bell, Daniel, 140, 141
Bennet, James, 166, 167
Bennett, Jackie M., 161
Bennett, Lerone, Jr., 100, 114
Bennett, William J., 162–63
Benoit, William, 152, 153, 166, 174, 175
Bhabha, Homi K., 92
Bittman, Robert J., 147, 157, 161
Black Anti-Defamation Association, 13
Black Power movement, 92–95, 110, 114, 115, 118, 187
Blaney, Joseph, 152, 153, 166, 174, 175
Blecher, Mari, 172
Bloodworth-Thomason, Linda, 163
Boyle, David, 6
Bracey, John H., 96
Bradley, Mamie, 69, 88, 89
Breland, J. J.
  cultural politics and, 77–79, 82, 85–88
  defense undertaken by, 84
  secret sessions with, 63–65, 70, 72
Breland & Whitten
  cultural politics and, 77–79, 82, 85–88
  defense undertaken by, 84
  secret sessions with, 63–65, 66, 70, 72
Brennan, John, 36
Breuer, Josef, 57
Brooks, Peter
  on authenticity, 13, 185, 186
  on confession, generally, 5, 6, 9, 122–23, 192n. 2
  on power, 10
Brown, H. Rap, 93
Brown, John, 106, 107
Browne, Stephen H., 118, 207n. 105
Brownell, Herbert, 74–75, 77
Brown v. Board of Education, 16, 79, 82–88
Bryant, Carolyn, 64, 68, 70, 76, 80–81, 83
Bryant, Roy
  secret sessions with, 63–66, 70, 72, 78
  Till murder and, 68, 73, 75–76, 80–81
  trial of, 63, 84, 85
Bywater, Michael, 172

Campbell, Melvin, 81
Carmichael, Stokely, 93
Caryn, James, 162
Cellini, Benvenuto, 11, 22
Chevrolet Motor Company, 50
Chrysler, Walter, 48
Citizens' Councils, 16, 67, 77–79, 83–84, 86, 87

civil rights. *See also* race; segregation
  The Confessions of Nat Turner (Styron) and, 92–95, 96, 110, 114, 118, 187
  Till murder and, 16, 73–77
Clark, Hubert, 81
Clark, Roy, 187–88
Clarke, John Henrik, 110–11, 112, 113–14
class
  authenticity and, 51–57
  confessional crises and, 3
  confessional genre and, 2, 47, 51–57, 60–62
  confessional hermeneutics and, 4, 15
  cultural politics, as element of, 2, 3–4, 12, 188, 190
  power and, 47, 60–62
  True Story Magazine and, 2–3, 15, 22, 44, 45–57, 60–62
Cleaver, Eldridge, 103–4
Clinton, Bill
  authenticity and, 152, 158, 160, 187
  coercion and, 160–62, 166–73, 187
  confessional anxiety and, 146–47, 162
  confessional crises and, 3, 146–50, 153–54, 162
  confessional genre and, 147–50, 154–79, 187, 191
  confessional hermeneutics and, 3, 7, 17–18, 147–50, 154–79, 187
  confessions by, specifics of, 17–18, 122, 147–51, 154, 155–56, 157, 159, 163–65, 176, 177–78
  cultural politics and, 3, 17–18, 148, 149–50, 153–79, 187, 191
  denial of affair by, 146
  Flowers and, 155–57, 159, 160, 162, 176, 177, 179
  grand jury testimony by, 148–50, 154–55, 156–62, 167–73, 173–74, 178, 179
  impeachment of, 160, 163, 166, 171, 177–79
  legal defense and, 148–49, 150, 151–54, 157–62, 163–65, 167–70, 173–76, 177–79
  Map Room speech, 147–48, 149–50, 151, 152, 153, 154–55, 162–65, 166, 167, 173–74, 175, 176, 178, 179
  My Life, 11
  power and, 10, 12, 149, 153, 171
  Prayer Breakfast speech, 147–48, 149–50, 150–51, 153, 165–67, 173–76, 178, 179

religion and, 148, 151, 152–54, 165,
    173–76, 179
  rhetorical style and, 150–54, 159, 165,
    167–68, 169, 171, 176
  Starr and, 147, 148–50, 151, 154–55,
    156–62, 163, 164–65, 166–73, 174,
    177–79, 191
  Swaggart compared with, 122
Clinton, Chelsea, 176
Clinton, Hillary, 155, 156, 176
coercion
  authenticity and, 13–14, 185–87
  Clinton and, 160–62, 166–73, 187
  confessional crises and, 13–14
  confessional genre and, 160–62,
    166–73, 185–87
  confessional hermeneutics and, 13–14,
    17, 160–62, 166–73
  The Confessions of Nat Turner (Styron)
    and, 187
  cultural politics and, 17, 160–62,
    166–73, 185–87
  Million Little Pieces (Frey) and, 185–87
  power and, 13–14, 17, 171,
    186, 187
  rhetorical style and, 171
  Swaggart and, 17, 120–22
Cohen, Lizabeth, 50, 55
Cohen, Richard, 187–88
Cole, Joanna, 166
Coleman, J. P., 1, 75–76, 77, 85
Coles, Joanna, 151
Collins, 81
Compelling Confessions (Diamond), 5
compulsion. *See* coercion
Comstock, Anthony
  Physical Culture Exhibition and, 23–26
  Physical Culture Magazine and, 27, 28,
    29, 30
  True Story Magazine and, 3, 14, 22–23,
    30–31, 34, 38, 39, 41–42, 44, 45, 54,
    55, 190
confessional anxiety. *See also* confessional
    crises
  authenticity and, 6, 105,
    188–89, 191
  Clinton and, 146–47, 162
  confessional crises and, 1, 105, 162,
    187–91
  confessional genre and, 8–9, 105, 162,
    187–91
  confessional hermeneutics and, 2, 8,
    162, 187–91

The Confessions of Nat Turner (Styron)
  and, 105
cultural politics and, 2, 8–9, 105, 162,
  187–91
Million Little Pieces (Frey) and,
  187–91
popularity of, 5–6
power and, 6, 105
reception history and, 8–9
Swaggart and, 137
confessional crises. *See also* confessional
  anxiety; confessional hermeneutics;
  individual crises
  authenticity and, 5, 13–14, 41–42, 93–94,
    188–89, 191
  Clinton and, 3, 146–50, 153–54, 162
  coercion and, 13–14
  confessional anxiety and, 1, 105, 162,
    187–91
  confessional genre and, 105–18, 145, 162,
    187–91
  confessional hermeneutics and, 1–5,
    93–95, 105–18, 162, 187–91
  The Confessions of Nat Turner (Styron)
    and, 3, 93–95, 105–18
  cultural politics and, 1–5, 41–42, 93–95,
    105–18, 153–54, 162, 187–91
  definition of, 1
  Million Little Pieces (Frey) and,
    187–91
  overview of, 14–19
  power and, 3–4, 5, 13–14, 105
  "The Shocking Story" (Huie) and, 1–2, 3,
    5, 66–67, 71–72, 74–77
  Swaggart and, 3, 145
  True Story Magazine and, 2–3, 22–23,
    41–42
confessional culture, 1, 5–6, 9, 42, 124,
  181–91. *See also* cultural politics
confessional genre. *See also* confessional
  hermeneutics
  authenticity and, 41–42, 43–44, 51–57,
    70–72, 78–79, 88–90, 93–94,
    100–105, 181, 184–87, 188–89, 191
  class and, 2, 47, 51–57, 60–62
  Clinton and, 147–50, 154–79, 187, 191
  coercion and, 160–62, 166–73, 185–87
  confessional anxiety and, 8–9, 105, 162,
    187–91
  confessional crises and, 105–18, 145, 162,
    187–91
  confessional hermeneutics and, 4–5,
    8–13, 100, 105–18, 187–91

confessional genre (*continued*)
  The Confessions of Nat Turner (Styron) and, 91–95, 100–118, 187, 191
  cultural politics and, 2, 4, 8–13, 18–19, 22–23, 28, 41–44, 47, 51–57, 60–62, 66–67, 87–88, 91–95, 100–118, 120–25, 129–36, 138–39, 140–41, 141–43, 144–45, 148, 150, 153–79, 181–87
  definitions in, 6, 7–9, 10–11, 17–18, 122–25, 129–36, 148–49, 153–54, 157–60, 174, 179, 184, 188
  democracy and, 2, 140–41, 144, 150, 154–79
  legal defense and, 148–49, 150, 151–54, 157–62, 163–65, 167–70, 173–76, 177–79
  Million Little Pieces (Frey) and, 181–87
  Physical Culture Magazine and, 28, 30, 31, 34
  political economy and, 4, 12–13, 19, 43–44
  popularity of, 1, 5–6
  power and, 5, 7, 10–13, 18–19, 47, 60–62, 67, 77, 78–79, 88–90, 103–5, 117–18, 149, 153, 171, 181, 186, 187
  race and, 2, 66–67, 87–88, 91–95, 100–118
  reception history of, 6–7
  religion and, 2, 120–25, 129–31, 138–39, 140–41, 141–43, 144–45, 148, 152–54
  rhetorical style and, 122–25, 135–45, 159, 165, 169, 171, 176
  sexuality and, 2, 22–23, 28, 41–44, 62
  "The Shocking Story" (Huie) and, 63–67, 70–72, 77–82, 87–90, 191
  Swaggart and, 120–25, 127–29, 130, 135–45, 191
  True Story Magazine and, 20–23, 28, 29–34, 41–44, 47, 51–62, 190
  violence and, 2, 91–95, 100, 105–18
confessional hermeneutics. *See also* confessional crises; confessional genre; genre criticism
  authenticity and, 13–14, 41–42, 78–79, 88–90, 93–94, 188–89
  class and, 4, 15
  Clinton and, 3, 7, 17–18, 147–50, 154–79, 187
  coercion and, 13–14, 17, 160–62, 166–73
  confessional anxiety and, 2, 8, 162, 187–91
  confessional crises and, 1–5, 93–95, 105–18, 162, 187–91
  confessional genre and, 4–5, 8–13, 100, 105–18, 187–91
  The Confessions of Nat Turner (Styron) and, 3, 7, 13, 16–17, 93–95, 100, 105–18, 187
  cultural politics and, 1–5, 7–13, 14–19, 22–23, 28, 41–42, 66–67, 73–90, 93–95, 100, 105–18, 121–25, 150, 154–79, 181, 187–91
  definitions in, 3, 6, 7–9, 10–11, 17–18, 117, 122–25, 129–36, 148–49, 153–54, 157–60, 174, 179, 184, 188
  democracy and, 4, 17–18, 150, 154–79
  legal defense and, 148–49, 150, 157–62, 163–65, 167–70, 173–76, 177–79
  Million Little Pieces (Frey) and, 181–84, 187–91
  Physical Culture Magazine and, 28
  power and, 3–4, 7, 10–14, 17, 18–19, 77, 78–79, 88–90, 117–18, 149, 171
  race and, 4, 15–17, 66–67, 73–90, 93–95, 100, 105–18
  reception history and, 8, 12
  religion and, 4, 17, 121–25
  rhetorical style and, 122–25, 159, 165, 169, 171, 176
  sexuality and, 4, 14–15, 22–23, 28, 41–42
  "The Shocking Story" (Huie) and, 1–2, 3, 4, 15–16, 66–67, 73–90
  Swaggart and, 3, 7, 17, 121–25
  True Story Magazine and, 2–3, 7, 14–15, 20–23, 41–42
  violence and, 4, 16–17, 93–95, 100, 105–18
confessions. *See also* confessional genre; confessional hermeneutics; disclosure
  Augustine on, 122–23, 129–31, 141
  by Clinton, specifics of, 17–18, 122, 147–51, 154, 155–56, 157, 159, 163–65, 176, 177–78
  definitions of, 6, 7–9, 10–11, 17–18, 117, 122–25, 129–36, 148–49, 153–54, 157–60, 174, 179, 184, 188
  Freud on, 57–60
  Rousseau on, 122–23, 129, 130–36, 136–37, 138–39, 140, 141, 142
  by Swaggart, 119–25, 127–29, 130, 135–45
  for Till murder, 63–66, 70–72, 74–76, 86–87
  by Turner, 91, 92, 106

Confessions (Augustine), 129–31, 152–53, 182, 183, 184
Confessions (Rousseau), 130–31, 133–34, 139
"The Confessions of Nat Turner" (Gray), 91, 92, 106, 107
The Confessions of Nat Turner (Styron)
  authenticity and, 13, 93–94, 100–105, 187
  coercion and, 187
  confessional anxiety and, 105
  confessional crises and, 3, 93–95, 105–18
  confessional genre and, 91–95, 100–118, 187, 191
  confessional hermeneutics and, 3, 7, 13, 16–17, 93–95, 100, 105–18, 187
  "The Confessions of Nat Turner" (Gray) and, 91, 92, 106, 107
  criticism of, 93–94, 95, 99, 105–17, 118
  cultural politics and, 3, 16–17, 91–95, 100–118, 187, 191
  history and, 92–93, 95–100, 106–10, 111–17, 118
  power and, 12, 13, 103–5, 117–18
  publication of, 91
  "This Quiet Dust" (Styron) and, 100–105, 106
Corsi, Edward, 45
Coryell, John R., 26, 29, 30, 31, 34, 38
Cothran, Ed, 81
Coxey, 49
Cruse, Harold, 201n. 12
cultural politics. *See also* class; confessional culture; democracy; race; religion; sexuality; violence
  authenticity and, 38–42, 43–44, 51–57, 78–79, 88–90, 93–94, 100–105, 181, 184–87, 188–89, 191
  Clinton and, 3, 17–18, 148, 149–50, 153–79, 187, 191
  coercion and, 17, 160–62, 166–73, 185–87
  confessional anxiety and, 2, 8–9, 105, 162, 187–91
  confessional crises and, 1–5, 41–42, 93–95, 105–18, 153–54, 162, 187–91
  confessional genre and, 2, 4, 8–13, 18–19, 22–23, 28, 41–44, 47, 51–57, 60–62, 66–67, 87–88, 91–95, 100–118, 120–25, 129–36, 138–39, 140–41, 141–43, 144–45, 148, 150, 153–79, 181

confessional hermeneutics and, 1–5, 7–13, 14–19, 22–23, 28, 41–42, 66–67, 73–90, 93–95, 100, 105–18, 121–25, 150, 154–79, 181–87, 187–91
The Confessions of Nat Turner (Styron) and, 3, 16–17, 91–95, 100–118, 187, 191
elements of, 2, 3–4, 12, 188, 190
genre criticism and, 2, 43
Million Little Pieces (Frey) and, 181–91
Negro Writing and, 103–5, 116–17
Physical Culture Magazine and, 24, 26–29, 38, 41, 42
political economy and, 4, 43–44
power and, 3–4, 10–13, 17, 18–19, 24–25, 47, 60–62, 67, 77, 78–79, 88–90, 103–5, 117–18, 149, 171, 186, 187
reception history and, 7, 8–9, 12
rhetorical hermeneutics and, 12
rhetorical style and, 138–39, 140–41, 141–45, 153–54, 165, 171, 176
"The Shocking Story" (Huie) and, 1–2, 3, 15–16, 66–67, 73–90, 191
Swaggart and, 3, 17, 120–25, 138–39, 140–41, 141–43, 144–45, 191
True Story Magazine and, 2–3, 14–15, 22–23, 29–32, 38–44, 45–57, 60–62, 190
culture. *See* confessional culture; cultural politics
Culture and Society (Williams), 8

Darsey, 205n. 23
Daschle, Tom, 152
David, King, 129, 130
Debs, Eugene, 49
Delany, Lloyd Tom, 112–13, 113–14
democracy
  Clinton and, 17–18, 149–50, 154–79, 191
  coercion and, 160–62, 166–73
  confessional anxiety and, 162
  confessional crises and, 3, 162
  confessional genre and, 2, 140–41, 144, 150, 154–79
  confessional hermeneutics and, 4, 17–18, 150, 154–79
  cultural politics, as element of, 2, 3–4, 12, 188, 190
  legal defense and, 177, 178–79
  Map Room speech and, 165
  power and, 149, 171
  Prayer Breakfast speech and, 176
  rhetorical style and, 140–41, 144, 165, 171, 176

democracy (*continued*)
    Rousseau on, 130–31
    Starr and, 18, 166–73, 191
    Swaggart and, 140–41
    True Story Magazine and, 46
de Quincy, Thomas, 22
Derrida, Jacques, 132, 133, 135, 138
Diamond, Suzanne, 5
Didion, Joan, 156
disclosure. *See also* privacy
    Bauer and Foucault on, 10–12
    Clinton and, 155–57, 158, 160, 167–73, 177–79
    Swaggart and, 120–21, 123, 129–43
Doubleday, 180, 182
Dowd, Maureen, 168
Downey, Sharon, 198n. 14
Duberman, Martin, 99
Durden, Robert F., 116
Dylan, Bob, 66, 89

Earle, Henry, 28–29
Eastland, James O., 83
Eberly, Rosa A., 18
86% of America (Macfadden), 48–52
Eisenhower, Dwight, 16
Elkins, Stanley M.
    The Confessions of Nat Turner (Styron) and, 106, 108–9, 110, 111, 112, 113, 114–15
    on Phillips, 96
    on slavery, 97–100
Ellison, Ralph, 207n. 105
Emanuel, Rahm, 155, 163
Emile (Rousseau), 133
England, O. H., 40
Ernst, Robert, 33
"Essay on the Origin of Languages" (Rousseau), 131–33, 135–36

Fabian, Ann, 20, 34–35
Falwell, Jerry, 126
Fanon, Frantz, 92, 95, 103, 106, 110, 111, 115, 116, 117
Faulkner, William, 100–101
Fawcett, W. H., 33
Federal Bureau of Investigation (FBI), 66, 67, 81, 82, 89, 90
Fineman, Howard, 162
First Assembly Church of God, 126
Fishbein, Morris, 59, 60
Fisher, Walter, 211n. 4
Fliegelman, Jay, 123, 139

Flowers, Gennifer, 155–57, 159, 160, 162, 176, 177, 179
Ford, Henry, 45, 48
Foucault, Michel
    Clinton and, 149
    on confessional genre generally, 7, 11–12, 18, 44, 117, 124, 144, 192n. 2
    on Freud, 60
    on power, 10, 24–25
    on violence, 118, 185
Franklin, Jean, 72
Franklin, John Hope, 105, 202n. 28
French, Scot, 92, 111
Freud, Sigmund, 18, 57–60, 117
Frey, James, 1, 6, 19, 180–91

Garsten, Bryan, 144
Garver, Newton, 135
Gay, Peter, 59
Gayle, Addison, Jr., 116–17, 202n. 19
Genovese, Eugene, 97
genre. *See* confessional genre
genre criticism, 2, 18–19, 43, 103–5, 116–17.
    See also confessional hermeneutics
genre politics, 183–84. *See also* confessional genre; cultural politics
Gephardt, Dick, 152
Gerbner, George, 20, 21, 36, 61, 62
Gilman, Richard, 103–5, 106, 110, 116–17
Gingrich, Newt, 173
Giuliano, Michael J., 119–20, 125, 136, 140, 142
glossolalia, 140, 142
Gorman, Marvin, 17, 119, 120, 121, 126–27, 128, 136
Gormley, Ken, 163, 164, 175, 176
Grafton, Anthony, 186
Graham, Billy, 126
Gray, Thomas, 91, 92, 106, 107
Greenblatt, Stephen, 170–73
Grimm, Friedrich Melchior baron von, 134
Grindy, Matthew, 81–82, 84, 85, 87, 88, 90
"Growing to Manhood" (Coryell), 26–29, 30, 31, 34, 38

Habermas, 141
Hahn, Jessica, 126
Hahn, Steven, 95
Hairston, Loyle, 93–94, 114–15, 118
Hall, Forrest, 121, 127–28
Halttunen, Karen, 69, 117–18
Hamilton, Charles V., 93, 94
Harding, Susan Friend, 125

Harding, Vincent, 113, 116–17
Harris, John F., 151, 161, 165, 174
Hart, Rod, 43
Hartman, Anne, 205n. 24
Hatch, Orrin, 158
Hatton, Jacqueline, 57
Heffernan, Virginia, 185
Heller, Karen, 183
hermeneutics. *See* confessional hermeneutics
Heyn, Ernest V., 22
Hicks, James L., 15–16, 66, 69, 71, 74–75, 77–78, 81
History and Magazines (Macfadden), 53, 54, 56
Hogan, J. Michael, 150, 151, 174–75
Honey, Maureen, 61
Hoover, Herbert, 48
Houck, Davis, 81–82, 84, 85, 87, 88, 90
Howard, T. R. M., 69, 71, 81
Hughes, Langston, 116
Huie, William Bradford. *See also* "The Shocking Story" (Huie)
  authenticity and, 70–72, 78–79, 88–90
  confessional crises and, 15–16, 66–67, 71–72, 75–77
  confessional genre and, 63–67, 70–72, 77–82, 87–90
  confessional hermeneutics and, 66–67, 73–74, 75–76, 77–82, 85–90
  cultural politics and, 66–67, 73–74, 75–76, 77–82, 85–90
  secret sessions with, 63–65, 70, 78–79, 80, 81–82, 85–88
Hunt, William, 23–24

Jakes, T. D., 172
Janway, Cecil, 126, 128
Jimmy Swaggart Ministries, 120, 126, 127, 143–44
Jordan, Arthur, 74, 76–77
Joseph, Peniel, 92
J. Walter Thompson Company, 49–50

Kakutani, Michiko, 175, 188–89, 190, 191
Karr, Mary, 189, 190, 191
Kazin, Alfred, 109–10, 111, 112
Kemble, Dorothy, 37
Kendall, David, 148, 157, 158, 159, 164, 168
Kennedy, Ted, 10
Killens, John Oliver
  Black Power movement and, 92–93
  The Confessions of Nat Turner (Styron) and, 111, 112, 113, 114, 115–16, 116–17, 187

King, Larry, 180
Kroft, Steve, 155–56
Kurtz, Howard, 146, 174, 185

language. *See* rhetorical style
Law, Bernard, 122
Lazare, Aaron, 5, 8, 9
Lee, Ronald, 148, 152, 153, 166, 174, 175–76
legal defense
  grand jury testimony and, 157–62
  impeachment trial and, 177–79
  Map Room speech and, 148, 150, 151–54, 163–65
  Prayer Breakfast speech and, 173–76
  Starr Report and, 167–70
Lewinsky, Monica
  in confessions generally, 3, 7, 17
  denial of affair with, 146
  in grand jury testimony, 154, 157, 158, 159, 160, 167–68, 169–70, 178
  in impeachment memorandum, 177–78, 179
  in Map Room speech, 150, 154, 163, 164, 178
  in Prayer Breakfast speech, 150–51, 166
  in Starr Report, 169–70
Lewis, Anthony, 172
Look article. *See* "The Shocking Story" (Huie)
Lorde, Audre, 89
Loughery, John, 59
Luxembourg, Mme de, 133–34

Macfadden, Bernarr
  authenticity and, 34–42, 43–44, 51–57
  confessional crises and, 2–3, 41–42
  confessional genre and, 20–23, 28, 29–34, 41–44, 47, 51–62, 190
  confessional hermeneutics and, 41–42
  cultural politics and, 2–3, 14–15, 22–32, 38–44, 45–57, 60–62, 190
  Macfadden Publications, 46, 48–52, 53, 54, 55, 56
  Physical Culture Exhibition, 23–26, 28
  Physical Culture Magazine and, 24, 26–29, 30, 31, 34, 38, 41, 42
  power and, 47, 60–62
  True Story Magazine and, 2–3, 14–15, 20, 21, 22, 23, 29–44, 45–62
Macfadden Publications, 46, 48–52, 53, 54, 55, 56
Mailloux, Steven, 3–4, 7, 8, 9, 12
Malcolm X, 103, 104

Mandziuk, Roseann M., 21, 61
Marchand, Roland, 46
Markus, Robert, 130, 206n. 45
Marx, Karl, 48
Matthews, Charles, 130
McCarthy, Joseph, 161, 170, 172
McChesney, Robert W., 4, 193n. 22
McCurry, Mike, 148
McGrory, Mary, 150, 152
McMillen, Neil, 83
Medhurst, Martin J., 125, 140
Meier, August, 92, 94
Mellon, Andrew, 48
Melville, Herman, 108, 109
Memoir: A History (Yagoda), 5
Mencken, H. L., 35, 42
Mendelsohn, Daniel, 1, 6, 182
Mich, Daniel D., 63–64, 65, 79, 80, 82, 87
Milam, J. W.
 denial of confession by, 71–72, 78
 secret sessions with, 63–66, 70, 78
 on "The Shocking Story" (Huie), 89
 Till murder and, 68, 73, 75–76, 80–82, 86–87, 90
 trial of, 63, 84, 85
Milam, Leslie, 66, 81
Miller, Arthur, 14, 149, 161–62, 170, 171, 172, 187
Miller, Donald Earl, 122
Miller, Thomas, 121
Million Little Pieces (Frey), 1, 6, 19, 180–91
Miranda v. Arizona, 5, 13, 186
Monteith, Sharon, 82, 89
Morris, Dick, 146
Mullins, Greg, 42
My Life (Clinton), 11

National Association for the Advancement of Colored People (NAACP). *See also* Wilkins, Roy
 confessional genre and, 16, 65, 74, 75–78, 88
 cultural politics and, 67, 74, 75–78, 84–85, 86, 87, 88
 Till murder and, 69, 73, 75–78
Negro Writing, 103–5, 116–17
Nelson, Lars-Erik, 162
New Masses, 45

O'Brien, Geoffrey, 161–62
O'Connell, Shaun, 108–9, 110, 112
Office of Independent Counsel (OIC). *See* Starr, Kenneth

On Apology (Lazare), 5, 8, 9
Oursler, Fulton, 29, 30, 31, 36, 40, 57

Paist, Mrs. Frederic M., 45
Parry-Gileses, 174
Paul, Saint, 139–40
Payne, Ethel, 69
Pells, Richard H., 50–51, 55
Phillips, Ulrich B., 96–97, 98, 99, 100
Physical Culture Exhibition, 23–26, 28
Physical Culture Magazine
 confessional genre and, 28, 30, 31, 34
 confessional hermeneutics and, 28
 cultural politics and, 24, 26–29, 38, 41, 42
Plimpton, George, 102
political economy, 4, 12–13, 19, 43–44, 183–84
postcolonialism, 103–5
Potter, Andrew, 5, 6, 184–85
power
 authenticity and, 5, 13–14, 78–79, 88–90, 103–5, 181, 186, 187
 class and, 47, 60–62
 Clinton and, 10, 12, 149, 153, 171
 coercion and, 13–14, 17, 171, 186, 187
 confessional anxiety and, 6, 105
 confessional crises and, 3–4, 5, 13–14, 105
 confessional genre and, 5, 7, 10–13, 18–19, 47, 60–62, 67, 77, 78–79, 88–90, 103–5, 117–18, 149, 153, 171, 181, 186, 187
 confessional hermeneutics and, 3–4, 7, 10–14, 17, 18–19, 77, 78–79, 88–90, 117–18, 149, 171
 The Confessions of Nat Turner (Styron) and, 12, 13, 103–5, 117–18
 cultural politics and, 3–4, 10–13, 17, 18–19, 24–25, 47, 60–62, 67, 77, 78–79, 88–90, 103–5, 117–18, 149, 171, 186, 187
 democracy and, 149, 171
 disciplinary, 11, 12
 Million Little Pieces (Frey) and, 181, 186
 psychoanalysis and, 60
 race and, 67, 77, 78–79, 88–90, 103–5, 117–18
 reception history and, 12
 religion and, 17, 153
 rhetorical style and, 10–11, 12, 133–35, 136–41, 153, 171
 sexuality and, 24–25

"The Shocking Story" (Huie) and, 5, 12, 77, 78–79, 88–90
Swaggart and, 10–11, 17, 119–20, 126–27
True Story Magazine and, 12, 47, 60–62
violence and, 117–18
Pressley, Nelson, 161
Printer's Ink, 46, 48, 55
privacy. *See also* disclosure
Augustine on, 130
Clinton and, 156–57, 158–59, 160, 163–65, 173–74, 177–79
Swaggart and, 127
Purdum, Todd S., 208n. 36

race
authenticity and, 78–79, 88–90, 93–94, 100–105
Black Power movement, 92–95, 110, 114, 115, 118, 187
civil rights, 16, 73–77, 92–95, 96, 110, 114, 118, 187
confessional anxiety and, 105
confessional crises and, 3, 93–95, 105–18
confessional genre and, 2, 66–67, 87–88, 91–95, 100–118
confessional hermeneutics and, 4, 15–17, 66–67, 73–90, 93–95, 100, 105–18
The Confessions of Nat Turner (Styron) and, 16–17, 91–95, 100–118, 187
cultural politics, as element of, 2, 3–4, 12, 188, 190
Negro Writing and, 103–5, 116–17
power and, 67, 77, 78–79, 88–90, 103–5, 117–18
scholarship on, 95–100
segregation, 77–79, 82–88, 100–101
"The Shocking Story" (Huie) and, 1–2, 15–16, 66–67, 73–90, 191
violence and, 91–100, 105–18, 172
Radway, Janice, 61
Raines, Howell, 64
Rapp, William Jourdan, 45
Reality Hunger (Shields), 6
Reception Histories (Mailloux), 7
reception history, 6–7, 8–9, 12
Redding, Saunders, 105
Reed, Willie, 81
religion
Clinton and, 148, 151, 152–54, 165, 173–76, 179
coercion and, 17
confessional crises and, 3, 153–54

confessional genre and, 2, 120–25, 129–31, 138–39, 140–41, 141–43, 144–45, 148, 152–54
confessional hermeneutics and, 4, 17, 121–25
cultural politics, as element of, 2, 3–4, 12, 188, 190
power and, 17, 153
rhetorical style and, 138–39, 140–41, 141–45, 152–54
Swaggart and, 17, 120–25, 138–39, 140–41, 141–43, 144–45, 191
True Story Magazine and, 40, 57, 60
Rentz, Jim, 121
rhetorical hermeneutics, 12
rhetorical style
authenticity and, 35–37, 140
Clinton and, 150–54, 159, 165, 167–68, 169, 171, 176
coercion and, 171
confessional genre and, 122–25, 135–45, 159, 165, 169, 171, 176
confessional hermeneutics and, 122–25, 159, 165, 169, 171, 176
cultural politics and, 138–39, 140–41, 141–45, 153–54, 165, 171, 176
democracy and, 140–41, 144, 165, 171, 176
power and, 10–11, 12, 133–35, 136–41, 153, 171
religion and, 138–39, 140–41, 141–45, 152–54
Rousseau on, 131–36
Swaggart and, 122–25, 135–45
True Story Magazine and, 35–37, 42, 45–46
Rich, Frank, 19, 172
Roberts, Oral, 125
Robinson, Cedric J., 95
Rosenthal, A. M., 156, 162, 176
Roth, Philip, 104
Rousseau, Jean-Jacques
on confession, generally, 18, 22, 129, 130–36
The Confessions of Nat Turner (Styron) and, 117
Swaggart and, 122–23, 129, 130, 136–37, 138–39, 140, 141, 142
Rowland, Robert, 153, 174, 208n. 8,
Rudwick, Elliot, 92, 94
Ruff, Charles F. C., 148, 157

Sartre, Jean-Paul, 92
Scarry, Elaine, 186

236 INDEX

Schiappa, Edward, 10, 192n. 3
Schudson, Michael, 140–41
Schuller, Robert, 126
Schultze, Quentin J., 119, 122
Scott, John T., 132
segregation, 77–79, 82–88, 100–101.
   See also civil rights; race
sexuality
   authenticity and, 38–42, 43–44, 54
   confessional crises and, 3, 41–42
   confessional genre and, 2, 22–23, 28,
      41–44, 62
   confessional hermeneutics and, 4, 14–15,
      22–23, 28, 41–42
   cultural politics, as element of, 2, 3–4,
      12, 188, 190
   Physical Culture Exhibition and, 23–26
   Physical Culture Magazine and, 24,
      26–29
   power and, 24–25
   prostitution, 17, 126–27, 141–43
   True Story Magazine and, 2–3, 14–15,
      22–23, 29–32, 38–44, 45, 54, 62, 190
Shales, Tom, 161
Shapiro, Walter, 146, 162, 172
Sheed, Wilfred, 202n. 28
Shields, David, 6
"The Shocking Story" (Huie)
   authenticity and, 5, 69–72, 78–79,
      88–90
   Citizens' Councils and, 16, 67, 77–79,
      83–84, 86, 87
   confessional crises and, 1–2, 3, 5, 66–67,
      71–72, 74–77
   confessional genre and, 63–67, 70–72,
      77–82, 87–90, 191
   confessional hermeneutics and, 1–2, 3,
      4, 15–16, 66–67, 73–90
   cultural politics and, 1–2, 3, 15–16,
      66–67, 73–90, 191
   Federal Bureau of Investigation (FBI)
      and, 66, 67, 81, 82, 89, 90
   Hicks and, 66, 69, 71, 74–75, 77–78, 81
   National Association for the Advance-
      ment of Colored People (NAACP)
      and, 16, 65, 67, 74, 75–78, 84–85,
      86, 87, 88
   power and, 5, 12, 77, 78–79, 88–90
   secret sessions for, 63–65, 70, 78–79,
      80, 81–82, 85–88
   Till murder and, 63–64, 67–70, 79–82
   Wilkins and, 1–2, 3, 4, 5, 65, 69, 70, 73,
      74, 75–78, 79, 80, 82, 84–85, 88

Shrum, Robert, 163
Siklos, Richard, 189, 190
Simons, Herbert, 152
sin
   Bauer on, 7, 205n. 21
   Clinton and, 151, 159, 165, 173–76, 177–78
   Swaggart and, 123, 129–30, 141–43
slavery, 92, 95–100, 106–10, 111–17, 118
Smoking Gun, 180, 183, 184
Sokolov, Raymond A., 109, 110
Soul on Ice (Cleaver), 103–4
The Sound and the Fury (Faulkner),
   100–101
Stampp, Kenneth M., 97, 99, 100
Starobinski, Jean, 131, 135
Starr, Kenneth
   authenticity and, 14
   coercion and, 166–73
   confessional crises and, 3
   confessional genre and, 148, 156–62,
      166–73, 174, 191
   confessional hermeneutics and, 3, 7, 18,
      156–62, 166–73, 174
   cultural politics and, 3, 18, 166–73, 191
   investigation by, 147, 148–50, 151,
      154–55, 156–62, 163, 164–65, 166,
      177, 178
   power and, 12, 171
   report by, 148–50, 157, 166–73,
      177–79, 191
   rhetorical style and, 169, 171
Starr Report, 148–50, 157, 166–73,
   177–79, 191
Stone, Albert, 94
Strider, H. C., 80–81
Strine, Mary, 93
Styron, William
   authenticity and, 93–94, 100–105, 187
   coercion and, 187
   confessional anxiety and, 105
   confessional crises and, 3, 16–17, 93–95,
      105–18
   confessional genre and, 3, 16–17, 91–95,
      100–118, 187, 191
   confessional hermeneutics and, 3,
      93–95, 100, 105–18, 187
   criticism of, 93–94, 95, 99, 105–17, 118
   cultural politics and, 3, 91–95, 100–118,
      187, 191
   history and, 92–93, 95–100, 106–10,
      111–17, 118
   power and, 103–5, 117–18
   "This Quiet Dust," 100–105, 106

Sullens, Frederick, 82, 84, 85
Sullivan, Andrew, 172
Sumner, John Saxton, 32
Sussman, Robert, 112
Swaggart, Debbie, 137
Swaggart, Donnie, 137, 143
Swaggart, Frances, 119, 137
Swaggart, Jimmy
  authenticity and, 140
  Bakker and, 126
  Clinton compared with, 122
  coercion and, 17, 120–22
  confessional anxiety and, 137
  confessional crises and, 3, 145
  confessional genre and, 120–25, 127–29, 130, 135–45, 191
  confessional hermeneutics and, 3, 7, 17, 121–25
  confession by, 119–25, 127–29, 130, 135–45
  cultural politics and, 3, 17, 120–25, 138–39, 140–41, 141–43, 144–45, 191
  ministry of, 120, 126, 127, 143–44
  power and, 10–11, 17, 119–20, 126–27
  prostitution and, 17, 126–27, 141–43
  rhetorical style and, 122–25, 135–45

Taft, William, 21
Taft, William Howard, 29
Talese, Nan A., 180, 182
Tannenbaum, Frank, 99
Taylor, Charles, 131
Terry, David, 198n. 14
Thelwell, Mike, 115–16, 116–17
"This Quiet Dust" (Styron), 100–105, 106
Thomason, Harry, 160
Till, Emmett, 1–2, 3, 15–16, 63–64, 67–70, 79–82. *See also* "The Shocking Story" (Huie)
Till, Louis, 86
Toobin, Jeffrey, 150, 152, 154, 157
torture, 185, 186–87
Tragle, Henry, 106–7, 201n. 1
Treeby, William, 128
Troubling Confessions (Brooks), 5, 6, 9
True Confessions, 33–34
True Story Magazine
  authenticity and, 34–42, 43–44, 51–57
  class and, 2–3, 15, 22, 44, 45–57, 60–62
  confessional crises and, 2–3, 22–23, 41–42
  confessional genre and, 20–23, 29–34, 41–44, 47, 51–62, 190

  confessional hermeneutics and, 2–3, 7, 14–15, 20–23, 41–42
  cultural politics and, 2–3, 14–15, 22–23, 29–32, 38–44, 45–57, 60–62, 190
  power and, 12, 47, 60–62
  religion and, 40, 57, 60
  rhetorical style and, 35–37, 42, 45–46
truth. *See* authenticity
Tsongas, Paul, 155
Turner, Nat. *See also The Confessions of Nat Turner* (Styron)
  confession by, 91, 92, 106, 107
  education of, 102
  rebellion led by, 16, 92–93, 106–10, 111–17, 118
Twentieth Century-Fox, 13

violence
  authenticity and, 93–94
  Black Power movement and, 92–95, 110, 114, 115, 118
  confessional crises and, 3, 93–95, 105–18
  confessional genre and, 2, 91–95, 100, 105–18
  confessional hermeneutics and, 4, 16–17, 93–95, 100, 105–18
  The Confessions of Nat Turner (Styron) and, 16–17, 91–95, 100, 105–18, 191
  cultural politics, as element of, 2, 3–4, 12, 188, 190
  power and, 117–18
  race and, 91–100, 105–18, 172
  scholarship on, 95–100
  torture, 185, 186–87

Walters, Basil, 65, 78, 79–80, 82, 85–86
Warens, Mme de, 133–34
Warren, Earl, 186
Watanabe, Teresa, 153
Waugh, Clifford, 25
Whitaker, Stephen, 83
White, Byron, 5, 187
White, Theodore, 21
Whitfield, Stephen J., 83, 84, 85
Whitten, John
  cultural politics and, 77–79, 82, 85–88
  defense undertaken by, 84
  secret sessions with, 63–65, 66, 70, 72, 80
Wilkins, Roy
  authenticity and, 5
  confessional genre and, 1–2, 3, 74, 75–78, 88

Wilkins, Roy (*continued*)
   cultural politics and, 1–2, 3, 75–78, 84–85, 88
   Huie and, 65, 70, 79, 80, 82
   Till murder and, 69, 73, 74
Will, George, 152
Williams, Brian, 182, 185
Williams, John A., 114
Williams, Raymond, 8
William Styron's Nat Turner: Ten Black Writers Respond (Clarke), 110–17
Winfrey, Oprah, 180–81, 182, 184–85, 186, 187–88, 189
Wisenberg, Solomon L., 158, 159–60, 161, 162, 163, 179
witch-hunt tradition, 149, 150, 154, 160, 161–62, 166–67, 170–73, 178
Withers, Ernest C., 69
Wood, James, 170
Woodward, C. Vann, 102, 107–8, 109, 110, 111, 112
Wretched of the Earth (Fanon), 92, 103
Wright, Moses, 80

Yagoda, Ben, 5, 6, 192n. 2
Yardley, Jonathon, 6, 189, 190

Zarefsky, David, 10

www.ingramcontent.com/pod-product-compliance
Lightning Source LLC
Chambersburg PA
CBHW021400290426
44108CB00010B/327